MAVERICK TALES
True Stories of Early Texas
J. D. RITTENHOUSE

Winchester Press

Library of Congress Catalog Card Number: 72-163-780

ISBN: O-876-91-052-5

Published by Winchester Press
460 Park Avenue, New York 10022

PRINTED IN THE UNITED STATES OF AMERICA

Introduction

THIS IS A COLLECTION of true tales from the country southwest of Red River, the stream that separates Oklahoma from Texas. That region includes western Louisiana, most of Texas, and a part of New Mexico — a land that probably has more curious history, that is less known, than any other section of America.

These stories are not entirely new to the people of the Southwest, although in some cases only half the story was ever told before. The historian Macaulay's famous line, "Every school-boy knows who imprisoned Montezuma and who strangled Atahualpa," could be paraphrased. Everyone, or nearly everyone, has heard of the Alamo and the Texas Rangers and Coronado. Not so many have heard of the Battle of Glorieta or the prison of Perote or the Red River raft.

The Southwestern history one gets in New York or Detroit or Seattle is apt to be like the Southwestern chili one gets there: lacking the flavor of the real thing.

Each of these episodes has been written from the old records. Nothing was invented. If there is dialogue, it was from the pen of someone who heard the words spoken. If there is description, it comes from the archives or from walking the earth itself. The plots are better than anyone could invent, and they are more strange. On some of the incidents entire books, sometimes whole sets of books, have been written, but they are known only to the *aficionados* of the Southwest.

This book was not written for professional historians, for they should have known all this before they won their degrees. It was not written for all native Southwesterners, but only for those few who are unfamiliar with the legends of their own land. It has been written as a sampler for the world, to be read for pleasure.

In the preparation of such a book, the roots of obligation run deep, over many years. Much credit must go to the men of the Houston Civil War Round Table, where we talked of Dick Dowling's Battle and the last campaign of Rip Ford. Credit is due also to Ed Bartholomew, for discussions of badmen and good beside Ed's fireplace in a Davis Mountains lodge, and to the inspiration of men such as J. Frank Dobie and C. L. Sonnichsen, both of whom have shown how to tell a good tale. Thanks are due to Morris Cook, the antiquarian bookdealer in Austin who let me borrow rare volumes from his private collection; to Martin Hardwick Hall, the historian who first sparked my interest in the Sibley Brigade; and to the Santa Fe Corral of Westerners, for whom history is not a profession but a way of life.

In these modern days when walls seem to close in upon men and the daily routine turns in a short radius, it is hard to conceive the vastness of the Southwest. There a man might start an adventure somewhere along a Texas bayou and end it on some far river. He might journey across a third of the continent and meet an old friend in an adobe hut in New Mexico or far to the south in a Spanish prison. Coincidence became natural and paradox became expected. Read, and see for yourself.

Albuquerque   JACK D. RITTENHOUSE
February, 1971

Contents

1

Cavalier on the Bayou

THE LAND that no one yet had named lay just beyond the thin fog. The man standing by the ship's starboard rail stared off to the north, his magnificently embroidered coat gleaming dully in the overcast January weather. At first you saw that he was built like a wrestler and seemed to wear the fine clothes as though he had to, not as if he enjoyed them. And then you noticed his eyes, large and deepset, burning with the intensity of either a great dreamer or a great leader.

Rene-Robert Cavelier, Sieur de la Salle, had much of both in him. Almost enough to win. But not quite.

Yet as he stood here on the deck of the thirty-gun man-o'-war *Joly* riding gently off the Texas coast, listening to the soft creak of the rigging, he was destined to change the history of New Spain, in this year of our Lord 1685.

For history, like men, stirs into action only when it must, moving in spurts and jerks, not steadily.

La Salle was staring, this thin January day, at the country men soon would call Texas, but which at the moment was marked on maps only as the Land of the Flesh Eaters.

It was here that La Salle would establish the first colony — a French colony in Spanish territory. History might forget this colony, but it would make Spain move into a region it had ignored for two hundred years and would start a new era that men would remember forever.

Give a few years, it was two centuries since Columbus found the new world, yet Spain had paid no serious attention to this part of

1

it. A shipwreck survivor or two had wandered across it, a few missionaries had trudged over it seeking souls to convert, or an occasional expedition seeking gold — these were the only visitors. Buffalo roamed in herds of five thousand head, and tattooed Indians lived in brush huts, but there were not, and never had been, any settlements north of the Rio Grande except around El Paso.

South of the Rio Grande it was a different story; there were silver mines there, with the mines at Santa Barbara not far below the great, twisting stream that then was called Rio Bravo del Norte. And the French knew those mines were there.

Louis XIV of France knew they were there and that they could be captured, possibly. So he agreed to La Salle's scheme. It had enough ring of assurance that it might succeed. And if it didn't? What would be lost? A few colonists that were a nuisance in France anyway, a little money — most of it from the pockets of the adventurers or of the merchants and nobles who backed them.

La Salle had given good proof that he might be the man who could do it. Just past forty years in age, the son of a merchant family but made penniless because he happened to be still in a holy order when his father died — ready to quit but technically still a Jesuit. And La Salle had since made a name for himself in Canada and on the Great Lakes, including the first voyage down the Mississippi to its mouth to plant the banner of France and claim all of Louisiana. Barely past forty, with nearly twenty years of it in the American wilderness!

La Salle had pointed out to the king that the motions of planting a banner did not really secure a territory. Only a colony could do that. And better still, it should be a settlement that could serve as a base of operations that ranged out in all directions. Particularly in the directions of mines, rich mines. Louis listened. He was fighting a war with Spain even then. Most of the fighting was close at hand in the Netherlands, but the Spanish troops were being paid with silver from the New World. And French troops had to be paid, too.

La Salle asked only for permission to make the attempt, for authority, and beyond that for any help the king might give in the way of ships and money. There were others ready to lend support and men ready to volunteer.

With a few small ships, perhaps four hundred soldiers, a few settlers and artisans, and a small store of ammunition and supplies he would get under way. (The king gave him one ship and the loan of another; he cut the troops to a hundred.)

Along the way La Salle planned to stop in the West Indies and recruit fifty tough buccaneers. (We know that he actually recruited at least one.) Once settled in the colony, he would call down four thousand Indians from the tribes he had united in the Illinois country (none ever came). To these he expected to add enough Indians from the Gulf Coast villages to swell the fighting force to fifteen thousand. (He found no such allies, only enemies.) And with this awesome might he would smash into the northern provinces of Mexico, just below the Rio Grande, capturing the silver mines and consolidating all America from the Great Lakes to the Gulf into a great French empire overseas.

Louis gave his approval, but secretly. There had been too many harebrained schemes such as this and Louis above all was sensitive about ridicule if the plan failed. Also there was no point in letting the Spanish know what was afoot.

At any rate, Louis felt safer with La Salle's proposal than with the ridiculous scheme advanced by that Spaniard with the impossible name of Don Diego Dionisio de Peñalosa Briceno y Berdugo. Besides, Peñalosa's idea might have been planted by the Spanish, for all Louis knew.

Peñalosa had been governor of New Mexico for two or three years, until he crossed up the Spanish Inquisition in the New World. You didn't get off lightly when you did that, and he found himself not only out of a job but out of a title and exiled from all Spanish possessions.

So he tried to peddle the idea of invading Mexico. He even went so far as to write a completely fictitious book about an entirely mythical expedition from New Mexico to the Mississippi.

All he did was pave the way for La Salle, who now stood gazing at the land he was to colonize.

Colonize with what? He turned to gaze across the water at the other ships: the little six-gun frigate, *Belle,* that Louis had given him, and beyond it the smaller supply vessel, *Aimable.*

There had been another, the ketch *St. Francois,* hardly bigger than a yacht and rigged like one. But the Spanish buccaneers seized it when it lagged too far behind as they approached Santo Domingo.

Santo Domingo! Or rather the miserable little seaport of Petit

Gouave, where they had put in for water, and where La Salle had lain sick with fever in a miserable room while the ships' crews drank in the taverns, yelled in the streets, and caroused in the brothels — until he had been compelled to stop all shore leave. That hadn't made them happy, any more than they had liked it when he refused to let them go through their absurd ceremonies as the ships entered the tropics. Threatening to duck the elegant gentlemen in a tub of sea water, just so they could collect a few coins for letting the gallants go free.

Well, here they were at the end of this dull voyage, and little did it matter now if every sailor from the cabin boy to Captain Beaujeu himself passed him with a surly look.

Soon they would land, as soon as they found the proper spot. There was the rub: what would be the proper spot? True, the plan — at least as it was announced — was to go sixty leagues up the Mississippi from its mouth. But where was the mouth? It showed on no maps. La Salle had been there two years before, but he came down from Canada and went back up the stream, knowing only the latitude of the mouth but not its longitude. How could you locate a spot if you knew only one measurement? Well, go to that line and follow it across. So now they were sailing west along the Gulf Coast.

A glance at any modern map of Texas will show how its coast is paralleled by long offshore islands, spits, and sandbars, broken here and there by entrances into bays and lagoons behind these natural breakwaters.

While La Salle was trying to guess which of these bays concealed the mouth of the Mississippi, one of his military engineers, named Minet, suggested that it might be better to put a detachment on shore to seek the river. La Salle at first rejected the idea with such insolence that Minet wrote home that "he treated me as if I were the lowest of mankind." In fact, Minet quit the expedition a few days later. Another example of how to lose friends and alienate people.

But Minet's suggestion was a good one, and La Salle finally put some men ashore on what today is Matagorda Island. They trudged along its shelving, sandy beach until they came to what is now Cavallo Pass, entrance to the bay. They signalled the ships and La Salle landed.

He proclaimed that this was indeed the place he sought.

La Salle stood watching the first vessel to enter: the supply craft

Aimable, moving slowly through the channel marked by men rowing ahead in boats.

Suddenly there was a shout from among the trees behind him. Indians had seized and carried off some of the men in the first landing party. La Salle and some armed companions hurried off in pursuit.

Pursuit was easy. The Indians feared guns and La Salle soon returned with the rescued men — only to find that disaster had fallen in his absence. The *Aimable* had struck a reef and lay rocking in the water with her side split open. Casks and bales tumbled in a sea whipped by a rising storm.

They saved what they could, but it was little enough: some gunpowder, some flour, and little else except what floated ashore — and the Indians stole all they could of that. Gone were nearly all of their medicines, most of the tools and personal baggage of the colonists, the major part of their provisions, together with cannon, cannonballs, more than two tons of lead, a forge and a mill, and boxes of arms.

In spite of this irreparable loss, La Salle decided to stay. Captain Beaujeu made ready to sail back to France in the *Joly,* leaving the little frigate *Belle* with La Salle, the vessel that Louis had given to the explorer as a personal gift.

Beaujeu was glad to turn back. Ever since the whole affair started, back in France, he had been at odds with La Salle. The captain had felt insulted by La Salle's demand for a naval salute so grand that there would have been no greater honors left for a marshal of France.

Beaujeu complained, to anyone who would listen, that this backwoods upstart knew nothing about handling men and changed his mind every few minutes. "He is so suspicious that I dare not ask him anything," Beaujeu wrote. The truth is that La Salle *was* suspicious. He knew that Beaujeu's wife was a strong supporter of the Jesuits, who were apparently anxious to hamstring La Salle's project.

The *Joly* sailed away. The engineer Minet went back with it, and so did some others who had lost heart either in the colony or in La Salle.

Now there were on shore less than two hundred men, women, and children. It was a temporary camp in an unhealthy, unpleasant place. Dysentery was prompt to appear; the water was brackish and bad; the only protection was a rough barricade made of driftwood stumps and rotten logs.

For this goal families had left their homes, artisans their benches, and young women with stars in their eyes had joined to seek a new life in what they believed would surely be an enchanted land.

It didn't take La Salle long to be convinced that he was far from the Mississippi — or maybe he had secretly known this all along and landed where he did just to be nearer the Spanish mines.

The first task was to find a more suitable place for his new settlement. About five miles inland he found a good spot. Some say it was on Garcitas Creek, not far from where Port Lavaca is located today; others say it was over between Menefee and Venada bayous.

Here they built a fort, in that summer of 1685. There was a barracks for the men and another for the women, plus a small chapel and other buildings, all surrounded by a wooden stockade. Every stick of lumber had to be dragged overland or floated upstream. La Salle himself marked off the mortises and tenons after finding that his master carpenter was little more than a wood butcher. The walls had two small cannon at each corner, and another cannon was given to the blacksmith for an anvil.

It was brutal work for unskilled amateurs, wrestling heavy timbers in the hell-hot days of a humid Texas summer. Matters continued to slide downward. Two men were killed trying to recover blankets stolen by the Indians. Another died of snakebite. Two more deserted, either to die or turn savage. A deserter was caught and hanged. Several fell ill after gorging on strange wild fruit. The only carpenter went after some game he saw on the prairie and was never seen again. By the end of October the little cemetery was full. Less than a hundred people remained alive.

There was plenty of game for food, especially buffalo. One man, Joutel, wrote later of his experiences in hunting buffalo and his account would be read sympathetically by any greenhorn hunter today. Like any beginner, Joutel did not know that a primitive musket would drop a buffalo in its tracks only if it were hit in the spine. Time and again he crept in to get a close shot, only to see the bulls go thundering away when they were hit.

"I fired again and again," he wrote, "But could not make one of them fall. I was not discouraged; and after approaching several more bands — which was hard work, because I had to crawl on the ground so as not to be seen — I found myself in a herd of five or six thousand, but to my great vexation I could not bring one of them down. They all ran off to the right and left. It was near night, and I had killed nothing. Though I was very tired, I tried again, approached another band and fired a number of shots, but not a buffalo would fall. The skin was off my knees with crawling. At last as I was going back to rejoin our men I saw a buffalo lying on the ground. I went towards it and saw that it was dead. I examined it and found that the bullet had gone in near the shoulder. Then I found the others dead like the first. I beckoned the men to come up, and we set to work to cut up the meat — a task which was new to us all."

A gun fancier would find little to interest him in the records of the colony. Joutel, who wrote the most detailed account, called his weapon a firelock, a musket, or a piece. He mentioned an inventory of two hundred firelocks and on another occasion spoke of eight hundred balls and three hundred flints. So the weapons were probably flintlocks and not matchlocks or wheellocks.

The French had been making good flintlocks for more than forty years before this trip began. They had sent a regiment to Canada in 1665, equipped with this new firearm. And Louis was at war, so the gunsmiths were busy.

La Salle knew the importance of a weapon on the far frontier. The chances are that he chose carefully. No fancy engraving such as Piraube or Gruché, the Parisian masters of the time, might have put on a royal fowling piece. Just a good sturdy flintlock.

If it followed the typical French design of that era — for those interested in such things — it had a barrel about four feet long, held by pins in a full-length stock that ended flush with the muzzle. There would have been a bit of brass pipe at the front and rear end of the barrel to hold the ramrod.

The lock plate would have had a concave curve in its lower edge, with a raised rim all around the lock plate except at its front. In general the stock looked clumsy; the butt seemed stuffed or inflated, almost leg-o'-mutton. The heel would have been concave and the trigger guard heavy and round, with a tang running down the butt halfway to the heel. If there were a sling, it would have been on the side away from the lock. The flint was probably gray or white, rounded at its heel in the French style. The piece fired a one-ounce ball. It might kill at a hundred yards or it might not.

Anyway, if you find one today it will bring enough to put your kid through a year of college.

Now that the walls were up and the storeroom stocked with buffalo meat, La Salle could start doing what he came to do, go after the Spaniards or the Mississippi or both. In October, 1685, he started off on the first of three trips he made from the stockade that he had named Fort Saint Louis.

He went with fifty men, well armed and wearing makeshift armor: a sort of corselet made of tough wooden splints laced together with thongs. Proof enough against most Indian arrows. From what we can gather, he went west to look for Spanish garrisons.

Six months later, in March, 1866, he was back, emptyhanded. About this time, the little frigate *Belle* met its end. First it lost part of its crew during a short excursion upstream. The men went ashore to sleep and were killed by Indians. Then the *Belle* went out into the bay, where it was wrecked and all but six of its crew drowned.

Now La Salle was cut off from the world. It was obvious that he must open a line of communication eastward to the Mississippi if the colony were to survive.

He started out with twenty of the remaining men and probably went as far east as the Trinity River, not too far from today's Texas-Louisiana line. When their ammunition ran low and their health turned poor, they backtracked to the little fort. Only eight of the twenty made it back. Four had deserted, one was eaten by an alligator, one became lost, and six others died of various causes, chiefly exhaustion.

Two who came back played a role in later events. One was an ex-buccaneer named Hiens: a German who had sailed with English pirates. La Salle had recruited him when they stopped at Santo Domingo, and the rugged Hiens found a sympathetic chord in La Salle, who preferred a fighting man to a city-bred weakling. The other man to remember was a Shawnee Indian named Nika, captured by the Iroquois and given by them to La Salle years before. Nika followed La Salle to the end.

It was now August, 1686. The colony had been in its stockade for more than a year. Now only about fifty persons remained. Morale was gloomy; it was harder and harder to keep the men and women from slipping away together on occasion. As the situation worsened, La Salle became even more stern and harsh, sometimes downright unjust. It wasn't that he had a mean streak in him, far from it. He simply couldn't understand why other people didn't have his devotion to the expedition, or why they couldn't muster the endurance he had.

Take the young Marquis de la Sablonniere for example. A nobleman, yes, but his entire estate rattled in the scabbard at his side. After a riotous interval when the *Joly* touched at Petit Gouave, Sablonniere staggered back on board broke. Even worse was the disease he acquired ashore. Now he couldn't march on any long trips. He had learned nothing — even at Fort Saint Louis, his supplies were issued in daily lots; if he were given more, he gambled or traded it all away. Useless.

La Salle's suspicions increased as the weeks passed. Finally it came to the point where not even a member of the small colony could be admitted to the fort without the day's password. Once Duhaut was out with a scouting party led by La Salle. Along the way Duhaut stopped to mend a moccasin and then took the wrong buffalo trail when he tried to catch up. A signal shot brought no reply. All Duhaut could do was to return to the fort. He didn't know the password but finally talked his way in. When La Salle returned there was an angry scene. To Duhaut it was one more of a long series of injustices, most of them in the presence of his young servant, Jean l'Archeveque, who shared his master's feelings.

Sometimes Duhaut compared notes with Liotot, a surgeon at the colony. On one scouting trip Liotot's brother was ready to drop from exhaustion. La Salle told him to go back to the fort by himself. On the way he was killed by Indians. From then on Liotot was convinced that La Salle had deliberately sent his brother to his death.

Supplies were running out; so was time and so were lives. La Salle decided to make one more try — this time not toward the Mississippi but toward Canada itself. As the year drew toward its end they made their preparations. On New Year's Eve they drank a toast in cold water — all wine and brandy was used or lost long before — and in January, 1787, they started on what would be the last trip.

There were seventeen of them, with five packhorses laden with trade goods, ammunition, and a few other supplies. They would live off the country as they traveled.

Next to La Salle in rank was his nephew Moranget, his brother the priest, and the Sieur de Marle. No matter how primitive the conditions might be, La Salle insisted upon formalities, deference, salutes, the recognition and privileges of birth and station. The men found it hard to pay such respects to Moranget, who matched La Salle in haughtiness and exceeded him in the art of verbal abuse.

The real number two man was Joutel, who wrote the whole story of what happened later.

This little group started northeast across Texas, crossing stream after stream. The cavalcade drew curious Indians like a Shriners' parade. There were always red men following or flanking the seventeen, observing and annoying the strange little column.

Anyone who has ever driven through that part of south central Texas that lies today between the towns of Victoria and Navasota knows that the countryside has a certain sameness. A level prairie broken at times by slight hills, scores of little streams and two major rivers (the Colorado and the Brazos), open meadows, belts of trees, and occasional marshland. The nights in January and February can drop to freezing, and rains are frequent — sometimes lasting three or four days. The days are not too uncomfortable except when a norther blows down from the Panhandle.

The seventeen moved along steadily, slogging in footgear of rawhide buffalo skin that had to be kept wet to stay pliable. Later they traded with Indians for some dressed skins that made more comfortable moccasins.

They made a crude bullboat of buffalo hide that could be carried on the packhorses, and with this they crossed the seemingly countless little streams, creeks, bayous, and rivers. There was little social conversation; two and a half years' common experience had not joined them together but had built walls of silence, suspicion, even hate.

In the Ides of March, 1687, they came to a certain fateful camp.

Today if you drive from Houston northwest toward Texas A&M University near Bryan, you pass through the little town of Navasota. At a jog in the main street, off to the right, you may see a statue in the esplanade about a block east. It commemorates La Salle's camp nearby. (There are those who say the camp was really somewhere else, but this makes little difference because you are remembering the man more than the place.)

La Salle chose the campsite. It seemed to be vaguely familiar. Then he recalled that the year before, on his unsuccessful trip to find the Mississippi, he had buried some grain and beans not far from this place.

The next morning he sent seven men to hunt for the grain. It took them the better part of the day, and when they found the cache the grain and beans were rotten. On their way back they spotted some buffalo, the first real game in some time. The Shawnee hunter, Nika, dropped two animals.

Also with the seven was another Indian, a Mohegan named Saget who had been with La Salle almost as long as Nika. Saget was sent back to the base camp with a message: did La Salle want them to bring in only a part of the meat or all of it for curing? If they were to bring it all they needed horses sent up from the main camp.

Knowing that the main camp was several hours' march away, the hunters decided to start curing the meat at once. They made a rough camp and built light scaffolds to hold the meat in the smoke.

Around the fire were Duhaut, his servant L'Archeveque, Liotot the surgeon, Hiens the ex-buccaneer, a man named Teissier, and Nika the Shawnee hunter.

The next morning, La Salle told his nephew Moranget and the Sieur de Marle to take horses and fetch the meat. Saget would guide them.

When these three reached the hunters' camp they found the meat only partially cured. The hunters were seated around the fire enjoying an age-long privilege of men who killed game: cooking the scrap bones to enjoy the rich marrow and the bits of remaining flesh.

Moranget, ignoring the traditional rights of hunters, "fell into a most unreasonable fit of rage, berated and menaced Duhaut and his party, and ended by seizing upon the whole of the meat" including even the marrow bones.

This was not the first time that Moranget's violence had fallen on the men, but it would be the last time. Liotot in particular remembered when he had doctored Moranget for an arrow wound, to be repaid only with insults.

As darkness fell the hunters moved off to one side and huddled in a discussion. Moranget paid little heed; surly grumblings were common.

In the group of five plotters were the two who hated La Salle the most: Duhaut and Liotot, together with Hiens. L'Archeveque, and Teissier. Back by the fire sat those who were still loyal: Moranget, De Marle, and La Salle's two devoted Indians, Nika and Saget.

The hunters agreed that there was no course open except to kill Moranget, and this meant killing Nika and Saget as well. It might even mean that La Salle must die.

Killing was not new to an ex-buccaneer such as Hiens; the necessity overruled his slight friendship for La Salle, who had given him occasional favors. Hiens voted for death.

Teissier abstained, saying he would neither aid nor oppose the plot. L'Archeveque, who at this time was only sixteen and a fledgling poet, and was possibly easily influenced, agreed to go along with the plans of his master Duhaut. All five returned to the campfire.

It was customary to stand guard by turns. Possibly as part of the plan, it was scheduled so that Moranget, Saget, and Nika would take the first three watches.

After the last had stood his turn, the conspirators arose silently. Duhaut and Hiens cocked their guns and stood ready to shoot anyone who moved.

Liotot picked up an axe, crept toward the sleeping figures, and in turn struck a deadly blow at Nika, Saget, and Moranget. The first two died instantly. Moranget tried to sit up but could not speak. De Marle was awakened and ordered to complete the death of Moranget or die himself. He did as he was told. The plotters felt this would involve De Marle deeply enough to guarantee his silence.

When morning came, the hunters started to load the meat on the packhorses, but the river had swollen enough during the night that a crossing would have been difficult. They decided to wait.

In the base camp, La Salle grew worried as the day passed and no hunters had returned. By evening he decided to go in search of the men, and arranged for one of the ever-present local Indian camp-followers to be a guide.

In the morning, La Salle told Joutel to stay in camp and to take charge, but he asked Joutel for his pistol, the best one in camp. Accompanied by the friar Anastase Douay and an Indian guide, La Salle left camp. The date was March 20, 1687.

Still some distance from the hunters' camp, La Salle saw carrion birds circling in the sky ahead. He fired his musket and his pistol as a signal to summon the hunters.

The men in camp heard the shots. Duhaut, Liotot, L'Archeveque, and possibly Hiens, quickly left camp and went upstream where there were trees and bushes to conceal their movement and where they could now cross the river to be on the same bank as the approaching La Salle.

L'Archeveque went on ahead, openly; the others hid in the under-brush along the bank.

La Salle was coming forward when he saw L'Archeveque and asked him if he had seen Moranget. L'Archeveque replied that Moranget was somewhere around, walking along the river. While making this reply the youth neglected, either deliberately or from panic, to touch his hat in the usual salute. La Salle at once broke into a severe rebuke, to which L'Archeveque made a rude answer as he moved back toward the bushes where the others were concealed.

La Salle continued forward. Duhaut fired a sudden quick shot and La Salle dropped.

It was over. Yet in another sense it had only begun.

Friar Douay stood beside the crumpled body, stiff with terror. The killers came out of the bushes, telling the priest he had nothing to fear. The men moved up and looked down at the dead man.

"There you lie, great Pasha, there you lie!" cried Liotot.

La Salle was only forty-three, one of the greatest men of his times, capable of overcoming any obstacles except his own haughtiness and harshness.

Joulet later recorded that the conspirators stripped his body, shouting insults upon it, and dragged it into the bushes without any pretense of burial.

During all this some Indians watched, astounded by the whole affair. Duhaut took them across the river and made the natives load the buffalo meat on the horses. Then the party returned to the base camp.

Father Douay rushed into the rough shelter occupied by La Salle's brother, the priest, to tell the story. The others at the camp begged for their lives, but Duhaut — now master of the little expedition — told them there was no need for more deaths.

When Duhaut and the others arrived with their terrible message, Joutel was not in the camp. He was off beyond a small hill, keeping watch over the small horse herd and tending a fire of dried grass so its smoke might guide La Salle's return.

History has named L'Archeveque as one of the killers. There are circumstances that indicate that he was probably no more than a youth who went along with the decisions of his elders. There is a further extenuating factor: he was a friend of Joutel and seeing that Joutel was not in camp went to tell him the news.

"I was very much surprised when I saw him coming," records Joutel. "When he came up to me he seemed all in confusion, or, rather, out of his wits. He began with saying that there was very bad news. I asked what it was. He answered that the Sieur de la Salle was dead, and also his nephew the Sieur de Moranget, his Indian hunter, and his servant. . . . The man added that, at first, the murderers had sworn to kill me too. . . . L'Archeveque assured me that they had changed their minds and had agreed to murder nobody else unless they met with resistance."

The party now numbered thirteen. The next day they held a council and decided to proceed, at least as far as some Indian villages reached by La Salle on his trip the previous year.

They moved out, the two factions apprehensive of each other. A week later they came near the villages they sought, which they called Cenis and were probably Caddo Indians. These Indians had horses, descendants of Spanish animals — possibly from DeSoto's expedition, and a few of the braves carried Spanish swords.

The venturers made camp a short distance before the village. Duhaut stayed in camp and sent Joutel, Hiens, Liotot, and Teissier ahead to find out if the Indians were friendly.

They found the Indians friendly enough, and some of the Frenchmen noticed the women: tattooed like the men, with charcoal powder rubbed into needle-pricked skin. Joulet recorded that the women tattooed the corners of their eyes and "made more particular show on their well-shaped bosoms," remarking that tattooing in that particular area must have been painful. He added that the women were generally virtuous, but their virtue was not always proof against the offer of a string of beads.

A Frenchman from Provence was living among the Indians as an equal. He was a deserter from La Salle's trip in the previous year, and he told Joutel there were two other deserters living nearby who feared to come forward if La Salle was in command.

On learning that La Salle was dead, the other two came into camp. One was a man from Brittany, a quarrelsome fellow named Ruter who later became a companion of Hiens. He was tattooed in the Indian fashion and had his hair trimmed to a scalplock.

The other, who later played a curious role in this adventure, was Jacques Grolet (sometimes spelled Groslet, Grole, or Grollet), born in La Rochelle, France, where he became a sailor and served in La Salle's fleet when it sailed from La Rochelle. As yet, Grolet had refused to be tattooed or to have his hair cut. He was perhaps five years older than L'Archeveque, and the two became close companions after their reunion.

The four men went back to Duhaut's camp with provisions, and the venturers rested for several days debating the best course to follow. The two groups cooked and ate apart: La Salle's friends around one fire, his enemies at another. Duhaut's group decided to return to the little colony; the others agreed among themselves to press on toward Canada, but they kept this secret from Duhaut.

Hiens and others went back to the Indian villages to trade for more horses. While they were gone, Duhaut learned of Joutel's plan to head for Canada. Instead of opposing the idea, he changed his mind abruptly and said he would go along. Joutel suspected he would go along only until he had an opportunity to kill them all.

Hiens came back with the horses and learned of Duhaut's change of mind. He strode up to Duhaut and said he would have nothing to do with the new plan, that he (Hiens) still intended to return to the little Fort Saint Louis and demanded his share of supplies and trade goods.

Duhaut said that he was in charge of the goods.

"So you won't give them to me?" answered Hiens.

"No."

"You wretch!" shouted Heins, in the dime novel language of the ancient records. "You killed my master!" At this Hiens drew his pistol and killed Duhaut.

Simultaneously Ruter — who had returned with Hiens from the Indian village — fired his musket at Liotot "who fell pierced by three balls." (As recently as the American Revolution, it was not uncommon for muskets to be loaded with more than one ball, although Washington's men usually preferred one regular ball and two to four large buckshot.)

L'Archeveque was at the moment off hunting. Aware that the youth was Duhaut's servant, Hiens said he would kill L'Archeveque as well. Joutel and the priests talked him out of it.

Now there was another interruption in their plans. When Hiens went back to the Indian villages to trade for horses, the natives had asked if he and the others would aid them in a war, and he had agreed. Hiens, L'Archeveque, Grolet, and another man went back to accompany the Indians. In a few days they were back safely, with news of a victory made easy by their firearms.

It was now time to end their indecision. Joutel and the other friends of La Salle made ready to head out for Canada. L'Archeveque begged to go with them if they would forgive him. La Salle's brother, the priest, said he would grant his forgiveness.

Hiens stuck by his intention to return to Fort St. Louis, but he agreed to divide the supplies. Then at the last minute L'Archeveque changed his mind again and decided not to go to Canada.

So seven men headed out for France: La Salle's brother, the nephew Cavelier, Joutel, the Sieur de Marle, a young Parisian named Bartholomew, Father Anastase Douay, and Teissier — the only one of the conspirators who went on to Canada. De Marle was drowned by accident while bathing; the other six made it to Montreal where Teissier, a Protestant, at once joined the Church. It took them almost eighteen months to reach France from the Indian villages.

Hiens, Ruter, L'Archeveque, Grolet, and two others turned back toward the little colony. Hiens was killed by Ruter in an argument; Ruter and two others disappeared to an unknown fate. L'Archeveque and Grolet still had a strange new life to come.

For there were still the Spanish to reckon with.

The Spaniards in the New World had not been ignorant of the fact that La Salle was up to something. There had been a leak at Santo Domingo, confirmed in 1685 when the crew of a captured French frigate blurted out mention of La Salle's colony near the bay.

In the next four years small Spanish search parties hunted for La Salle. No luck. Then they captured a French deserter named Jean Gery, living with the Indians. He was taken to Mexico City and to the viceroy, where he described the location of the settlement in detail.

The result was immediate assignment of Alonso de Leon to head an expedition to clean out the French colony. De Leon moved out in March, 1689. La Salle had then been dead two years.

The remnant of the colony near Lavaca Bay had been in pitiful shape when La Salle left. Then there were perhaps a score of adults and several children. Some of these died of smallpox. Three months before De Leon's men arrived, the Karankawa Indians ambushed and butchered most of the remaining settlers, carried off a few captives, and pillaged the fort.

L'Archeveque and Grolet, living in nearby Indian villages under conditions delicately balanced between death and friendship, could do nothing to warn the settlers. After the massacre the two men went to the fort and buried fourteen bodies.

When De Leon's men approached there was only the silence of death hanging over a half-ruined stockade. No sentries, no banners. One account says, "The Spaniards spurred their reluctant horses through the gateway, and a scene of desolation met their sight. No living thing was stirring. Doors were torn from their hinges; broken boxes, staved barrels, and rusty kettles, mingled with a great number of stocks of arquebuses and muskets, were scattered about in confusion. Here, too, trampled in mud and soaked with rain, they saw more than two hundred books, many of which still retained traces of costly bindings. On the adjacent prairie lay three dead bodies, one of which, from fragments of dress still clinging to the wasted remains, they saw to be that of a woman."

The first settlement in Texas was ended.

L'Archeveque and Grolet knew when the Spaniards reached the fort. They knew, too, that their lives were at risk. Still, they sent a messenger with a curiously inscribed document to De Leon, who replied with an offer of good treatment if they came forward.

Two "Indians" approached the Spanish camp, wrapped in buffalo robes and with tattooed faces. They were L'Archeveque and Grolet.

In a letter written at this time by one of De Leon's soldiers he mentioned the surrender of these two Frenchmen who had been living with the "Texas Indians." It was the first known use of the word *Texas* in written history.

And before De Leon started back, he left on the banks of Garcitas Creek a bull, a cow, a stallion, and a mare. The start of the Texas livestock industry!

A year later De Leon returned to Texas to establish a Spanish colony. On this trip he rescued from the Indians three French youths who had been held captive by the Indians. One of them was Pierre Meusnier, then aged twenty. Pierre's father had been court treasurer to Louis XIV and the youth had been in La Salle's special care.

But the story did not end there; the strange chain of events that began when Duhaut hired young L'Archeveque was destined to run for three more decades.

L'Archeveque and Grolet were taken to Mexico City, before the viceroy. Then they were sent to Spain, but were back in Mexico in 1693.

In that year L'Archeveque started out on another expedition to a distant colony—this time into New Mexico.

Thirteen years earlier, in 1680, the Indians of New Mexico rose in revolt, killed many of the priests in the pueblo missions, and drove all Spaniards south to El Paso. In 1692 an expedition under Diego de Vargas reconquered the province and then returned to El Paso to escort settlers returning to Santa Fe.

With them went Jean L'Archeveque, now known as Juan de Archibeque (or sometimes Archibec). In El Paso he had a reunion with Pierre Meusnier, now Pedro Munier, a settler recuited to go north. Jacques Grolet, now known as Santiago Grole (or Gurule) was still on the scene but not as a soldier. Archibeque and Grole still bore traces of Indian tattoo marks on·their faces. The men ranged in age from twenty-two to twenty-nine.

Grole settled down as a farmer at Bernalillo and was still mentioned in records in 1705. Meusnier was still in Santa Fe in 1699. All three men married, and on at least two of the occasions the others of the trio turned up to sign the wedding documents.

To appreciate what happened next, it is important to understand that men of the early West were not tied to their hearths. The traders, trappers, and adventurers ranged over vast distances. In total numbers the population was small, yet its members encountered each other time and again in the most remote and unlikely places.

There were no real boundaries of states or provinces. The claims of France, Spain, and England were vague and overlapping. A border was "over yonder". Except for El Paso, where Juarez is today, Santa Fe was the only significant town in the entire West. There was nothing in California; even Saint Louis and New Orleans did not exist in A.D. 1700.

The few people in the new Spanish settlements in Texas were oriented toward Mexico City, but they considered the Platte River in present Nebraska as still within their rightful sphere. The small French settlements in Illinois similarly looked west and southwest.

Archibeque became a successful merchant in Santa Fe, also a member of the militia and at one time served as a junior alcalde or vice-mayor. In those days citizens often took part — voluntarily or otherwise — in Spanish military expeditions to keep the Indians under control. In 1702, Archibeque went on such a trip with Captain Juan de Uribarri to the pueblos of Acoma and Zuni.

Some Indians from the pueblo of Picurīs had gone over into what is now Kansas to settle at a place called El Cuartelejo, a few miles below

present Scott City. In 1706 Captain Uribarri led a force to El Cuartelejo and took possession of it for Spain. Archibeque went along. In
that same year he became the official post trader at El Cuartelejo —
the first Indian trader on the great plains.

After a short time in this lonely but profitable outpost, Captain
Archibeque went back to Santa Fe. By now he had two children, plus
a son "by an unwed woman." Sometime before 1719 his wife died.
Archibeque married again, but in the interim he had another son by
a servant girl. At his second marriage in 1719 his best man was none
other than Governor Antonio Valverde y Cosio.

During these years the French were making excursions toward New
Mexico from various directions. In 1719 it was reported that a group
of armed Frenchmen were at a camp of Pawnee Indians on the Platte
River, in Nebraska, where it forks to form its northern and southern
branches. Governor Valverde was ordered to send a force to drive out
the intruders.

Lieutenant Colonel Pedro de Villasur was ordered to take the field
with a force of about forty men. With him went Archibeque in a
triple capacity: first as the confidant of the governor, to keep an eye
on Villasur; second as an able interpreter if they needed to parley
with the French; third as a trader, for he loaded ten horses and six
mules with packs of trade goods, just to do a little good business on
the side if the chance arose.

The chance never arose. On August 15, 1720, Villasur's men came
in sight of the Pawnee camp where hundreds of braves waited, fully
aware of the approaching Spanish. With them were said to be several French equipped with firearms.

The Spanish forces camped for the night. Next morning as they
arose to lay plans for the battle they were surprised by the Indians.
Two-thirds of the Santa Fe men fell in the first volley. One of the
first to die was Archibeque, just mounting a horse held by his servant
Santiago Giravalle. It was practically the Custer fight — more than
a hundred and fifty years ahead of its time. Only a half dozen of the
Spanish lived to carry back the message of defeat.

One version of this tale, not well documented, says that among
the French was young Cavelier, La Salle's nephew, bringing a
strange retribution for his uncle's death. Even if true, he could
hardly have known in advance that his old foe, L'Archeveque-
Archibeque would be facing him.

But one result was sure: the Spanish would never again maintain real power as far north as the Platte. The borders were now closing in upon Texas. In 1718 — while the French were approaching the Pawnee village on the Platte — the Spanish established a mission at San Antonio, where six years later they would select the site for the Alamo.

La Salle's lost colony had spurred the Spanish into settling the land that was now to be known as Texas.

2

Filibusters West

IN THE GOLDEN AUTUMN of 1812 a young Mexican general rode southwestward out of Louisiana. His trail roughly backtracked the route taken long before by La Salle's leaderless men when they fled to Canada. General José Bernardo Gutiérrez de Lara, then thirty-eight, was on his way to proclaim the first Republic of Texas and give the new state its first constitution.

His green banner flaunted ambitiously for less than a year, but it was the first gambit in a game where the pieces moved inexorably toward Mexican independence from Spain, then Texas' independence from Mexico, and finally to the United States' conquest of the Southwest.

Gutiérrez' rank as general had been conferred only through election by his followers, but it was not a tavern revolution inspired by a fanatic. He had a strong base of support in Mexico; Washington circles had given their tacit approval, and one of the first secret agents of the United States helped guide his strategy. Beside the general rode a brilliant ex-officer of the American army.

Bad luck and worse judgment, combined with an ignorance of the odds against him, would doom Gutiérrez' uprising but it could never sully what became a legend of patriotism.

What history called the Gutiérrez-Magee Expedition was an extension of an uprising that already had started. A revolution had begun throughout all Mexico in 1810, with the *padre* Hidalgo as its central figure. It had spread, with varying success, to all of the Mexican states including Texas.

One of Hidalgo's provincial leaders was young José Bernardo Gutiérrez de Lara, an ironworker in the village of Revilla (today Guerrero), just below the Rio Grande. The revolutionists twice had been unsuccessful in getting an emissary through to Washington, and Gutiérrez was named for the third try.

Late in July, 1811, the thirty-seven-year-old insurgent left with several companions on his trip across frontier America. His diary describes his experiences. Across Texas the men rode the back trails to avoid capture by the royalists. Just before they reached the United States' border of Louisiana they were nearly caught. As it was, they escaped without funds or documents.

They headed for the Louisiana town of Natchitoches, but word of their coming had traveled ahead. A party of armed men came out from the village to escort them safely. There he met Dr. John Sibley, a United States Indian agent who kept an eye open for anything of significance to his country. Sibley recognized Gutiérrez as a man of possible historical importance and helped the young Mexican proceed, with a boy companion, along his route east. He went to Natchez and then over the outlaw-infested Natchez Trace to Nashville and on to Virginia and the nation's capital.

It was a journey filled with strange sights: Indians dining off china plates, using a knife and fork "with amazing dexterity;" town jails with pillories in front; ferryboats; children "as white as the very snow, so that I wondered at seeing them;" water-powered gristmills, and a thousand curious novelties.

Gutiérrez' opinions of the frontier people were enlightening: Americans make their wives work incessantly; the very rich and the very poor are friendly and hospitable, but the middle classes, especially innkeepers, treat strangers with contempt; husbands and wives often fight; but, in general, the Americans are a happy people.

In Washington the young representative from Mexico was given the full treatment of hospitality, intrigue, and promises. He met Secretary of State James Monroe and spent a great deal of time with Secretary of War Eustis (to whom Dr. John Sibley reported regularly) and with John Graham, the chief clerk of the State Department.

All of these visits were actually quite unofficial, for the United States was still on formal good terms with Spain. Hidalgo was dead and the revolution apparently crushed, but the United States was aware of the smoldering sentiment of the people.

Gutiérrez asked for military aid. This, said the officials, could not be given, but if war were to start between the United States and Great Britain, Monroe said he probably would approve sending fifty thousand soldiers to help Mexico secure its independence.

The young Mexican also asked for freedom of trade across the border and for American resistance to intervention by any other power in the internal affairs of Mexico. On both points he received smooth replies that he accepted as encouraging, although he realized they were not formal commitments at the time.

In reality, the men at Washington wanted to drain Gutiérrez of all possible information that might give them a clue to the trend of events in Mexico. To keep their options open, they treated him with all possible friendliness. And at the same time they were sizing him up as a figure of possible importance in future affairs in the Southwest. Although they did little at the time beyond advancing him funds for expenses on his return trip, Gutiérrez was to learn later that steps would be taken to aid his cause — within limits.

And so, for a month in Washington and another in Philadelphia, he enjoyed the scenes of the eastern capitals. He visited an arsenal, a hospital, an art gallery, a madhouse, and saw a street parade of Freemasons.

His diary contains two curious entries, incomplete in themselves, but the sort of thing a man might write to help him recall strange events:

(Washington, Dec. 24, 1811.) "... At night we returned home and had supper. My grand doctor [acquaintance] and other gentlemen asked me to get into the carriage and accompany them to the house of one of them; I did not go there, however, because they took me to another place where I saw things which in all my life I had never seen before. O what formidable mirrors there are in here in which to see the monstrosity of the world. Note: The Doctor was also a contemptible runt."

And another, when he was in Philadelphia: (February 3, 1812.) "At night I went to pay a visit to a handsome young woman, one of the principal women of the city, who did me the distinguished honor to admit me to her boudoir. This is a mark of distinction which is shown to very few persons — this is the custom of the country — be their rank what it may."

But Gutiérrez would return with more than curious memories. Before his journey ended, he made two new friends — one of whom would become his deadliest rival and the other his closest counsellor.

The first of these he met in Washington: a thirty-three-year-old Cuban exile named José Alvarez de Toledo y Dubois. Toledo was aflame with zeal for independence in the Americas, and the two men spoke eagerly in Spanish of their dreams.

Toledo had been born in Cuba, and educated in Spain, at the Spanish equivalent of Annapolis. When Spain tried to offer concessions to its colonies by inviting delegates to sit in the Cortes, Toledo had been the representative from Santo Domingo. He soon saw that there was no substitute for independence, or at least for home rule, and his fiery remarks put him in disfavor. The American consul at Cadiz helped him flee from Spain, and in 1811 he arrived in Philadelphia.

Toledo was more concerned with freedom in the West Indies than in Mexico. He went to Washington to talk with Secretary of State James Monroe, and there he learned that Gutiérrez had already arrived with news of a ferment below the Rio Grande.

After the two young revolutionists had met and exchanged enthusiasms, each reinforcing the other's spirit, Gutiérrez sailed for New Orleans, via Havana. Toledo went back to Philadelphia and began to build plans in a new direction, toward Mexico and especially toward Texas.

Gutiérrez had an uneventful voyage, with only a single day in Havana. He reached New Orleans on March 23 and went at once to present his letter of introduction to Governor Claiborne of Louisiana.

At the governor's mansion Gutiérrez met his second new friend, William Shaler, who was outwardly a United States consul visiting in New Orleans. In reality he was a secret agent of the State Department, waiting intentionally for Gutiérrez. Before the first day ended, the young revolutionist was Shaler's house guest.

Shaler was a remarkable individual, worthy of a biography that could easily equal any modern tale of counter-espionage. His father had commanded a privateer in the American Revolution, and young William was himself a captain before he was thirty. He sailed on

venturesome voyages to South America and then entered the profitable trade of carrying furs across the Pacific to Canton. Sailing in
those warm, blue waters, he stopped at Hawaii and won the confidence of King Kamehameha.

That slight venture into international relations brought Shaler to
the attention of the American government, especially because of the
detailed report he wrote for the *American Register* in 1808 about
his experiences. The officials at Washington asked him to take a
consular post in Mexico, and Shaler agreed.

He went first to Havana, only to learn there that Mexico refused
him admittance to Vera Cruz. For three months he stayed in the
Cuban port, and then word came for him to proceed to New Orleans. There his new assignment was to report on (and guide if possible) the activities of Mexican revolutionaries operating out of
Louisiana. Since his new orders reached him only a few weeks after
Secretary of State Monroe had first talked with Gutiérrez in Washington, it is probable that a calculated directive had been sent by
fast packet ship.

About two weeks after his arrival in New Orleans, Gutiérrez was
ready to leave for Natchitoches in northwestern Louisiana. Shaler,
of course, went along. Their boat sailed leisurely up the Mississippi
to the mouth of the Red River, and then they sailed and rowed as
far up the Red as it was navigable. They went the rest of the way
overland and reached the border outpost in late April.

Only months before, Gutiérrez had come out of Mexico to the
same town almost as a fugitive. Now he had a mysterious aura about
him, an importance that hinted of high approval from Washington.
He was wined and feasted by military and civil officials; he had
time to inspect the town, which had stores and businesses that were
surprising for a backwoods village in 1812.

Two things were unusual enough to be mentioned in his diary:
one was a printing plant that produced with amazing ease a thousand
copies of a proclamation he could send into Texas; the other was
a visit to a Methodist church.

In the Protestant service he found the congregation "praying to
the All-Powerful in a manner at which I wondered. The priests
preach with shouts, making gestures with their hands as if in applause; all to the end that the people be moved to pray to God for
forgiveness of their sins. This they do so entirely from the heart

casting all their eyes to the ground they utter loud cries, shed tears, and the women faint. I, though evil, prayed to God our Lord, of His mercy to be pleased to shed upon these people a ray of His Divine light."

Gutiérrez then settled down to the business of organizing his invasion force. There were frequent meetings with Shaler and Dr. Sibley; strange visitors came and wer⁺ The little town took these events calmly, because Natchitoches had long been the crossroads of intrigue and turmoil — although never before had there been so many cross-currents of political influence.

Foremost, of course, was the continuing rumble of revolution in Mexico. For the Americans this was matched in importance by talk of a coming war between the United States and England. The start of the War of 1812 was only weeks away.

In Spain itself, the French under Bonaparte were fighting a combination of English and loyal Spanish. There were reports that French agents in the Americas were seeking to swing Mexican support to Bonaparte, or at least to neutralize Mexico. There were other reports that Spanish elements, both in Spain and in Mexico, who were pro-French, were seeking to turn Mexico completely over to Bonaparte's growing empire.

Nor was there complete assurance in Mexico that the United States itself did not have designs on Texas. The Louisiana Purchase was not yet ten years past, and the French had once claimed all of Texas to the Rio Grande. Might not the U.S. feel it already owned Texas? There was also the mystery of General James Wilkinson of the U.S., who was supposed to have sinister ambitions although he had exposed Aaron Burr's conspiracy to carve out a new and separate empire in the Southwest. In Mexico, people were still arguing over the real purpose of Zebulon Pike's excursion into the Rockies a few years before.

Altogether it was a highly charged atmosphere, in which any man — Spanish, English, French, Anglo-American, and even Mexican — might be on either side. Letters were constantly going off to Washington, Madrid, London, Paris, and Mexico City. There were agents, double agents, and men who might be recruited as agents.

In such a situation, Gutiérrez could not openly mobilize a force in Natchitoches. Men were being assembled in the country west and southwest of the town, ready to flow together on command.

The largest of these units was being organized by an ex-officer of the U.S. Army, Augustus William Magee. He was a tall, handsome Bostonian, twenty-three years old, three years out of West Point (where only two classmates had graduated with higher standing), and he had served more than two years on the Louisiana frontier as an artillery officer.

Just why Magee chose to resign his commission on June 22, 1812, and start recruiting a corps of filibusters was never revealed. A requested promotion had been denied, and that was given as the reason for his dissatisfaction. But he had been a protegé of General Wilkinson, a politically astute officer, and may have had his own ambitions stirred by the acquaintance. And Wilkinson's own son was with this expedition.

At any rate, Magee threw himself enthusiastically into the work of mobilizing an invasion force, unaware it was an expedition from which he would not return. In six weeks he built a formidable group of perhaps a hundred and fifty men, and it was increasing rapidly.

Magee knew how to deal with frontiersmen on their own terms. While stationed at frontier army posts he had used severe tactics on captured brigands, not hesitating to put them to the lash — a common practice in armies and navies of that period — but on at least one occasion even ordered hot coals placed on the back of one bandit who would not name his accomplices.

Some of the renegades Magee had once punished were ready to join his new army, enticed by the chance for loot. Others sought the promised pay, which was good: forty dollars a month and a square league of land for all who served six months. Not all recruits were frontier bravos. Some were genuine Mexican patriots seeking home rule. Others were Anglo-Americans sympathetic to the cause, and some of these were prominent men who traveled long distances to join. They included such men as Warren D. C. Hall; Samuel Kemper, who had helped bring Spanish West Florida into the United States; a Louisiana sheriff named James Gaines; a physician, Forsythe; Owen, a merchant; together with such experienced fighters as Reuben Ross and Henry Perry.

One of his best men was Peter Samuel Davenport, a man in his late forties, born in Pennsylvania but with a score or more years' experience along the Louisiana-Texas border as a freighter. Davenport had been a trusted agent for the Spanish at nearby Nacogdoches in Texas but was ready to quit their cause. As Magee's quartermaster officer he was invaluable in acquiring supplies.

Gutiérrez remained at Natchitoches during this recruiting, knowing what his eventual course would be but waiting for the precise moment to move. He discussed each move with Shaler, who dutifully sent reports back to Washington. Gutiérrez also talked with a French agent named Despallier.

Magee's men moved out first, on August 12. Gutiérrez stayed back at Natchitoches. Magee's men hit the first Mexican border outpost at dawn, and only one of the twenty men there managed to get away to carry the warning ahead to Nacogdoches; five other were killed or wounded.

The commander at Nacogdoches tried to rally his people for defense; they showed little interest. Finally the commander, Zambrano, had to ride out of the town, followed by only ten loyal men.

Magee's men marched in unopposed, seizing six hundred mules and horses, plus a fair amount of silver coin, together with an ample supply of lances, gunpowder, and food.   Gutiérrez came at once from Natchitoches. Shaler remained behind.

For the next three or four weeks, the forces remained at Nacogdoches and became a unified force when they could operate openly. They called themselves the Republican Army of the North. Gutiérrez was named general; Magee became colonel. The Americans were formed into five infantry companies, with Ross, Perry, Hall, Gaines, and a man named Luckett as captains. Kemper became major. Gutiérrez sent handwritten proclamations into Texas, as far as Bexar (San Antonio). These proclaimed the new republic and said that the cause was aided by American volunteers who were "free descendants of the men who fought for the independence of the United States."

More men came in constantly to augment the companies. Many from the former Spanish garrison joined the new colors and were formed into a mounted unit. Gutiérrez later reported that the force had included four hundred men when it entered Nacogdoches and grew to seven hundred by mid-September. These figures may have included many who were not fighting men, because Gutiérrez said that out of the seven hundred last-named only four hundred and fifty were "well armed and united." The green flag of the first Texas

Republic was ready to wave over the new state.

In October, Gutiérrez was ready to move deeper into Texas. It was easy to choose an objective, because there were really only two towns of any importance: San Fernando de Bexar, then usually called Bexar and today known as San Antonio, and the settlement of La Bahía, today's Goliad. Except for a small Spanish post of log buildings at Trinidad de Salcedo, about ninety miles beyond Nacogdoches, the trail lay open and straight to the capital at Bexar.

Gutiérrez' advance guard rode into Trinidad, deserted of all troops except a handful who remained to join the triumphant new army. The Republican Army of the North was moving smoothly, well equipped, and with enthusiasm rising as each new mile was gained.

The column, which grew daily as more volunteers came in from the sparsely-settled countryside, continued down the road to Bexar. Beyond the Brazos river they were joined by a deserter from the Spanish forces. He brought news that the royalist commander, Salcedo, had pulled his troops out of La Bahía to build the strongest possible garrison at Bexar. If that were the case, Gutiérrez decided, La Bahía should be seized while it was weak.

And so the men took a fork that led southwest to La Bahía, where there was a square fort built of stone. There the story of Nacogdoches and Trinidad de Salcedo was repeated: the small garrison fled at the approach of the Republican army, and the victors rode in, scarcely needing to cock their muskets.

La Bahía made the army feel that its conquests were improving. The massive walls, the fine barracks, and the big church were impressive. There were cannon, too, a couple of ancient pieces that the historian Yoakum says were those found a century and a quarter before by the Spanish troops who marched into La Salle's dead fort, a few leagues from where La Bahía was later built.

It was mid-November, 1812. Gutiérrez' men settled down for a short rest and a long feast, gorging on the captured supplies. Their picnic was brief, for as soon as the Spanish commander at Bexar heard that La Bahía had become the objective he took the offensive and sent a strong column to retake the stone presidio. Their first attack was thrown back by the sharp fire of the American riflemen.

Salcedo's army, roughly equal to the Republicans in numbers, went into camp around the stone fort and laid siege to it. For the next four months there were charges and repulses, sallies and skirmishes. Salcedo waited for reinforcements; word had gone months before to Mexico City and even to Spain; help was only a question of time.

Inside the fort the problem was not time but indecision. Gutiérrez had written back to Shaler in Natchitoches, urging the American agent to come to La Bahía. Shaler replied that it was unwise at the time to do anything that might give the impression that the United States agents were seeking to take control of Texas. He decided to stay in Louisiana, but it was a useless precaution. The rumors of American intervention were already loose, even among Gutiérrez' own men to some degree.

Inside La Bahía fortress, Magee was stumbling around more than half sick with a fever that had started a few days out of Nacogdoches. His own morale, like that of his men, was at the balance point: no longer rising, not yet ready to fall. Few new enthusiastic volunteers came to join them. In fact, some of the local recruits slipped out the back way. Gutiérrez grew aloof and suspicious. It was obvious that some, at least, of the cheers on their arrival had been cries of hope rather than confidence.

Magee called a council of the officers. Several voted to discuss possible terms with the royalists, and Magee went out with a flag of truce to parley. The terms did not include amnesty. Magee's men decided to fight, come what may, in a scene that was an early rehearsal of Travis' hour of decision at the Alamo. They sent their quartermaster, Davenport, back to Shaler with the news.

Shaler sent the gloomy reports on to Washington, but to the men at La Bahía he wrote encouraging replies, urging them to stiffen their resolve.

It was too late as far as Magee was concerned; on February 6, 1813, he died. Gutiérrez, who had become convinced that Magee tried to sell him out during the parley over terms, reported that Magee had taken poison. Magee's own men were equally sure that it was fever or perhaps tuberculosis.

The new American leader was Samuel Kemper, a huge man of great courage but, as Shaler reported in confidence to Washington, "of no education and of doubtful capacity for chief command."

Outside the walls, Salcedo's own men also were hungry, impatient, unenthusiastic. Their commander decided on a final, storming attack.

They fought from dawn until late afternoon, with terrible losses from the fierce return fire directed by Kemper and Gutiérrez. Then Salcedo took his exhausted troops back to Bexar.

To Gutiérrez and Kemper, the road to Bexar lay open, or so it seemed. Their spirits lifted even more with the arrival of a hundred reinforcements from the east. And in mid-March the Republican Army of the North marched out of La Bahía on its way to Bexar. The column then numbered six hundred resolute men, with half again that many coming along to lend a hand if things went well.

Five leagues from Bexar they found twelve hundred of Salcedo's men ready for battle at Salado. It was a short fight but a hot one, and a victory for the Republicans. The victors chased the royalists into Bexar itself, while they halted a mile or so outside.

Three days later Salcedo and his men surrendered. The green flag of the first Texas republic flew over Bexar.

Two days after the surrender, a squadron of silent horsemen rode south out of the city, escorting as prisoners Salcedo and thirteen of his staff. That night the captives were decapitated, stripped, and left where they fell.

This event, born of local hatreds long nurtured, left the Americans aghast. None of them had ridden with the squadron of death, nor could they share the passions that burned inside the executioners. They felt only revulsion.

The Americans' attitude dropped still more when Gutiérrez proclaimed his new constitution, the first issued in Texas. True, it was based on the laws and customs of Spain and thus differed from that issued by the Continental Congress. But the essential difference was that it proclaimed Texas to be a Mexican state — of, by, and for Mexicans, although the American volunteers were each to receive the promised square league of land in grant. Gutiérrez sent a letter of thanks back to Shaler, but there was an ominous lack of any promised alliance with the United States.

Samuel Kemper quit as field commander of the Republican Army and went back to Natchitoches. Scores of other Americans rode with him. Reuben Ross took over the military command. Gutiérrez relaxed in his new capital, discussing vague plans of developing his new state.

Back in Louisiana, Shaler was alarmed. From the news brought back by Kemper, it seemed as though Gutiérrez had been guilty of the horrible executions, the "all-Mexican" constitution, and the fumbling that continued at Bexar. True or not, the picture was disturbing to Shaler. He decided that Gutiérrez was not a commander who deserved support.

But a new leader was at hand, in the person of José Alvarez de Toledo, and Shaler brightened at the new possibilities.

Toledo had stayed in Philadelphia after Gutiérrez sailed for Havana and New Orleans. There the Cuban exile began to organize men for his own expedition to Natchitoches and on into Texas. He spoke to men of wealth who might have an interest in such a venture, and he recruited followers such as Aaron Mower, a printer with his own equipment.

When news of the executions and the isolationist constitution reached Philadelphia, Toledo's financial supporters turned cool. Their attitude was solidified still more against his plans when Governor Claiborne of Louisiana issued a formal proclamation condemning Gutiérrez' whole venture. That was a diplomatic necessity, in view of American relations with Spain, but it dampened Toledo's financial hopes. He had no choice but to go ahead with the small sums he could raise here and there.

In December, 1812, while Gutiérrez and Magee were celebrating in the stone fortress they had captured at La Bahía, Toledo started out with a handful of men. They went overland to Pittsburgh, then by river boat down to Natchez, and again by land to Natchitoches. Toledo put on the uniform of a full general before he rode into the town.

Shaler and Sibley were courteous to the newcomer, although at first they considered him a useless fifth wheel as far as affairs in Texas were concerned. But as events moved toward utter confusion in Bexar, Shaler brightened toward Toledo. Influential men heading west into Texas were advised to put in a good word for the energetic young "general," to pave the way for his entry into the drama at the capital of the new republic.

In May, while Gutiérrez lounged at Bexar, Toledo and his contingent moved west to Nacogdoches, inside Texas. There they started to set the type for Texas' first newspaper, *Gaceta de Texas*, with the dateline of May 25, 1813. It proclaimed the need for more energy in the cause of freedom. The type was set slowly, toward the future date on the masthead.

Then came a blistering letter from Gutiérrez, who suspected Toledo of being either a Spanish or French agent, at least, if not an American agent or even a double-agent. In alarm, Toledo had the type forms packed for transport back to Natchitoches. The first newspaper typeset in Texas was really printed in Louisiana. Shaler had been along on the trip to Nacogdoches; it was one of only two times he ever went beyond his country's border during the entire episode.

In Bexar, affairs continued to drift, in spite of indication that a Spanish counter-offensive was being planned. The new council set up to guide affairs in Texas debated about the conditions facing them. The Spanish government in Mexico City had placed General Arredondo in charge of the "internal provinces," which included Texas. Under him was Lieutenant Colonel Ygnacio Elizondo, who had gained fame as the captor of Hidalgo in the early months of the Mexican revolution.

Arredondo ordered Elizondo to advance toward Bexar in a show of force. Instead, the colonel tried to go the whole way. Gutiérrez' soldiers went out to meet the advancing enemy and defeated him in a brisk encounter. The fact that the Republicans did not continue the pursuit caused even more dissension in their councils.

Matters finally reached the point where the American volunteers threatened to pull out en masse unless something was done. After several votes, the Council decided to invite Toledo to come to Bexar and take charge.

Gutiérrez left a few days before Toledo arrived. The former commander rode east, his bitterness increased by rumors that Toledo had set paid assassins on his trail.

Toledo reached Bexar early in August, bringing with him a hundred recruits from Nacogdoches. His first task was to reorganize the army, which took a new name: Republican Army of North Mexico. Ross had resigned, and the Anglos were put in a separate division under Colonel Henry Perry. The Mexicans and Indians were in another division commanded by José Menchaca, a native of Bexar. The regulars under Toledo then had a total of about nine hundred men, plus an undetermined number of Indians. This figure was tripled in later enemy reports.

There was little time for Toledo to do anything else in the way of organization and training. On the day he first reached Bexar the scouts brought in reports that a large Spanish force was coming up from the south under General Joaquín de Arredondo.

Arredondo had started from Laredo and was joined along the way by Elizondo's division. The total force then included roughly twelve hundred cavalry and six hundred infantry. Not only were the odds two to one in his favor, but Arredondo's army included a thousand battle-trained regulars that had been sent from the Napoleonic wars in Spain and landed at Matamoros.

A few miles southwest of Bexar was the Medina River and beyond that the Atascosa River. When Toledo learned that the Spanish forces had ventured close enough to cross the Atascosa, he decided to move out to meet them. Whether or not he might have successfully resisted a siege by staying in Bexar is still debatable. What happened when he marched west and crossed the Medina to meet Arredondo is beyond argument.

The royalist general moved forward cautiously, probing for signs of the Republican army. From his camp near a place called Rancherías. Arredondo sent a corporal and four men ahead to scout. They came back to report signs of enemy activity, although they had failed to observe the main body of Toledo's Republican troops, who had crossed the Medina and were camped in a good position on the southwestern bank of that river.

The next morning, August 18, 1813, Arredondo prepared to move the Spanish army toward Bexar. The old Spanish road between Louisiana and Mexico was not far away, but Arredondo avoided taking that route. There was a canyon there, surrounded by enough timber to provide a perfect ambush.

Instead, the Spanish general sent out Lieutenant Colonel Elizondo with a hundred and eighty cavalrymen as an advance guard by a different route toward the Medina. Elizondo was told to move carefully and not to engage the enemy unless their forces were small. If he were attacked by a large force, he was to retreat slowly in a holding action while the main Spanish force could move up in support.

Elizondo and his men rode out in the early light, around five o'clock. Three hours later one of his men, who had ridden off separately to some distance, was seen by the Republican pickets. Firing began at once. Elizondo saw that he was facing a large force, perhaps the enemy's entire army, and was in danger of being surrounded. His men returned the Republican fire and moved back, giving ground slowly, while a messenger rode back to notify Arredondo.

The Spanish commander immediately moved his troops forward. At the same time he rushed a relief unit of a hundred and fifty cavalrymen, supported by two small pieces of artillery, to the aid of Elizondo. This relief unit was commanded by Zambrano, the same officer who a year before had fled from Nacogdoches at the first approach of the invaders under Magee and Gutiérrez.

Toledo's army had the mistaken idea that Elizondo's small advance unit was the entire Spanish army. When they saw Zambrano's relief column ride up they compounded their error by assuming that the arrivals were the total reserve forces available on the Spanish side. They redoubled the energy of their attack on the Spanish until Zambrano's little guns were unlimbered and took a heavy toll. That slowed the Republican advance briefly, but they soon overran the guns. At that point they were confident they had won the battle.

General Arredondo later wrote a complete report of the battle that followed, and his document was analyzed in recent years by Harry McCorry Henderson, a modern United States Army officer.

Arredondo's force had been marching in column. When they came up to the action they spread out into a battle line. The infantry were in the center, with units of cavalry on both wings, and artillery on both flanks outside the cavalry.

The sudden appearance of an immensely larger force jolted Toledo's Republican troops. They paused in a fringe of oak trees and straightened their own line. Then they determinedly kept advancing. The two lines were firing at each other only a pistol shot distance apart. The cannons were slugging it out forty paces from each other.

This kept up for two hours without a decision. Some of Toledo's men managed to get around behind the Spanish troops, but Arredondo organized a rear guard that dealt effectively with that menace.

Then it seemed that the Republicans were about to send out units to their right and left to outflank the Spanish. Arredondo promptly sent forward an advance unit on each of his own wings, with the result that Toledo's men were themselves outflanked and boxed in on both sides as well as in front. From that point on it was little less than slaughter. To stimulate his troops, Arredondo ordered his drummer to beat the reveille and ordered his band to play. The Spanish troops stiffened and started to push forward, and the Republican forces shuffled back in confusion, abandoning their cannon. Arredondo sent a detachment forward to seize the guns.

Toledo's troops broke in retreat, and Arredondo turned his horsemen loose upon them. All the way back to the Medina the cavalry pursued the fleeing Republicans, killing any they caught. No prisoners were taken; they were killed. Hundreds of Americans died. Ninety-three escaped, among them Col. Perry and Dr. Forsythe.

It was the end of one of the most decisive battles in Southwestern history.

There was a curious sidelight in Arredondo's official report. He took pains to praise most of his officers individually. One sentence in part read, "I recommend . . . Don Antonio [Lopez de] Santa Anna . . ." Some twenty years later the same officer would be back again fighting before the town of Bexar, against Travis at the Alamo.

The Republican leaders escaped back to Natchitoches; their native followers were pursued and butchered when caught. The American volunteers who survived the Battle of Medina were allowed to make their way back to Louisiana unmolested, for the Spanish victors said the Anglos were only "offending vagabonds." One small group of Americans set up an independent colony for a while on Galveston Island; some were still there four years later when Jean Lafitte also founded a settlement there and called it his "Republic of Mexico."

Gutiérrez, Shaler, and Toledo moved to new ventures. José Bernardo Gutiérrez de Lara reached Natchitoches safely, in spite of his fears that Toledo's men might assassinate him. He stayed on the Louisiana scene for several years. During the Battle of New Orleans he fought beside the troops of Andrew Jackson, as did others of the old Republican army. When Mexico won its independence from Spain in 1821, Gutiérrez was useful in Texas, but in 1824 he went back to the village of Revilla he had left thirteen years earlier. The returning hero was made governor of the state of Tamaulipas and served in other capacities until his death in 1841.

William Shaler left for Washington a few weeks after the defeat on the Medina. In 1815 he was sent with Stephen Decatur's naval squadron to Algiers, where he helped negotiate a treaty. Algiers fascinated him, and he stayed there for the next thirteen years. During his stay he wrote a book about Morocco that was useful when the French occupied their new colony.

José Alvarez de Toledo y Dubois loitered around Nacogdoches for a while, trying to reorganize a counter-offensive with a mixed band of patriots and brigands. In time he drifted on to new enterprises, returned to Spain, changed sides, and became useful to his old enemies — advising them on how to suppress revolutions.

In the years between 1813 and 1821 there were other insurgent drives into Mexico, but they never marched again under the legendary green banner.

3

Sailing the Texas Main

THE TEXAS trading schooner *San Felipe* rode easily in the swells of the Gulf of Mexico, heading on a southwesterly course from New Orleans. Her destination was the little port of Quintana at the mouth of the Brazos river, about forty-five miles beyond Galveston.

It was a new command for Captain William A. Hurd. Back of him lay years of experience in the merchant marine. It is an interesting question whether he was at that moment a merchant captain, a naval commander, or a pirate.

In a purely technical sense he was a merchant captain, for the *San Felipe* was owned by the firm of McKinney, Williams and Company, merchants at Quintana, Texas. Their money, $8,965 of it, had just purchased the schooner. It was not the first vessel owned by Thomas F. McKinney and Samuel M. Williams. They owned a little river steamer, the *Laura*, and other trading ships.

In another sense the *San Felipe* was the first vessel of what was soon afterward the first Texas Navy. The date was September 1, 1835, and there was as yet no Texas Republic. There had been movements in that direction, and conferences had been held to discuss the idea. For more than a year the colonists in the Mexican state of Texas had been aroused over various persecutions, not the least of which were unfair customs duties. Yet, at the moment, the wisest men were trying to work out a solution based on rights for Texas as a state within, not outside, Mexico. A month earlier, Santa Anna had formally announced his intention to enter Texas with a disciplinary force.

If Santa Anna's intentions were sincere, and no one doubted them, then the *San Felipe* might be considered a pirate schooner. The two six-pounder guns mounted on its deck behind cotton bales did not indicate a peaceful merchantman.

Captain Hurd's most important passenger was no ordinary traveler taking a cruise on a freighter. He was Stephen F. Austin, the founder of Anglo-American Texas. For two years Austin had been in a Mexican prison, suspected of inciting toward insurrection. He had been given his freedom and passage to New Orleans in July; now in September he was almost home. Inside him was the smouldering conviction that only through force of arms could Texas assert and protect its rights. The *San Felipe* was carrying munitions, and if there was ever a foetus of the Texas Navy, the *San Felipe* was it.

Beyond the horizon was waiting the Mexican schooner-of-war, *Correo de Mejico*, scouring the Gulf for just such vessels as the *San Felipe*. She was commanded by Lieutenant Thomas M. "Mexico" Thompson, a sailor of fortune in the service of Mexico.

On that morning of September 1 Thompson had already captured the American brig *Tremont*. She was moving out of the Brazos River, destined for Florida with a cargo of lumber, when the Mexican schooner ordered her to lay to for investigation.

Some say Thompson suspected the *Tremont* of being involved in the slave trade; others said it was only Thompson's malicious nature that caused the seizure of the vessel; no definite reason is known.

At any rate, the Texans were not ready to surrender the lumber brig without a fight. McKinney, Williams and Company had their steamboat *Laura* at Velasco just across from Quintana at the mouth of the Brazos. The *Laura* took on board a posse of armed Texans, got up steam, and headed out — firing as she came.

Thompson was no coward and was ready for any proposed action. He recalled his men from the *Tremont* and did what he could to return the fire. There was only the slightest breeze, and movement was slow and difficult. The *Laura* towed the *Tremont* to safety.

At that moment Thompson's attention was caught by a new sail approaching: the *San Felipe*, making little headway in the near-calm. The newcomer was unknown to Thompson but must have been familiar to its new owner, McKinney, for the steamer *Laura* promptly headed to the *San Felipe* and took it in tow.

The breeze freshened slightly and Thompson decided to make a fight of it. He had the *Correo* cleared for action and put Lieutenant Carlos Ocampo in charge of the small party of marines. Ocampo had been en route from the Mexican garrison at Anahuac and was carrying government funds.

In an effort to discover the identity of the new ship, Thompson ordered a ship's boat lowered and sent off with a party of armed men.

The *San Felipe* had the best of the small wind and sailed into a position to attack. The *Correo's* boat rowed past the *San Felipe* and fired several musket shots. There were many riflemen on the latter, taken on board from the *Laura*, which had also transferred Stephen Austin and other passengers to safety. The Texans held their fire.

Thompson hailed the *San Felipe* in English, feeling certain the newcomer was not a Mexican vessel. When the reply was in English his doubts vanished, and he ordered a shot sent across the bow of the *San Felipe*. She did not halt but instead returned the fire.

There was an exchange of cannon and musket fire that lasted almost an hour. The *Correo's* rigging was damaged, and the *San Felipe's* rudder was hit, making it impossible for the Texans to come close enough to board the *Correo*.

Thompson managed to tack beyond the range of the enemy guns and headed south all night, toward Matamoros. With only slight wind and damaged rigging, the *Correo* made little headway.

Daybreak found the *Correo* still near the Texas coast. The *San Felipe*, towed by the *Laura*, was within half a cannon shot. Thompson's ammunition was almost gone, his rigging was crippled, several men were wounded, and those sent out in the longboat had mysteriously never returned. The Mexican schooner's captain realized that even with sweeps he could not row out of danger, so he decided to surrender.

Thompson sent Lieutenant Ocampo in a boat to the *San Felipe* to discuss terms. He was told by Captain Hurd that the *Correo* was beaten and there was no occasion for any discussion of terms.

The *San Felipe* then sent a whaleboat with a boarding party to take charge of the *Correo*. Most of its crew and all of its marines were ferried ashore. Captain Thompson, Lieutenant Ocampo, the *Correo's* engineer Edmund Hogan, and three others of the crew were taken aboard the *San Felipe* and put in irons.

Captain Hurd had to decide upon his next course. The Texans

knew and hated Thompson; there was no wish to let him go. To free the *Correo* was strategically unwise. The Texas ship had, in a very real sense, won the first Texas naval victory at sea, but it was completely unofficial. There was not even a temporary or provisional Texas government to whom Hurd could turn over the *Correo*. In this regard, his own position was shaky. His only solid base for action was self-defense, because he had fired only when fired upon. To dispose of the *Correo* as his own prize would make him a pirate.

Piracy! That was a possibility for a charge against Thompson, and it was supported by the thinnest of evidence. The captured Mexican commander could not produce any document to prove that he was a commissioned officer in the navy of Mexico. The oral confirmation by others on board the *Correo* meant nothing; it was a long-standing rule of the sea. So Captain Hurd decided to send the *Correo* and its officers to New Orleans, to stand trial in a United States court on the charge of piracy. Like any modern motorist, if Thompson could not produce his driver's license he must go to court.

It took Captain Hurd three days to come to this conclusion. On the fourth day he had the six captives from the *Correo* transferred back to it from the *San Felipe*. Hurd called the commander of the steamboat *Laura*, Lieutenant Thomas W. Grayson, and put him in charge of the *San Felipe*, which was to remain in port.

Hurd put a Texan crew on the *Correo*, hoisted the United States colors, and started on the eight days' voyage to New Orleans with himself in command.

Off New Orleans the *Correo* was intercepted by a United States revenue cutter. Its captain ordered the irons removed from Lieutenant Ocampo but otherwise kept him a prisoner. They arrived in New Orleans on September 15, 1835. The six men of the *Correo* were jailed, and Captain Hurd entered formal charges.

The experiences of men involved in this naval engagement, together with the adventures of others who became implicated, show how the "web" of history is more than just a fancy word. Those primarily involved were Captain William A. Hurd of the Texan vessel, Lieutenant Thomas M. Thompson of the Mexican *Correo*, and the Mexican officer Carlos Ocampo. Also involved were Thomas F. McKinney and Samuel May Williams, the merchants who owned the Texan schooner, together with Felix Huston and Pierre Soulé, who were involved in legal affairs at New Orleans during the trial of Thompson. The story involved other schooners, brigs, and most of the Texas Navy; the web was entangled with duels, piracy, shipwrecks, and mutiny.

There were strange parallels between the Texas Revolution and the American Revolution sixty years earlier. Much of the spirit of John Adams and John Paul Jones, much of the Gaspee affair and the Boston Tea Party, and much of the Sons of Liberty and the Continental Congress all seemed to be echoed in Texas. It was as if the United States had a spiritual frontier as well as a geographical one, and that the ghosts of 1776 moved across Texas in 1836.

History can be understood only in terms of men; not in their names alone, nor in concepts of men as stuffed figures in a lifeless diorama — but in the realization that the men of history were men who had ambitions, desires, jealousies, and weaknesses. In short, they were human.

Take Thomas M. "Mexico" Thompson as an example. He was a young English seafaring man when he came to New Orleans and sailed as a mate on ships of the J. W. Zacharie firm. That company had a profitable business shipping supplies to Mexico and, for that matter, to anyone with good credit. Thompson came to know the waters of the Gulf of Mexico and the ports of Mexico. Not all was success; he had one period "on the beach" when he ran a low-class tavern at New Orleans, on the levee. Some of the debts he incurred at that time came back to cause him trouble later.

Early in 1835 Thompson signed on with the Mexican Navy, such as it was, and became a *Teniente Segundo* and a Mexican citizen. Along with his routine duties that involved coast guard and revenue officer activities he also began to make excellent maps of the Gulf. These were captured later by the Texas Navy and put to effective use against Mexico.

His main action was against smuggling. At that time, in early 1835, much contraband was being landed at the port of Anahuac, not far from Galveston. A tough Mexican customs inspector with the Anglo name of Bradburn was resented by the Texans. He was replaced by a new officer, Antonio Tenorio, who was no easier.

Thompson was ordered to Anahuac to reinforce Tenorio. While in the port Thompson issued a proclamation warning the townspeople against formation of a local militia. When they ignored his order he threatened to burn the town. As a result, the name of

Thomas M. Thompson was not popular in Texas, and it was no wonder that Captain Hurd pushed for a charge of piracy.

The day after the officers and crew of the *Correo* landed at New
Orleans and were imprisoned, the local Mexican consul, Francisco
Pizarro Martinez, sent a written message to Henry Carleton, United
States attorney for the district of Louisiana, demanding immediate
liberation of the men.

Martinez had a reply from Carleton on the following day. It said
that because Captain Hurd had filed a formal affidavit before Justice
Preval in New Orleans the men could not be freed until legal proceedings had been completed. The men soon were freed on a writ of
habeas corpus, but they were rearrested within two hours and jailed.

Consul Martinez then moved the matter to a higher diplomatic
level by writing to the Mexican chargé d'affaires at Philadelphia,
J. M. de Castillo y Langas. Castillo y Langas added his own forceful
comments and forwarded the message to Asbury Dickins, the acting
Secretary of State. The Mexican position was that Thompson's vessel
was part of the *guarda costa* and therefore an official vessel of the
Mexican government.

The United States countered with the technicality that regardless
of the nature of the *Correo* itself, its officer in command at the time
of the battle could not produce a commission or any other document
proving that he was an authorized Mexican government officer. Thus
the charge of piracy was still maintained by the United States.

The case of "United States *vs.* Thompson" came to court on January 12, 1836, in the U.S. court for the eastern district of Louisiana,
with Judge Harper presiding. For the prosecution was District Attorney Carleton and his assistant, Randall Hunt, and another young
attorney named Felix Huston (not related to Sam Houston). One of
Thompson's defense attorneys was Pierre Soulé. Both Soulé and
Huston had colorful careers after the trial.

It was really Texas *vs.* Thompson, or Texas *vs.* Mexico if you wish.
"Truth, justice and civil liberty" were words used often by the
prosecution. Attorneys Carleton and· Soulé exchanged hot words,
to the point where charges of "liar!" were followed by the hurling of
inkwells and books between the rivals.

When the case went to the jury a decision was reached in a single
night on Lieutenant Ocampo, who was freed. But the jury was unde-
cided about Thompson. Judge Harper was ready to dismiss the case

because of the hung jury and said he would declare a new trial. At this point District Attorney Carleton interrupted to enter a motion of *nolle prosequi,* or dismissal of the charge, and the judge agreed to this motion. It was a diplomatic solution. If Thompson had been acquitted, it would have been an admission that the *San Felipe* had done wrong. The simple withdrawal of the charge and dismissal of the case did not precisely indicate wrong on the part of the Texans.

To maintain the dignity of the court, Judge Parker gave brief jail sentences to Carleton and Soulé for their uproar during the proceedings. Thus an alleged pirate went free, while the lawyers were jailed.

Supporters of Texas visited Carleton in jail. They also presented an inscribed gift to Randall Hunt as a testimonial of their "approbation and esteem . . . [for his] . . . sympathies for their oppressed and struggling country."

Countersuits followed promptly. Lieutenant Ocampo filed a suit against Hurd, claiming that the captain had taken $1,000 from him after the capture of the *Correo.* Hurd denied that any such sum had been aboard the vessel when taken.

Lieutenant Thompson found no complete freedom, for he was no sooner released from the first trial when he was again arrested. This time it was on a charge filed by some of his old creditors. The Mexican government protested this new trial and asked that any claims against Thompson should be directed against the Mexican government.

Thompson and Ocampo went back to Mexico. Ocampo resumed his duties as an army officer, and Thompson was assigned to sea duty on the Mexican schooner-of-war *Bravo,* which formerly had been named the *Moctezuma.*

The two schooners, *Correo* and *San Felipe,* involved in the original incident had short and undistinguished histories thereafter. The *Correo* had been taken to New Orleans and impounded. It was released after the trial and returned to Mexico. There it was renamed the *Rafaelita* and again put to sea. It was captured by the Texas Navy ship *Brutus* in August, 1837, but was lost at sea about two weeks later.

The *San Felipe* had been left behind off Texas in command of Lieutenant, now Captain, Grayson. While Hurd was still in New Orleans a Mexican war vessel appeared off the Texas coast and Grayson gave chase in the *San Felipe,* which had been armed with an additional heavy gun. In the engagement that followed, the *San Felipe* ran aground and was wrecked. Its heavy gun was salvaged, but it was the end of the first war vessel equipped by Texas.

During the last quarter of 1835, while the *Correo* was impounded at New Orleans and its captain was awaiting trial, Texas had moved closer to independence. In early October, Texas colonists opposed a Mexican military force at Gonzales, and the first shots of the open revolution were fired on land, a month after guns had spoken at sea.

In November there was a consultation of delegates from settlements in Texas. They voted to set up an independent state government but to remain within the Republic of Mexico. One of their actions was the writing of a provision for handling naval affairs.

Mexican blockade vessels still harassed the Texas coast. Determined to protect their own interests, a group of nine men at Matagorda raised $3,500 among themselves and bought the schooner *William Robbins*. It was then armed, equipped, and sent to sea as a privateer. For its commander the Texans chose Captain Hurd, who had returned to Texas while the court case was in abeyance at New Orleans.

Hurd had only one important bit of action as captain of the *Robbins*, but it was a curious affair. A Mexican warship, the *Bravo*, had driven a Texas gunrunner ashore and had placed a prize crew on the wrecked ship. News of this came to Hurd and he sailed at once.

The wrecked ship was the *Hannah Elizabeth*. At the time it was forced onto the beach it had been carrying three cannon: two six-pounders and a four-pounder, as well as two cases of rifles and a good supply of powder. Fearing that they faced a Mexican penalty for gunrunning, the crew jettisoned all of the arms.

The captain of the *Bravo* ordered an officer, Lieutenant Mateo, to go with a dozen men in a ship's boat and take possession of the beached vessel. They were to bring off any prisoners, take any items of special value, and burn the wreck.

Lieutenant Mateo's boarding party were surprised at the lack of any resistance. Not a shot was fired. In several trips they transferred most of the passengers back to the *Bravo*.

During one of these trips, a strong norther blew up and the *Bravo* had to stand out to sea; it was unable to return. Lieutenant Mateo's men fared little better, for their own boat was upset as they returned to the wreck. They managed to scramble aboard the beached *Han-*

nah Elizabeth, but their boat washed ashore. There it was captured by a Texan named Somers and two companions. These three managed to take possession of the wreck; apparently Lieutenant Mateo's men had lost their own weapons during the spill. It might also have been that any of the Mexican boarding party left on the *Hannah Elizabeth* were more than comfortably drunk by then. There were twenty-two barrels of whiskey on board, plus five casks of gin and as many of brandy. One of the Mexicans died shortly afterwards of exposure suffered while drunk.

Somers asked the Mexican officer to surrender, but Mateo replied stiffly that he would give up his sword only to a Texas officer. This perplexed Somers, who knew that help was coming, but he decided to guard the prisoners whether they surrendered formally or not. For the next two days Somers and his friends stood watch in turn over the Mexicans.

When Hurd and his crew, aided by more than a score of enthusiastic volunteers, arrived at the wreck they accepted the lieutenant's sword and Mexican honor was preserved.

The wreck of the *Hannah Elizabeth* was in sad condition. She had rolled in the heavy breakers, snapping her masts and splitting her deck. All hands fell to and quickly transferred the remaining cargo to the beach, the principal items (in addition to the liquors) being two hundred bales of tobacco and a hundred barrels of flour.

Hurd then found himself in a dilemma no less confusing than the one that had faced him when he captured Thompson's *Correo.* Hurd's own vessel, the *William Robbins,* was sailing as a privateer, under a letter of marque. This entitled its captain to sell any captured enemy cargo and retain the money received. Without hesitation, he sold most of the merchandise except one large portion that he allowed its original owner, a passenger still on the wrecked *Hannah Elizabeth,* to buy back at half its invoice value on the ship's manifest.

A genuine wrangle arose then in Texas. There were those who claimed that because the *Hannah Elizabeth* was originally a Texas-chartered ship it had only been freed and was not truly a prize of war. Hurd maintained that the Mexicans had taken it and placed a prize crew aboard; that made it a Mexican vessel.

There was as yet no Republic of Texas, but affairs were being handled by a General Council. The ticklish question was referred to them. A committee was set up, motions were made and tabled, and the matter eventually became lost in a tangle of red tape. Hurd apparently was cleared, for during this period the Council gave him a naval commission.

By the end of 1835, the Texas government had managed to scrape together enough funds to buy four schooners, which were to become the first official Texas Navy.

One of these was the *William Robbins*, which was renamed the *Liberty*. Another was the *Brutus*, a slow-sailing schooner of about a hundred and twenty-five tons burden, that was bought in New Orleans late in December. There she was outfitted with six cannon and one heavier pivot gun.

The underwriters of the *Brutus* in New Orleans, a group of twenty-eight men, protested against insuring a warship. They petitioned U.S. District Attorney Carleton, who was at that moment still involved with the case against Thompson. Carleton said he could take no action on mere suspicion, but if the underwriters could come forward with affidavits, witnesses, or other proof that it was planned to use the *Brutus* in an illegal manner, he would act. No further attempt was made to stop the ship from sailing.

Shortly after the Thompson-Ocampo trial in New Orleans was ended, the *Brutus* arrived at the port of Matagorda, Texas. William Hurd was promoted to become its commander, the only Texas naval officer who had seen action in three levels of naval service: wholly unofficial on the *San Felipe*, as a privateer on the *William Robbins*, and as a commissioned naval officer on the *Brutus*. His career was destined to have an unhappy ending.

Captain Hurd had departed from New Orleans under difficulties. The *Brutus* was anchored some distance from New Orleans, fearing that she might be seized by U.S. customs officials if she ventured into the river port. But the *Brutus* had to get a crew. Sailors were hesitant to sign on a ship without seeing it. Others had second thoughts because of a recent order by Santa Anna of Mexico, announcing that he would treat as pirates the crew of any vessel found aiding Texas. In time the *Brutus* signed on a full crew in spite of these problems.

Another of the four ships in the original Texas Navy was the schooner *Invincible*. In April, 1836, she captured the Mexican war vessel *Bravo* off the mouth of the Rio Grande. This was the same

Bravo that had driven the gunrunner on the beach and had been blown out to sea by a strong north wind.

What happened during and after this capture of the *Bravo* was almost unbelievable coincidence, except to those who understand how really small and far-ranging was the community of men in the Southwest.

The *Invincible* was pursuing the *Bravo* when the latter lost its rudder and lay helpless. The Texans sent a boarding party to the *Bravo*, where they found their old foe "Mexico" Thompson trying to repair the damage. Only three months after the end of his trial in New Orleans he again found himself a prisoner on a Texan ship.

At that moment a new sail appeared at sea, and the *Invincible* left the *Bravo* to pursue and capture the newcomer, an American brig carrying Mexican troops. And there with the troops was Lieutenant Ocampo, who rejoined his old cellmate Thompson, again as a captive. They were landed in Texas.

Affairs in Texas had proceeded to a complete break with Mexico. On March 2, 1836, Texas declared its independence. On March 6 the Alamo was taken by the Mexican forces. On the night of March 16-17 the Texas Constitution was signed, and on March 21, the Texan army under Sam Houston defeated and captured Santa Anna at the Battle of San Jacinto. There was a sort of armistice in the Treaty of Velasco, but there was never — then or later — a final treaty of surrender ending the war. As far as Mexico was concerned, Texas had only seceded and was still subject to military action. Hostilities on land grew less, but the fighting continued at sea.

During the period before Santa Anna's defeat, another steamboat belonging to the firm of McKinney, Williams and Company became involved in Texas history. This was the *Yellow Stone*, which had started as a riverboat on the upper Missouri River serving the fur trade!

It had been built at Louisville for Pierre Chouteau, Jr., in 1831. Its first return trip down the Missouri gained international notice when on July 5, 1831, it steamed to Saint Louis with a cargo of furs. For the next four years it operated up and down the Mississippi during the cold months. When the weather warmed in the upper reaches of the Missouri and the Yellowstone rivers, the little steamboat went upstream to Fort Tecumseh and Fort Union with a cargo of trade goods and trappers' supplies, returning with bales of furs.

At the end of December, 1835, it was bought by McKinney and Williams and made its first trip to Texas, transporting volunteers from Mobile. It went up the Brazos River as far as Stephen Austin's colony at San Felipe de Austin. It transported Houston's army across the Brazos River when he was en route to the Battle of San Jacinto, After the battle it carried the wounded Houston and his captive, Santa Anna, with their staffs, down to Galveston.

In its day it carried muskets, refugees, supplies, messages, and even a newspaper press, up and down the rivers and bayous of Texas. Its last major historical connection was when it carried the body of Stephen F. Austin down to Peach Point for burial on December 29, 1836. A short year in Texas but a remarkable one. The little wood-burner ended its days on some Texas stream, and its bell was given eventually to the Alamo Museum.

While all these battles, alarms, and excursions were occurring on land in Texas, the navy was busy at sea.

The *Brutus* under Captain Hurd was busy convoying transports of volunteers, doing blockade duty, capturing prizes when any appeared, and being generally useful. On one confused night in May the *Brutus* fired a shot at another Texas warship, the *Invincible,* and a small uproar ensued between the commanders until tempers were soothed.

By this time Mexico was also acquiring new and more powerful vessels. One of these bottled up the *Brutus* in Matagorda Bay in June, 1836, and it looked for a while as though Captain Hurd had seen his last voyage. Then he was rescued when the Mexican ship was driven off by the approach of two Texan vessels, one of which was a little steamer, the *Ocean,* commanded by Captain Thomas W. Grayson, whom Hurd had last known as the young lieutenant he transferred from the *Laura* to the *San Felipe* ten months before.

Early in July, Hurd suddenly and without official orders set sail in the *Brutus* for New York. President David Burnet of the Republic of Texas was "vexed and astonished" by Hurd's unexplained and hurried departure. He wrote to Thomas Toby, the Texas agent in New Orleans, for any news of the *Brutus*.

Toby replied that the ship apparently had sailed for New York and urged that Hurd be broken at once as captain. This Burnet hesitated to do. He felt that there might have been a necessity for some repairs and that Hurd had taken the *Brutus* to New York for them as repairs there cost much less and, even including round trip sailing time, could be done more quickly than along the Gulf Coast. Burnet also hesitated to have the *Brutus* left in New York without a commander. He considered the further possibility that there might have been trouble with the crew on the ship during its voyage east.

Burnet was partly right. Hurd apparently did have some sort of a mutiny on the trip to New York and had to shoot two of the crew. But Hurd was also becoming displeased with several government officials in Texas, according to Thomas Toby's report, and apparently was considering his own future. Meanwhile, repairs and back pay for the crew piled up an $8,000 debt in New York. Burnet sent a peremptory order to New York, instructing Hurd to return promptly with the *Brutus*.

Funds were raised, the bill paid, and Hurd arrived back in Galveston in April, 1837. He was promptly relieved of duty on the *Brutus*. His defense of the New York trip was not recorded, or all records of it have been lost. This was the end of Hurd's naval career, and in October, 1838, there was news that he had died in New Orleans.

Under a new commander, the *Brutus* had only four months' more service afloat. In August it was in Galveston Bay when another Texas ship was attacked offshore by two Mexican men of war. The *Brutus* set off to help its sister ship but became stuck on a shoal. A steam tug went to aid but succeeded only in getting a hawser entangled in the *Brutus'* rudder, making the ship helpless. A few weeks later a strong storm blew in and the *Brutus* was torn apart as it lay helpless.

But that was not the end of the story of the Texas Navy men whose fortunes had become interwoven. The smallest of the four vessels in the first Texas Navy had been the little *Liberty*, known as the *William Robbins* when Hurd commanded her. The *Liberty*, under Captain George Wheelwright, was ordered to convoy a ship carrying Sam Houston to New Orleans during his convalescence after the Battle of San Jacinto. The *Liberty* reached New Orleans badly in need of repairs and was laid up. When it came time to pay the bills Texas' purse was empty, and the little schooner was sold to satisfy the debt for repairs, in July, 1836.

But still the legend continued to build. When the *Liberty* was sold, its captain, Wheelwright, was assigned to the *Independence,* another of the four original Texas Navy ships. That ship was destined to be captured with strange consequences.

William H. Wharton had been named Texas' first minister to Washington. There he won U.S. recognition of the Texas Republic in March, 1837. He started for home and part of his trip was on board the *Independence,* commanded by Wheelwright. The ship was captured in a classic running fight with two of Mexico's best warships off the mouth of the Brazos in April. Wheelwright and Wharton, along with others, were imprisoned at Matamoros.

This was an important Mexican naval port, and the prisoners soon were visited by a Mexican naval officer.

He was none other than "Mexico" Thompson.

By now Thompson was beginning to have a change of heart and offered to make a deal. He would help Wheelwright and Wharton escape and would also defect to the Texan side, in return for their help in getting him a commission in the Texas Navy.

Wheelwright agreed to the proposal and plans were laid. Before the men could escape, Thompson learned that the Mexican officials were aware of his intention to desert and he had to flee. The escape went off as planned, but Thompson received a hostile reception when he arrived in Texas ahead of the escaped prisoners.

Matters were smoothed over when Wharton and Wheelwright arrived. Thompson apparently never received a commission for sea duty, but his name appeared on the rolls of Texas officers and there are reports that he was assigned to Navy Yard duties at Galveston for a time. He was last reported in 1840 as a beachcomber along the Caribbean coast of the Mexican state of Tabasco.

It was the end of the saga of the ships and captains of the first Texas Navy, assembled from second-hand ships and commanded by men of varied backgrounds. The other individuals on the fringe of the story remain to be chronicled; Huston, Soulé, McKinney, and Williams. All of them left their legends, but not in the records of the sea.

Felix Huston was thirty-six and a successful attorney from Natchez when he sat in the New Orleans courtroom during Thompson's trial. Perhaps the fervent pleas for Texas' freedom convinced a mind already half inclined. For the next four years he devoted his whole energy to the Texan cause.

He returned to Natchez that spring and raised a regiment of five hundred men, putting all of his own wealth and $40,000 of borrowed money into the venture. He reached Texas in the early summer of 1836 and in July was made quartermaster general of the republic's army. By December he was the junior brigadier general and, while awaiting official action in naming his senior brigadier, Huston was temporarily in command of the whole force. He became embittered when his new superior turned out to be Albert Sidney Johnston. He challenged Johnston to a duel; Johnston was wounded, but the pair were quickly reconciled. After four years in Texas, Johnston returned to the States. He died at Shiloh in the Civil War.

The Texas Army was suffering from barracks fatigue, with no enemy to fight and no pay coming from a depleted treasury. Felix was a popular commander, partly because he allowed celebrations he called "saturnalias," in which murders sometimes occurred during heavy drinking. He also clamored for action, proposing a counter-offensive that would thrust into Mexico itself by way of an attack on Matamoros.

Sam Houston did not approve of either the riotous saturnalias or the sword-rattling. He dared not dismiss a popular commander, nor could he disband the army because there were no funds to pay the men. Houston found an ingenious solution: he gave indefinite furloughs to most of the regiments, sending each unit to a different port to start their leave. Most of the men did what Houston expected: they then made their own way back to the States and never returned. Felix Huston suddenly realized what had happened, when he found his army down to six hundred men, and at that point he resigned. Sam Houston neither accepted the resignation nor protested it. Felix went back to Natchez and continued to agitate for Texas' annexation. Later he was a strong secessionist.

Pierre Soulé, who had defended Thompson, took no recorded part in the Texas Revolution. His defense of Thompson was not his first appearance in a case involving piracy: ten years earlier he had defended the officers and crew of the ship *General Bolivar*, including some men who had served under Jean Lafitte.

The ladies of New Orleans loved Soulé, who physically resembled Napoleon Bonaparte, with the added charm of Southern gallantry, long black hair, and flashing eyes.

When Franklin Pierce became president in 1852, he named Soulé minister to Spain. Soulé clamored for annexation of Cuba, by peaceful means or otherwise. When a dispute arose in 1854 over seizure of an American ship at Havana, Pierce's secretary of state suggested that three U.S. ministers in Europe meet at Ostend, Belgium, to discuss the general topic. At that meeting were Soulé from Spain, James Buchanan, minister to Great Britain, and John Y. Mason, minister to France. The trio issued the "Ostend Manifesto," stating that if the U.S. could not acquire Cuba by peaceful means then "by every law, human and divine, we shall be justified in wresting it from Spain if we have the power."

The result was an international uproar. President Pierce disclaimed all responsibility and recalled Soulé from Spain. His career ended with that dismissal.

The two Texas merchants who had financed the purchase of the schooner *San Felipe* continued to aid the Texas cause. As the years passed, the firm of McKinney, Williams and Company became prominent in banking, cotton, and shipping.

Of the two partners, Williams was the better financier but McKinney was more colorful. Thomas F. McKinney was a Kentuckian who had traveled with caravans to Santa Fe before he was twenty-two. Later he freighted cotton over the old Camino Real from Natchitoches to San Antonio and down to Chihuahua, where he traded the cotton for horses. At one time he was a partner of Michel Menard, a Texas lumber dealer who was a nephew of Pierre Menard, the famous fur trapper at Kaskaskia, Illinois. McKinney supported Texas independence. Later, during the Civil War, he did not favor secession but went along with majority opinion. For a while he served as an agent for Texas, cooperating with Simeon Hart, who was located near El Paso.

McKinney's partner, Samuel May Williams, had been a bookkeeper in New Orleans when Andrew Jackson went there during the War of 1812, and for a time he was Jackson's secretary. Williams went out to join Stephen Austin's colony, and in 1835 he was one of nine prominent Texans who had a price on their heads, offered by Santa Anna. He died poor as a result of the Civil War and unwise speculation.

The Texas Navy continued, of course, until the republic was annexed to the United States. As the original fleet was wrecked or fell apart by rot, there was—for a time—little effort made to maintain a navy. Then during the administration of Mirabeau B. Lamar the Navy became a popular project.

Lamar went after better ships and better men; he found both. Superb officer material was available in the United States Navy, where competent young men were held back from promotion by mossbacks who started their service in the War of 1812 and were still in command.

One of the best new men in the Texas Navy was Edwin Ward Moore, only twenty-nine but with fourteen of those years at sea with the American navy. He became commodore of the Texas Navy and guided its achievements for the rest of its years.

By mid-1839 there were several new vessels, some of them built especially for naval service. These included three fine schooners, a brig, and a full-rigged ship. There was also a single steamer, and in that aspect the Texas Navy was an equal match for the United States' fleet, which also had but one.

But as the months went by, and Mexico came to accept Texas' independence as a fact of life, there was less and less for the navy to do. The state of Yucatan was having its own quarrels with Mexico, and Yucatan offered to rent the Texas Navy for $8,000 a month — and Texas accepted the deal. That turned out to be short-term employment, and Commodore Moore again had to struggle with infrequent paydays, lack of money for repairs, slow recruiting, and one mutiny.

In 1843 the Yucatan arrangement was revived, and during that period the navy saw genuine action in three major engagements.

Sam Houston, always economy-minded, was back in office as president by then, and when the Yucatan business ended Houston ordered the ships to return to their home port. Moore hesitated, afraid Houston might scrap the fleet.

In fact, Houston had precisely that idea in mind, and when Moore did not bring the fleet home Houston declared his own navy to be pirates. Moore broke out all sail to return home, hotly indignant over the charge. Houston then tried to sell the entire navy at auction, but popular opinion blocked the sale.

The fleet saw no more action. Texas was annexed to the United States in 1845. A year later its ships were to be transferred to the American navy, but there was not a single seaworthy vessel left to transfer — only a few hulks.

Still, it had been a proud service while it lasted, and no corsairs of the Caribbean or the Gulf ever hoisted sail with more gusto than did *los diablos Tejanos,* the Texas devils who sailed the sea that had truly become the Texas Main.

4

Draw Black for Death

IN TROPICAL MEXICO, motorists driving west from the port of Vera Cruz along the old Highway 140 toward Mexico City pass a rugged volcanic mountain. It is crested with a formation resembling an old treasure chest. This is the peak named *Cofre de Perote*, the Coffer of Perote. A mile or so beyond, in a dreary, windswept plain is the little town of Perote. Near the village and hulking over it is a sombre old fort, the Castle of San Carlos. To the men of three luckless Southwestern expeditions the castle was known as the Prison of Perote.

First were those taken prisoner when an expedition from Austin attempted to extend Texan influence toward Santa Fe in 1841. Next were the prisoners taken when Mexico sent a punitive raid in return, into San Antonio. The third group were those captured when Texas retaliated to the San Antonio foray. The last of the three expeditions saw one of the deadliest episodes in Southwestern history: the drawing of the beans, where a black bean meant execution within minutes. That expedition also saw a dramatic escape.

When the viceroy of Mexico, Marquis de Gruillas, started construction of the palace two hundred years ago, he designed a fortress that was intended to keep every foe out and every prisoner in. By the standards of 1770 he built well. First there was the essential fort itself, about eight hundred feet square with a long bastion projecting at each corner. The walls were at least thirty feet high, built of honeycombed volcanic rock of a brittle hardness. Fourteen feet thick were the walls at their base, tapering as they rose, with battlements for cannon along the top. Around the inside of the walls ran a wide platform for the guns; the floor of this platform was also a thick ceiling for cells beneath — cells about eighteen by thirty feet.

Within the walled area, separated from the outer walls by a space of sixty feet, was an inner square structure, two stories high. In it were the living quarters for those at the castle: barracks on the ground floor, officers' quarters above. And in the center of this structure was a central patio about five hundred feet square. Beneath its thick, paved surface was a massive reservoir for water, filled by an underground stream.

Outside the main walls ran a moat, about a hundred feet wide and perhaps twenty deep, dry until the massive watergates were lifted to flood the ditch in an emergency. There was only one entrance, entered by a drawbridge over the moat.

But the fortifications did not end there. Around the outside of the moat ran a low stone wall, and fifty feet beyond that was the *chevaux de frise,* the horse-stopping fence of pointed wooden posts about twelve feet high. Outside the fence was another ditch fourteen feet wide, its outer bank piled almost as high as the posts. The total area within this ditch was about twenty-six acres.

The original purpose was to serve as a secondary defense back of the port of Vera Cruz. As a practical matter, most of its years saw it used as a prison.

Whether castle or prison, it is doubtful that a certain Texan colonel named Hugh McLeod had ever heard of the place when he rode from Austin in June, 1841. Even if he had known about Perote it would have been unimportant at that moment, for he was heading north, not south. His column of three hundred and twenty men, with fourteen heavy wagons loaded with merchandise and followed by a brass six-pounder cannon on a field carriage, was headed toward Santa Fe, New Mexico.

Or it might be better to say Santa Fe, *Texas.* When Texas won its independence from Mexico five years earlier, the young republic had claimed all of the land west to the Rio Grande. And Santa Fe lies east of that river, by a few miles.

Was the Texan Santa Fe Expedition a convoy of pioneer settlers moving to new lands? A military expedition sent to establish Texas' authority over a remote corner of the republic? A good-will tour of

merchants who hoped to open a southern branch of the Santa Fe
Trail? Or a highly-publicized project of President Lamar of Texas, to
take the people's minds off the depression that was plunging Texas
into financial difficulties?

Anyone who seeks can find affirmative evidence and negative
proof on any of these points. Officially the men were known as the
Santa Fe Pioneers. One thing was certain, it was a company of
gentleman adventurers heading, each with his own purpose, out
across a land unknown to all but a few guides. And even the guides
would become lost before the journey ended.

They thought the distance was about five hundred miles. By
today's highways it is just over seven hundred miles and is often
driven in a single day. But they took a wide detour, and were about
four months on the trail. Even today, a trip across the Llano Estacado, the Staked Plains of the Texas Panhandle, is no pleasure
jaunt in July.

Hugh McLeod was twenty-seven and a West Pointer. At the start,
the choice of him as commander seemed wise enough; the men
moved smartly and with military discipline. Before the last water-
hole was reached, months later, there was proof that West Point in
McLeod's time had offered no courses in prairie travel.

But they were on their way gaily, with their own small band of a
few fifes, four bugles, a couple of clarinets, and drums. They moved
easily, under no pressure to make fast time. A day's march was anywhere from four to seventeen miles across the rolling countryside.

Around the campfires the men came to know each other's life
story: a common topic in remote places, where men either tell a
great deal about themselves — or nothing at all. A newspaperman
named George Kendall, from the New Orleans *Picayune*, was along
to record everything. He was a Richard Harding Davis, a Floyd
Gibbons, or an Ernie Pyle, ahead of his time.

Archibald Fitzgerald probably was the most colorful in the expedition. Born in Ireland, he had fought as a soldier of fortune in
Spain, Persia, Brazil, and at the Cape of Good Hope. On the Santa
Fe trip he was a merchant, with a wagonload of trade goods. He
would survive his first trip to Perote but would die avoiding a
second.

Thomas Hancock, only twenty, was also going as a merchant. He had been in Texas only five years and already had been captured four times by Indians. He would see Perote twice; so would George F. X. Van Ness. And there was Richard F. Brenham, a thirty-year-old physician from Kentucky, headed for Santa Fe to become the Texas collector of customs there. He too would return once from Perote only to die fighting against a second imprisonment there.

The men — many of them actually teen-agers — had much to learn, and sometimes they learned the hard way. Once a few coals were dropped when a man borrowed some to start a new blaze. Instantly the prairie grass exploded into fire, terrifying the group as flames rose quickly to become a searing wall. Fortunately it blew to the side and rear, not ahead.

Later they found their first buffalo and then bear; there was wild honey, too. But no delicacies made up for the sheer labor of travel through one rough strip, known as the Cross Timbers. There the land was criss-crossed with so many gullies that the column might twist along twenty miles of trail to reach a point five miles away. Wheels broke, wagons upset; each mile was an ordeal.

Then they broke out onto the open country. Travel was easier, but their supplies began to thin out. There was no more sugar; they were using mesquite beans to make coffee; they still had beef from their herd of meat cattle but the flesh was stringy. The men, too, were lean and brown after two months in the open sun. Their hair was long and matted.

Late in August, they decided to split the column into two parties. One group of a hundred mounted men proceeded under Captains H. Sutton and William Cooke; the rest followed with the wagons, led by McLeod.

Two weeks later the Sutton-Cooke party, which had moved fast, met their first New Mexicans. There was no welcoming celebration — the Texans soon found themselves prisoners.

McLeod's party, moving more slowly, also encountered New Mexican troops and surrendered on October 5, 1841, at a point not far from the modern city of Tucumcari, New Mexico.

New Mexico had been aroused against the *Tejanos*. The governor ordered them treated as invaders, to be marched as captives down the Rio Grande and on to Mexico City. More than a thousand miles of hot, dusty trail lay ahead of them.

Under heavy guard, the Sutton-Cooke party moved south, through El Paso, Chihuahua, and into Mexico City. The McLeod party straggled in about two months later, on February 9, 1842. There they were parceled out into groups assigned to different prisons.

McLeod and fifty-one of his men were sent to Perote.

It is significant that during most of their journey they were treated with kindness by people along the way; the only cruelties came from their guards. In El Paso, a priest, Father Ramón, did all he could to help them. (Padre Ramón was still in El Paso thirty-five years later during a local "war" over rights to the salt lakes.) Businessmen and even the governor of Chihuahua gave the prisoners money, clothing, and food. Americans working in Mexico as stage drivers or wagon freighters gave generously. So did women of all classes, who cared for the sick, brought food, and did washing.

In the fortress at Perote the men found their quarters spacious but cold. February in central Mexico, even though in the tropics, can be chilly at an altitude of seven thousand feet. There was little light in the large cells: only a small grating over the ponderous wooden cell door, or through the loophole slit that penetrated the main wall of the fort. The floor was of cold stone.

But the prisoners at Perote were not locked in with nothing to do but brood. They were set to work in a nearby stone quarry and at labor on road-building.

The Texas Republic had, of course, no diplomatic representatives in Mexico City. Waddy Thompson, the American minister to Mexico, at once began to work for the men's freedom. Santa Anna, still smarting from his defeat by Sam Houston six years before and with his irritation renewed each time another foreign power recognized the Texas Republic, resisted all demands that the Texans be freed.

In the end, diplomatic pressure won out, although Santa Anna made it appear a magnanimous gesture. On July 13, 1842, all were freed except one man, José Antonio Navarro. He was held for three more years, partly because he had once been a Mexican national who joined the Texans' cause during their revolution.

The prisoners made their way to Vera Cruz and by ship back to Texas. Some got back in August, others in September. They had been gone at least fourteen months when they reached Galveston on a brig flying a white flag on her foremast and the Mexican flag atop her main. The smell from the ship was strong, the men moved in a slow mass coming ashore, although most seemed well enough.

Some announced that they had a bellyfull of "expeditioning," but others were ready to start out again right away. Some of them would be back in action sooner than they thought.

Even before he released the men of the Santa Fe Expedition, Santa Anna in Mexico had decided to send a punitive expedition into Texas. Nothing massive or drawn out; perhaps a good force of a thousand men, with a couple of cannon. Let them go in with strict orders to be back out within thirty days. Keep the discipline good; shoot any deserters.

Santa Anna selected one of his most professional officers, General Adrian Woll. He was a soldier's soldier, a Frenchman who had learned his trade under Bonaparte but had been in Mexico for twenty-five years and was loyal.

Woll started from Presidio a couple of weeks after the first men from Perote landed at Galveston. The Mexican column followed an old smugglers' trail part of the way, and in about ten days they were just outside San Antonio.

That night Woll split his column, and the Mexicans encircled the town. Fighting began early the next day, and the outnumbered Texans soon surrendered. Unknowingly, Woll had picked the most strategic day to attack. The court was in session, and among Woll's forty-two prisoners were so many local officials that the city government was in confusion for the following year and a half.

If the battle had continued to the death, it could have been a bloody affair on both sides. Instead, casualties were light. One report said the Texans killed only a Mexican drummer, and the Mexicans killed only one enemy rooster who got in the way of a stray bullet. Later reports credited the Mexicans with killing seven Anglos.

Among Woll's prisoners was Samuel Maverick, a prominent Texan, who later had a slight connection with the Salt War near El Paso; other captives included George Van Ness, Archibald Fitzgerald, and Thomas Hancock, who had been with the Santa Fe men and were recently returned from Perote.

A couple of days later Woll, sent the contingent of prisoners on their way, first to Presidio and eventually to Perote. Woll's thirty days still had not expired, so he stayed around San Antonio to mop up a few details. He was very nearly mopped up himself before he got away. The counter-attack was being organized.

One of the first Texans to ride in from the countryside and size up the situation was John Coffee "Jack" Hays, head of that relatively new force known as the Texas Rangers.

The word *Ranger* did not start in Texas; it was an old term for any border-warfare fighting man. Stephen F. Austin had used the word in his writings as early as 1823, but it was not until late 1835 that the provisional government of Texas officially created the force.

From 1836 to 1840 there was little action for the Rangers, whose primary duties included guarding the frontier against Mexican raiders and Indians. Funds were short in those years.

In 1840 the Rangers began to build a strong organization. Men such as Captain "Jack" Hays, Ben McCulloch, Samuel W. Walker, and W. A. A. "Bigfoot" Wallace joined.

At the time Woll rode down on San Antonio, the Texas Army was virtually non-existent, and there were only about a hundred and fifty Rangers to guard the entire Texas frontier. This lack of protection had caused concern among the Texans, and in nearly every community of any size some sort of minute-man organization was formed, ready to repel any raid or attack.

These local, spontaneous groups were on the move quickly when Captain Hays spread the news that Woll was in San Antonio. The mayor of San Antonio had escaped during the fight and had sent word to Colonel Mathew Caldwell, another Santa Fe-Perote man who had returned to Gonzales, not far from San Antonio. Caldwell hurried to a rallying point and took command of units that were riding in from the countryside. Bigfoot Wallace arrived with a keg of powder. The Battle of the Salado was about to open.

One week to the day after Woll attacked San Antonio, he found himself faced by a formidable Texan force on the Salado River just outside the city. He sent his main body of troops out to meet the enemy. Fighting was strong until Woll's men retreated late in the afternoon. Two days later the Mexican column was in retreat, back toward Presidio.

In the Battle of the Salado, Woll had lost about sixty men. The Texans had lost only one man killed in the main fight, but they had a tragic loss in a contingent from the town of LaGrange.

This unit of fifty-three men rode under the leadership of Nicholas Mosby Dawson. Before the "Dawson Men" could join the main Texan force fighting on the Salado, they were surrounded in a small grove by a force four or five times their size. The Mexicans also had a cannon. In the fighting that followed, thirty-five of the Dawson Men were killed, two or three escaped, and the remaining fifteen were captured. Woll took them with him when he left for Presidio. Most of the men from LaGrange were wounded too badly to send as far as Perote, but at least six were sent on to that sombre prison. After Woll's departure, most of the Texans dispersed. A few remained and laid plans to follow Woll, or at least to send a counter-expedition in revenge. President Sam Houston authorized such an expedition, under the leadership of Brigadier General Alexander Somervell. In two months, a force of seven hundred enthusiastic volunteers was organized.

The expedition marched to the Rio Grande and took the town of Laredo without difficulty. They continued downstream on the Mexican side and occupied Guerrero — the village that had once been named Revilla and had been the home of José Gutiérrez de Lara.

At that point, Somervell's force had dwindled to about five hundred men. The Texas government could not support even such a small force for any extended campaign into Mexico. Somervell saw that in a choice between "go for broke" and go home, it was wiser to go home.

The Texans were disappointed and angry at Somervell's decision. Only two-fifths of his command obeyed his order to return to San Antonio. The other three hundred decided to continue the campaign entirely on their own, and the Somervell Expedition overnight became the Mier Expedition — headed for the town of Mier, the next village downstream. The men elected William S. Fisher their new colonel, commandeered some barges, and floated down to Mier. They found the town without a military garrison.

The Texans laid a levy on the town for food, shoes, and blankets. The people of Mier asked for five days in which to gather the materials. The Texans went into camp a few miles from the town.

When the supplies were slow in coming, the Texans sent out some scouts to investigate. They found that General Pedro de Ampudia had arrived in Mier with a superior force of Mexican troops.

Still, the Texans decided to fight. They moved toward the town at dusk on Christmas evening, 1842. Some advance Texan scouts included Samuel Walker, whose name later became connected with a famous model of a revolver.

A drizzling rain was falling. There was almost no chance for surprise; the Texans could hear the rattle of cavalrymen's sabres and accoutrements as they neared a unit of Mexican cavalry posted to intercept the invaders. The Texans had some advantage in the darkness: they could see the town ahead, had been in it a few days before, and knew just where to move in the darkness. The Mexicans could shoot only when fired upon. In a short time, the Texans were inside some stone buildings on a street in the small village. The steady drizzling rain made it imperative for them to seek shelter. It took more time to unload a wet rifle than to unbreech a wet musket.

Dawn revealed the extent of the odds facing the Texans. Against about 300 men from San Antonio the enemy were at least eight to one. Nevertheless, tough street fighting began at once and continued for most of the day, with vicious losses for the Mexicans, who had to fight through the streets.

The Mexicans advanced a white flag and offered the Texans a chance to surrender. The Lone Star men opposed the idea strongly, but Colonel Fisher saw that the end could only be the loss of two-thirds, and perhaps all, of his force. Col. Thomas J. Green, his second in command, still wanted to fight. After long arguments, they did surrender, but it is still possible to get an argument going in Texas as to whether or not they did the wise thing.

One of the Texan guards, left back at their camp, was killed in a bit of action there. He was Major George Bonnell, and he had been with the Texan Santa Fe Expedition.

On December 31 the Mexican army marched out with its prisoners, headed for Matamoros, down toward the mouth of the Rio Grande. The first day's march was twenty five miles, with no stop for water. It took about ten days to reach Matamoros. Each night the prisoners were herded into a cowpen or corral if one were available.

From Matamoros, Colonel Fisher, Tom Green, and a few others, were sent on ahead of the others, headed for Mexico City, as hostages to ensure good conduct on the part of the prisoners. The main body followed at a slower pace.

Fisher, Green, and the small group were taken to Monterey and on to Saltillo. There they found six of the prisoners who had been taken by Woll at Bexar and on the Salado, and had been left at this place while the others went on. The group included three who were wounded, plus the three Santa Fe Expedition men: Fitzgerald, Van Ness, and Hancock.

At Saltillo the main body of prisoners caught up with the vanguard, but they were quartered separately, and when the march was resumed the main body was held back for a day. By this time, the men in the main contingent were already laying quiet plans for a mass break at the first opportunity.

It presented itself a few days later, when the main body and vanguard were again rejoined at a large rancho called Salado. This could scarcely be called a village; it sat in the middle of a bare desert plain and consisted of an old rambling hacienda around a large walled patio or courtyard. A deep well furnished brackish water, drawn by mules working a contrivance of leathern buckets.

The Mexican officer in charge of the vanguard had fallen sick, and while he was recovering the main body caught up with the leading group.

The next morning, the advance party left at dawn. The main body made ready to try a break. A few armed guards lounged on housetops around the courtyard. Through the doorway the prisoners could see a couple of sentinels, and beyond that were visible the muskets of other guards, stacked against a wall while the guards themselves finished breakfast and got their gear ready for travel. Everyone waited for a signal from Ewen Cameron, their acknowledged leader.

Cameron laid aside his hat.

"Now, boys, we go it!" he cried, as he jumped through the door and seized a sentinel's musket.

The others poured in a flood through the exit, jamming the narrow gateway. Others picked up pieces of broken brick and felled the guards on the rooftops. In a few minutes, the prisoners were outside and armed with captured muskets.

The vanguard heard the shots and knew a break was in progress.

For a moment, it looked as though they, as hostages, might be executed, but then the officer commanding the advance guard decided that he had to carry out his specific orders to deliver the most important prisoners. At the next town, the advance prisoners were turned over to the local authorities, who were told to take them on ahead while the military guard returned to see what could be done about the escaped men.

It was night, but the local militia, actually little better than a posse, took the prisoners on ahead. Later they were rejoined by the military guard, which had changed its mind about going back after the escaped main body.

The mass break was not going too smoothly. Five Texans, including three who were Santa Fe Expedition men (Brenham was one), were killed. Fitzgerald died of wounds a day or so later. But the cavalry soon were routed and the Texans were free, at least for the moment.

They made ready for their travel back to Texas. Most of them were armed, many were mounted; they filled gourds with water. They made seventy miles in the first eighteen hours and continued to travel by day and night.

Then they made a fatal error by leaving the main road and taking to the wild country. They became more or less lost, their water and food gave out, their shoes were worn to bits, and the organization fell apart as stronger individuals left to make it on their own. The remnants finally surrendered to a Mexican cavalry camp in order to get water.

In small groups and singly, the rest of the men were also captured, and again they formed their line of march, south, back to Salado in irons.

Some Americans working as teamsters on wagon freight lines in that part of Mexico came along to pass the news that an order was out to execute every tenth man. The guard knew nothing of such an order, so the prisoners passed it off with a shudder as just another rumor. They knew their guard well: if there had been such an order, he would have delighted in repeating it.

About two weeks later the column straggled into the walled yard of the old rancho at Salado, on March 25, 1843. Only six weeks earlier they had been victors at the same place. Their return was under ominous, cloudy skies; a strong wind was whipping up clouds of dust. Bigfoot Wallace observed a small peculiarity: no birds were singing, even the insects were silent.

Just before they entered the enclosure, the men were allowed to drink all the water they wished at the tank outside. Then about two o'clock they filed in. The wind lessened, as though it had given up the chase now that the prisoners had reached some sort of shelter. The men noticed several strange officers outside the gates, and soon a group of them came in. One, a little more richly dressed than the others, carried a document in his hand. He called for an interpreter, who addressed the men.

The prisoners crowded close, hoping that the news might be some order of clemency. They were due for a jolt. The proclamation stated that there had been a change in orders: whereas a previous order had been issued for execution of all, the new decision was that only every tenth man would be shot.

For a few seconds the men stood quietly, stunned, and then they shook their chains in frustrated anger. There could be no thought of escape. Files of armed soldiers faced them; more guards stood on the rooftops, their muskets at the ready. The men were ordered back into line. There was to be no waiting; the ceremony of selection started at once.

An officer came forward bearing an earthenware jar or mug. Behind him followed a private carrying a small bench, which he placed on a low wall inside the courtyard.

Another officer counted out one hundred and fifty-nine white beans and dropped them into the jar. He added seventeen black beans on top, covered the bowl with a small cloth, and handed it to the commanding officer. He lifted it, shook it slightly, and placed it back on the bench.

One hundred and seventy-six beans altogether, one for each prisoner, and every tenth bean a black one, for death.

An officer handed the interpreter a list of prisoners' names, written when they were recaptured. The first names called were those of the officers.

Thomas J. Green, one of the prisoners, saw a foreboding connection in some of the moves: the black beans were dropped in last, on top of the white ones; they were not mixed energetically; the officers were called first. Perhaps this was an intentional device to make sure the officers drew the deadly markers.

The men were warned to draw only a single bean. Should any man draw more than one, and his drawing included a black bean, the black would rule.

Cameron's name was called first, as the ranking Texas officer.

"Well, boys, let's be at it," he said and reached inside.

A white bean.

He came back to the line of prisoners. "Dip deep, boys," he whispered to those near.

The others stepped forward as their names were called: Wilson, Ryan, Gibson, Eastland. All drew white except Eastland, whose hand came out from under the cloth with the first black counter.

Then the enlisted men moved forward, chained in pairs, as their names were read. There was no panic; each seemed determined to strengthen the others by his own appearance of calm. They made casual remarks after they drew:

"Boys, this beats raffling all to pieces."

"They've taken my sign in at last."

"This is the tallest gambling scrape I was ever in."

"Well, boys, the jig is up with me."

Each handed his bean to the Mexican officer, who put the black beans in his waistcoat pocket. The white ones he laid on the low wall.

The drawing continued. At one point, twenty-four white beans were drawn in unbroken succession. Some men drew nonchalantly; others learned over the jar, anxious to see quickly what their fate would be.

The Mexican officers murmured among themselves at the courage of the prisoners; a few officers were obviously emotionally disturbed by a process they considered offensive to their national honor.

One officer was not disturbed; he seemed to enjoy the whole process. There are such men in any army. He spoke with soothing irony to those who hesitated slightly.

"Take your time, my boy," he would say. "Be careful, you know if you get a black bean you will be taken outside and shot in ten minutes. Ah! That's unfortunate (a black bean)! Better luck next time."

Bigfoot Wallace was among the enlisted men, and his name ranked low on the alphabetical list. He told his biographer later, "I thought I could perceive a slight difference in the size of the black and white beans — that the former were a shade larger than the latter. This difference, I know, may have been purely imaginary, but at any rate, I was eventually decided by it in my choice of a bean.

"When I first put my hand in the pot I took up several beans at once in my fingers, and endeavored to distinguish their color by the touch, but they all felt precisely alike. I then dropped them and picked up two more, and after fingering them carefully for an instant, I thought that one of them seemed a little larger than the other. I dropped that one like a hot potato, and drew out the one left. It was a white one, of course, or I should not now be here to tell my story — but not a *very* white one, and when I cast my eyes upon it, it looked to me as 'black as the ace of spades.'

"I felt certain for a moment that my fate was sealed, but when I handed it to the Mexican officer, I saw that he put it on the wall with the white beans . . . I knew then that I was safe."

After Wallace came Henry Whaling, who drew a black. "Well, boys, they won't make much off me, anyhow, for I know I've killed twenty-five."

By four o'clock the drawing was ended. The total number of beans drawn, both black and white, was counted formally.

Those who drew black beans were ordered to step apart from the others. Then they were marched outside the compound. Those who remained inside were warned to remain still during the execution, on penalty of death. Dusk was falling.

At least four survivors had their stories published later, and the variations indicate the sort of puzzle that historians often face, as well as demonstrating the chance for error when working from a single source.

One account said that the prisoners, after being taken outside the compound wall, were made to kneel. Another said they were forced to sit on a log near the wall, with their backs to the firing squad. A third said they sat facing their executioners. One said the condemned men were shot in two parties; others said they were in only a single group, but that the squad fired several volleys. Most agreed that the firing took about fifteen minutes. The interpreter later told the Texans that it took fifteen shots to finish Henry Whaling.

Then there was silence.

Next morning the surviving prisoners were herded together and continued their march. Outside the gate they passed the crumpled bodies of their comrades.

But there was one body missing: that of James L. Shepherd.

He was hit in the first volley, a slight wound on the cheek. He dropped to the ground and pretended to be dead. In the twilight and excitement, his ruse was successful. Before daybreak he was gone. But it was an unsuccessful escape; a few weeks later he was recaptured and taken to Saltillo. There he was executed by a firing squad in the public square.

A month later, while the prisoners were on the march, Ewen Cameron was executed by a special order. It was stated that four men had been absent at the drawing, requiring an eighteenth man to complete the proper decimation. As leader of the Texans, Cameron was taken out and shot.

By April 26 the main party was in Santiago, at an old convent. They had been on the road four months, and counting the doubling done by their attempted escape had marched seven hundred miles.

They had been in irons since their recapture at Salado rancho. At Santiago they were put to work making roads and were kept at this until early September.

The vanguard had reached Mexico City on March 15. They were given brief interviews with the American minister and a British diplomat and were then sent on to the prison at Perote, where they arrived on March 25. The main body were still doing road gang work, back in Santiago; later they too were brought to Perote.

As the weeks went by in the prison with only discouraging news about any release, one group of prisoners determined to try to escape. Thomas Jefferson Green, one of the most prominent of the Perote prisoners, wrote a detailed story of what happened.

Essentially, their plan was to make an opening through the back wall of their cell: the outer wall of the castle itself. Once through its eight-foot thickness, the men could drop into the moat and scale the outer defenses.

They first experimented with the loophole, about two feet wide on the inside and tapering to a slit about four by twelve inches. The men found, after a desperate trial, that the stones around the opening were too hard and their fastening too firm.

It was decided to make a new opening, straight through the full thickness of the wall. A spot was selected at the left of a loophole. The new opening could be concealed by swinging back the inside shutter of the loophole, draped with a carelessly hung blanket.

Prisoners who worked in the castle's carpenter shop smuggled in some chisels — inferior, but the only ones available. When the tools grew dull, they were taken back surreptitiously for sharpening.

Only one man could work at a time, lying prone, his ear alert for a warning tap by the lookout standing at the door. Using the chisel, a small hole was drilled into the mortar and a bit of stone pried off. Green wrote that "after a hard day's labour, not more than a hatful could be disengaged." The fragments were buried under loose stones on the cell floor or smuggled out to the privy.

Working in relays, the men dug until there was only a thin shell left to be broken when the moment arrived for the escape. The digging took a little more than two weeks.

While the diggers were at work, others gathered the supplies and equipment needed for a successful escape. Green had managed to secure a good map of that part of Mexico, smuggled in as a casual wrapping around some shaving articles. Friends on the outside in Mexico also provided money, and the prisoners bought a stock of sugar, coffee, chocolate, and bacon. Purchases were made from the castle's sutler, in small lots to avoid suspicion. Two weeks' rations were secured for each man in the group.

Prisoners who went into the town of Perote in work parties were able to buy short lengths of rope. An old seaman quickly spliced the pieces into a useful length, which was concealed under a pile of straw.

Sixteen men decided to make the attempt. Prison guards were rotated every few days, and the men waited until the officer on duty was one known for being indifferent and careless. When his tour arrived, the men packed their makeshift knapsacks and waited until the evening count was completed.

Those who were staying behind improvised elaborate methods of diverting the attention of the sentinel at the door. First they passed him several drinks of *mescal*, using an eggshell for a cup.

Others then spread a blanket on the floor inside the door, lit a pair of candles, and began a game of monte. For chips they used small squares of soap, worth a cent and a half. They passed a few of these counters to the sentinel and invited him to bet on cards of his choice. This alone riveted the attention of the sentinel, a confirmed monte player.

A thin air of panic swept the room when it was found that the opening was still too narrow to allow escape. The rough opening tapered slightly toward the outside, and two more hours' work were needed to widen the hole.

To cover the noise of this last-minute effort, eight or ten prisoners engaged in a rowdy, shuffling "bull dance," although they were chained together in pairs. When the dancers tired, others took their place or at intervals all joined in a noisy chorus.

By nine o'clock the first prisoner wriggled feet first into the breach and out into the darkness, where a thin rain was falling. It was slow, careful work — out the hole and down the rope thirty feet to the bottom of the moat. Three and a half hours passed before all·were out. The rain had stopped, and the moon was down.

Gathered in the darkness of the moat, the men listened to the guards calling their routine signals as they paced the top of the wall. In Indian file the men crossed to the far side of the moat and felt their way along until they came to a narrow stairway cut in the bank. They went up on hands and knees.

The next barrier was the twelve-foot *chevaux de frise* of wooden posts. Fortunately there was a horizontal stringer about six feet up, to hold the posts together. The men climbed up by means of this and over the top, then down into the outer ditch and over the last embankment.

Free! They couldn't cheer, but they jumped, really jumped, up and down a few times in their joy. The bell in the castle tolled a half hour past midnight.

By a pre-arranged plan, the men separated into twos and threes, each group heading off in a slightly different course toward east, northeast, or north.

There was no risk of pursuit before the morning count, so the men moved briskly. By daybreak, Tom Green and his partners were well into the mountains. For the next week they traveled by night and slept hidden during the day. It was the rainy season, and chilling showers were frequent. Once they inched down a narrow trail in the darkness into a thousand-foot canyon. In a dark hollow by a waterfall they paused one night to brew cup after cup of hot coffee.

When they came to the first town, Jalapa, they sent one man ahead. He spoke Spanish and was able to reach the house of a known friend. The others were then guided to safety.

For five days they stayed in the hideout, treated with kindness. They bought good shoes and all the gear of ordinary *rancheros*. On the sixth night their host took them, with a deep air of mystery, to a ravine where they found mules waiting. There was also a strange new guide, a robber who had been engaged to lead them to the seaport of Vera Cruz.

There was honor in this thief, at least, and he took his contract seriously. All night they rode, part of it in a howling rainstorm, and at daylight they dropped to sleep instantly in a marshy spot.

At noon they were awakened by their guide, who brought from under his *serape* a hot, cooked chicken, plus eggs and tortillas. A new guide appeared to replace the first, and by relays of such strange friends the Texans were led to Vera Cruz. There they waited another two weeks, crowded into a tiny lodging in the center of a district where yellow fever was rampant.

Once they spotted another Perote prisoner passing on the street and hastily called him inside. From him they learned that five of their friends had been retaken and four others were apparently still moving toward full freedom. One had already managed to leave on a ship. The other six, including Green, by now were gathered in the hideout.

Finally an American ship came into port. Green knew the mate, and that night the Perote men managed to board the vessel. Six days later they landed in Texas.

Tom Green's party had escaped on July 2, 1843. On the following March 25, exactly one year to the day from the time when they drew beans at Salado for life or death, another group of sixteen prisoners escaped from the same cell! They had dug down through the floor and out, following a gopher hole that provided thin ventilation.

If the castle had been in an uproar after the first escape, it was nothing compared to the excitement that followed the second escape. Santa Anna stormed with anger, but the forces of diplomacy were also growing more firm as talk of Texas' annexation to the United States began to circulate. On September 16, 1844, the last Texans were released from Perote.

The castle was not to disappear, as in some Iberian legend; history came again soon to Perote, and yet again a century after that.

In 1847 war was on as the United States invaded Mexico. In May, advancing American troops came to the old rancho at Salado, where the black beans had been drawn. With the unit was Captain John Dusenberry, who himself had fought at Mier. The bodies of most of the executed men had been given a rough burial; a few bones were still visible. The remains were removed carefully and sent back to Texas. They are now interred at Monument Hill, near the town of LaGrange, beside the Dawson men who fell in the fight against General Woll, outside San Antonio.

A week or so after Dusenberry returned to the Salado rancho, Samuel Walker, another Perote prisoner among the Mier men, rode back into the old castle as captain of a company of mounted riflemen with General Twiggs' division. To prove he knew the place, Walker dug up a small coin he had buried before he left Perote.

The Texas Rangers went to Perote, too, with the American army. It was the only time the Rangers served as a unit in the regular forces.

As the United States' troops plunged deeper into Mexico, they had found their lines of communication disrupted by effective Mexican guerrillas. To keep the routes safe, the top command decided to organize a regiment of Texas Rangers.

The job was turned over to Colonel Jack Hays, back in Texas. Hays decided to leave his older, experienced Rangers on guard along the border and to form a new regiment. He opened a recruiting office in San Antonio, and men flocked to join. Within weeks the new unit was on the march, back along the old road of the Mier men: to Presidio, Mier, Matamoros. In the outfit were men from the Santa Fe Expedition, men who had been captured by General Woll and sent to Perote, and veterans who had been taken to the old castle after the fight at Mier. They reached Perote in October, 1847.

The Rangers did good work, and their taut discipline in Mexico proved them to be forerunners of such fighting outfits as the Mexican *rurales*, the Rough Riders, Merrill's Marauders, and the Green Berets.

In a curious sidelight on American culture, the Perote prisoners brought back to Texas much of the first cowboy lore, and men from other states who served in the Mexican War took home the start of the Western gunfighter legend.

There was really no cattle industry in Texas before the Mexican War, but livestock raising had long been a Mexican occupation. At a rest stop in one hacienda along their march to Perote, the Mier prisoners had watched Mexican officers having sport with a lasso. Merely flinging a loop around an animal's neck was considered too simple; the real accomplishment was to lasso a beast by one foot while it was running. Even children used little ropes to lasso ducks and chickens. The Mexicans roped everything, even wild bulls. The prisoners remembered one small incident in the street fighting at Mier: a Mexican gun crew had been forced to abandon their cannon in the street, and no one dared venture into the open to retrieve it. Then the Texans saw a lasso whirl out from behind the corner wall and loop neatly over the gun, which was drawn back to safety.

In those weeks as prisoners, the Texans looked upon such antics as a ridiculous pastime. But when longhorns began to roam the ranges north of the Rio Grande, Texans were quick to adopt the useful *lazo*.

American army recruits who came from the eastern states to fight in Mexico returned with a definite memory of the Texans. Most of Jack Hays' Rangers were at least six feet tall. They were quiet men, superb riders, and each man had one or two of the new six-shot revolvers — the first American military unit that was so equipped. And when the war was over, and the other soldiers went back to their home states, they carried with them that image of a Southwesterner. From then on, all the Western men had to do was live up to the legend.

Jack Hays had helped to start the legend. When the war ended, he left the Rangers. He served on a commission that helped settle a border dispute and was for a time an Indian agent in New Mexico.

Then he went to California, became that state's surveyor-general, and laid out the town of Oakland. He remained in Oakland, except for time out to fight Indians in Nevada in 1860, and died in California in 1883.

Perote saw Santa Anna at least once more. In 1855 when his regime at last collapsed, he rode from Mexico City to flee on a ship from Vera Cruz. He made his farewell political address — at the village of Perote.

In 1933 the Mexican government classified Perote as a monument. It is still a military installation and may not be visited or photographed by any casual tourist. During World War II it was used as a detention center for German and Japanese nationals in Mexico. A hundred years after the Mier men, there were prisoners again at Perote.

5

Confederates on the Rio Grande

"WHEN I go to another war, I'm goin' to it a way I can get to it quicker than I can this 'ere one," a cavalryman of the Texas Mounted Volunteers, CSA, wrote back to a San Antonio newspaper in 1861. He had been in the saddle for six hundred rock-strewn miles and still was far from the scene of action.

What he had just been through was a pleasure ride compared to what lay ahead.

The Confederate plan to seize New Mexico was a dream that almost came true, a dream that is almost forgotten. Tourists who today stop at a bronze plaque in a rocky cove beside an old road in New Mexico often are amazed to find that in this remote spot was fought a battle that some tacticians call the Gettysburg of the West.

In the Far West, the Civil War began only a week after the first battle of Bull Run, and it was all over before the Battle of Shiloh, the first great combat east of the Mississippi. In the West the Confederate forces were almost entirely Texan.

From San Antonio to San Francisco, the whole West was in turmoil after Lincoln's election. There were new governors, new commanders, and new troops on both sides. It was the worst conceivable time to start a game for high stakes; a game with a short deck and deuces wild — to say nothing of more than one joker in the pack.

As the year 1861 opened, General Albert Sidney Johnston was named commander of all Union forces in the Department of California. Robert E. Lee was a Union officer stationed in Texas.

The uproar in Texas had already begun, within days after Lincoln's election the previous November. George Baylor, a rough and ready Indian fighter, had been making vigorous speeches in central Texas. John S. "Rip" Ford, who already had fought with distinction in the Texas Revolution and in the war with Mexico, was one of a group demanding that Texas secede.

On February 1, a state convention voted for secession, with their action subject to a popular vote scheduled for February 23. In Washington, Congress ordered a halt to the Butterfield stage service across the Southwest.

Without waiting for the public vote, the secession convention commissioned Rip Ford and two others as colonels of cavalry, with orders to start immediate recruitment. By mid-February Major General David E. Twiggs surrendered to the Texans all of the U.S. military posts and supplies located in the state.

When the popular vote was taken on February 23, Texans voted overwhelmingly for secession. Five days later the U.S. Congress voted to establish Colorado as a new territory. Thirteen months later, to the day, men from Texas and Colorado would clash to decide the fate of the West.

On March 2, Congress cancelled the Butterfield mail contract and the stage line operators began to demolish its stations. On March 4, Texas' secession became effective, and twelve days later the new officials took their oath of office. On that same day a meeting was held in far-off Tucson to declare that the mood of Arizona favored the Confederacy. A few days later the pro-Southern Colonel William W. Loring was named Union commander of the Department of New Mexico. And on the last day of March all of the buildings and supplies at Fort Bliss, near El Paso, were turned over to a local committee of Southerners.

Back in the East, rebel guns opened on Fort Sumter on April 12. Three days later Lincoln declared that a state of insurrection existed. Now the game opened officially for both sides, and players began to draw new cards. Robert E. Lee declared himself for the South. So did Albert Sidney Johnston in California. During May and June other officers in the West began to resign, many to reach fame later with the Confederate forces: Henry H. Sibley, Joseph Wheeler, Richard S. Ewell, George B. Crittenden, and James Longstreet — most of them from posts in New Mexico.

Lincoln made a few changes too. He appointed Henry Connelly as governor of New Mexico and named William Gilpin as the first governor of Colorado. Both men started to recruit their own territorial forces. The Texans had several weeks' head start in building their own military units.

Rip Ford had been organizing his 2nd Regiment, Texas Mounted Rifles, gathering at San Antonio and intended for combat in deep south Texas around the mouth of the Rio Grande.

In May, four companies of Ford's new outfit were ordered detached and sent west to El Paso, under Lieutenant Colonel John R. Baylor and Major Ed Waller. A few days later, Colonel Loring resigned as commander in New Mexico, and he was replaced with E. R. S. Canby. Three names mentioned so far carried the New Mexico conflict to its end: Baylor and Sibley for the Confederates, Canby for the Union.

As the Texas cavalry rode west from San Antonio to El Paso, roughly six hundred miles with water and shade scarcer every furlong, what was their objective? Surely not defense, for the few troops left in the west were no menace to Texas.

The reasons for the cavalry's westward ride were never found in any written orders that remain. They were revealed in a few quiet talks around bivouac campfires and mentioned in a few letters found in the archives. Nothing official, but still with a ring of truth to them.

There were, first of all, a few old scores to settle: the treatment given by New Mexicans to the men of the Texan-Santa Fe Expedition; also Texas' old claim to lands west to the Rio Grande. And Santa Fe lies east of the Rio Grande, within the area Texas claimed. Texas men had always had a tradition of answering any call to arms. A Texan was always ready for action, and this was action ready at hand, here and now.

There is some evidence that the Confederate leaders saw bigger stakes. For one thing, there was gold in California, in Nevada, and in Colorado. Gold was badly needed for the European arms and ammunition the South would have to buy.

Others had a dream of a Western Confederacy of states, expanding the Southern empire to the shores of the Pacific. Long before the Civil War began there had been national interest in a railroad from Texas to the Pacific. Along such an artery lay New Mexico, Arizona, and California. And why not go farther and annex, through conquest or purchase, the northern Mexican states of Sonora, Chihuahua, Durango, and Tamaulipas.

Such an expedition for gold and territory might well supply itself from abandoned army posts. There were plentiful signs of Confederate sympathy in every Southwestern state.

When Baylor's four companies reached El Paso, they were at once reinforced by local units. There were only forty-four Anglo-Americans in El Paso, but men came in from the hills and from up the Rio Grande, men such as Enrique D'Hamel, twenty-six years old and working at Hart's Mill, a mile or so upriver from El Paso. D'Hamel joined a unit of scouts recruited by Bethel Coopwood and known as the San Elizario Spy Company. D'Hamel later wrote that "all the members of the company were Texas backwoodsmen, ranchers and cowboys who knew the country from San Antonio to Santa Fe, and from mountain to mountain on both sides of the Rio Grande. Most of the men had been Indian fighters."

While Baylor was gathering his men at El Paso for a push into New Mexico, Henry H. Sibley was in Virginia where, on July 8, he was made a brigadier general by Jefferson Davis, with broad orders to organize troops in Texas and move west for the complete conquest of New Mexico. Baylor's quick dash to the west was only the preliminary; Sibley's steam roller would be the decisive effort.

Over in Arizona, the few Union outposts felt the local Confederate sympathy. In July the officers at Fort Breckenridge decided to burn their post rather than let it fall into Southern hands. They put the torch to their barracks and marched down to Fort Buchanan. On July 23 they burned Buchanan and headed east toward New Mexico.

That same night Baylor's men rode north toward Fort Fillmore. Before the next eight months had passed the Texans would meet the enemy in three major engagements: at Fillmore, at Valverde, and at Glorieta.

On paper it looked as though Fort Fillmore should have been a Union victory. It was a frontier fort manned by nearly seven hundred trained regulars. Baylor had less than half that many Texans, hastily trained and armed with shotguns, bear guns, navy revolvers, Minie muskets, and almost every other type and caliber of weapon found in the West.

Actually Fort Fillmore was no fort at all. It was a garrison of adobe barracks around three sides of a square, baking in an open plain on the east bank of the Rio Grande across from Mesilla and about forty miles above El Paso. The fort had no walls. It was surrounded by sand hills from which any foe, Indian or Confederate, could observe or attack. Its original function was to be a base of operation for troops guarding against Indian attacks on settlers or emigrant trains. The commander was an old veteran, Major Isaac Lynde, whom Canby had sent to Fillmore from another fort about five weeks earlier.

When Baylor left El Paso the night of July 23 he had 258 men in the column. His plan was to move quietly into position between the fort and the river, cut off the horses as they came down for water, and then attack the fort by surprise.

This was a good plan, but it didn't work. Baylor got close, but in the middle of the night one of his men, a former Union trooper named Brown, deserted the Texans and took the alarm to the fort. Instantly the drums sounded the long roll and the post garrison was alerted. The chance for surprise was gone.

The Texans backed off downriver a short distance and waited until morning. Then they splashed across a shallow ford into the village of Santo Tomas. Here they picked up eight Union solders, left behind either during the confusion or by their own choice. There had been two companies of the U.S. 7th Infantry at Santo Tomas, but the commandant had called them into the fort when the alarm rolled.

Baylor questioned them about the Union troops said to be riding east from Fort Breckenridge in Arizona. No troops, only supplies, had arrived, was their answer.

The Texans rode on into Mesilla, through the zig-zag dirt streets between one-story adobe houses and into the plaza. From all corners people were pouring into the square bringing food and even hay. The village had mushroomed a few years before, when the Mexican War ended and many northern New Mexicans thought they could leave U.S. territory by moving down to Mesilla. But the boundary commissioners, together with the Gadsden Purchase, placed Mesilla in New Mexico. Therefore, the war sympathy in Mesilla was strongly Southern, or at least anti-Union.

The Confederate flag had been flying in Mesilla two days before Baylor rode in, although it was not flying when he arrived. A lieutenant and fifty men from Fort Fillmore had just left after coming in to inspect the town. It was now about nine o'clock in the morning.

Baylor dismounted and chose his headquarters: a big, roomy place on the west side of the dusty plaza. (It is still there today, now a bookshop.) His men took advantage of the saloons, one of which would soon be operated by a man named Roy Bean, later a sort of judge, over "West of the Pecos" in Texas.

Shortly before five o'clock a Texan scout came to Baylor with word that the Union troops had crossed the river and were advancing toward Mesilla. This was it; the fighting would start here. One place was as good as another, and this one might be even better than some. Baylor posted his Texans out at the eastern edge of Mesilla: Hardeman's company off at the right behind a three-foot adobe wall topped by another three or four feet of ocotillo cactus stalks — good for protection against both musketry and cavalry. The other Confederates evened themselves out across the center and left wing, some in or behind buildings and some in cornfields.

There came the Federals, about three hundred by Lynde's later report. Cavalry, a couple of howitzers, and plenty of infantry. They stopped about three hundred yards off. Two men, unarmed, rode forward with a white flag. Baylor told Major Waller and a second man to go out for the parley. The two Texans rode forward, their double-barreled shotguns held casually.

The two Union men introduced themselves as Lieutenant Brooks and Surgeon McKee. They said Major Lynde demanded the unconditional surrender of Mesilla. Waller listened politely and asked them to wait while he relayed the message to his own commander.

"We will fight first and then surrender," said Baylor.

Waller rode back to Brooks and McKee with the message; both pairs then returned to their own lines.

The Union troops made the first moves, in textbook fashion and in perfect obedience to orders. Their infantry moved off the road to left and right, into the cornfields. The two brass howitzers were made ready in the center. Behind them waited the cavalry.

The mountain howitzer was a popular gun in the West. It was a stubby little piece with an almost cylindrical barrel, looking almost as though it were made of pipe. It threw a shell with low muzzle velocity, lobbing in a high arc, and the howitzers were usually mounted on a stub-tailed carriage to allow greater elevation. The gun had a large caliber in proportion to its weight. Most mountain howitzers were rated as twelve-pounders, measured by the weight of the projectile. Yet a twelve-pounder howitzer weighed a hundred pounds less than a cannon firing a six-pound ball. The difference was due to the smaller charge used in a howitzer: three-quarters of a pound of black powder to hurl a can (canister) containing small balls. In a mountain howitzer the shell nearly always contained musket balls. A small chamber at the back of the bore received and held the powder. Canister shot was most effective at ranges up to four hundred yards, against massed bodies of the enemy.

Lynde had four of these little beauties and brought two of them to Mesilla. The weapon on display today in the plaza in Albuquerque Old Town is probably one of Lynde's.

There was no waiting. Both howitzers fired, with no great effect other than to stampede the Texans' horses and to be the first shots of the Civil War in the Far West.

Then the Union cavalry moved up about fifty yards closer to the town, preparing for a charge. Baylor ordered Hardeman's riflemen to fire. The volley from their first rank hit the center of the Union cavalry. Lieutenant McNally was heading the horsemen; one shot shattered his saber, another went through his chest. Altogether perhaps four Union men were killed and seven wounded. The gunners at the howitzers dropped to the ground for safety. The Union cavalry were thrown into confusion, moving back into their own infantry. Lynde at once ordered a retreat, and the Union ranks formed for the march back toward the fort.

Baylor couldn't believe the retreat was genuine. He suspected a feint of some sort and held his men ready as night fell. They stayed in place that night.

Both sides stayed in position all the next day. Baylor had sent a messenger back to have the Confederate guns brought up from El Paso. Lynde debated within himself concerning the next Union move. He knew the Texans had no artillery in Mesilla, but he also knew they probably would bring up some pronto from El Paso. Fillmore could not withstand any siege — the only walls were those of the adobe barracks, and those sand hills around the place offered ideal positions for artillery. There were a hundred women and children in the fort. The men under his command were at least a fourth of all Union forces in New Mexico — and Lynde felt that men were more important than mud buildings. So he decided to retreat, away from the Rio Grande, across a short strip of desert, over the pass through the Organ Mountains just east, then past the Great White Sands and over to Fort Stanton.

Night fell, with Baylor still waiting for that second attack that never came. And at one in the morning the garrison with all its women and children started trailing out of Fort Fillmore.

Shortly after dawn on July 27, Baylor's outriders came tearing into Mesilla to report a column of dust rising in the air above Fillmore. Baylor took a telescope and climbed on a rooftop to verify the news. At once he ordered his men to saddle up and ride for the fort.

About a mile from the Rio Grande Baylor met another messenger reporting that the enemy had fled, leaving the fort on fire. The scout added that some Texans were already in Fillmore and had extinguished the flames before much damage was done.

Baylor ordered Major Waller to take a detachment and head directly into the fort, to occupy it and leave a small guard. He, Baylor, planned to head for the retreating Union forces, and Waller could catch up with him on the way.

The sun now was well up over the craggy Organs, and in July any part of lower New Mexico gets hot early in the day. The first fourteen miles had been easy for the Union garrison, but now the trail up to the pass was steeper. For some reason that no official report ever mentioned, the Union men had no water. Lynde himself had never ridden this trail and may have overlooked that need. Soon a hundred and then more dropped by the wayside, collapsing from the heat.

The Texans in pursuit were not having a picnic either, but they were traveling light and had learned about desert riding on their long trip across West Texas.

A detachment of Union reinforcements rushing south from Fort Craig saw Lynde's column climbing toward the pass and swung eastward to join up with him. The new men first caught up with the rearguard wagons, which were accompanied by two of the mountain howitzers. Those guns might have stopped the Texans but no one could find the ammunition.

When Baylor's men reached the summit of the pass, they saw the main body of Lynde's troops clustered below at San Agustin Springs.

Behind Baylor and ahead of him, along the trail down toward the springs, were hundreds of stragglers begging for water.

Baylor ordered Major Waller to ride ahead and cut through the line of stragglers, isolating Lynde's remaining main body. Waller did this neatly and rode directly into Lynde's camp. It took little more than a brief, formal conversation to complete the surrender. Only one thirst-crazed soldier fired a shot.

Less than three hundred Texans had won out over seven hundred Union regulars.

Any war is full of ifs, worth no more than the curious pleasure they provide for armchair generals. There is little point in guessing what would have happened if Lynde had fought — he didn't and was cashiered. There is little point in predicting what would have happened if Baylor had gone on then and hit Fort Craig. He didn't.

For the next six months Baylor stayed around Mesilla, carving his name in history. In August he declared formation of the Confederate Territory of Arizona, comprising the lower halves of present New Mexico and Arizona, with Mesilla as its capital and himself as governor.

By mid-August Sibley was back in Texas from Virginia, and he began forming a brigade. Up in Colorado, volunteer Union companies were starting to drill. Late in October Sibley's long column started west. Two weeks later a menacing column of Union volunteers started to move eastward from California to reinforce the fort at Yuma and to reoccupy Arizona. Baylor adopted drastic policies to control the Indians, and for this was relieved of his command.

As 1862 ended, Sibley was in El Paso, with Baylor's old units added to the Brigade. Only two major forts remained between Sibley and the gold mines of Colorado. These were Fort Craig, just below the center of the Territory, and Fort Union, up in the northeast corner near Colorado.

Fort Craig would be the first objective, of course, and near there Sibley was destined to fight the Battle of Valverde, beyond question a Confederate victory in any sense.

In January, Sibley began moving his men north. There were few roads, really only one that was practical, and this meant he had to move his men in sections. They had orders to rendezvous about a third of the way up the hundred and twenty miles from El Paso to Fort Craig. They would regroup at the site of old Fort Thorn.

By February 4, the main units were assembled at the rendezvous: the 4th, 5th, and 7th Regiments of the Army of New Mexico (or the Sibley Brigade, as it was later known). The sutlers unpacked their wagons and did a lively business in liquor, tobacco, preserved fruit, and candy. To clinch the Confederate claim to Arizona, Sibley detached Captain Sherod Hunter and several men to ride the 280 miles west to Tucson, Arizona and occupy that pro-Confederate town. The rest of the men made ready to move on Fort Craig with no further halts.

At Fort Craig, General Edward R. S. Canby was making ready to receive his expected visitors. By this time he had about 3,800 men at the post. Twelve hundred were his old regulars, another thousand were miscellaneous unreliable militia, and the remaining sixteen hundred were territorial regiments such as those headed by Kit Carson and Miguel E. Pino. One of his best units was a new little outfit of hard riding volunteers headed by Captain James "Paddy" Graydon, an independent company of scouts ready for any unusual and exciting assignment. This group got all it asked for and more before the action was over.

As a military post, Fort Craig was everything that Fort Fillmore was not. It was completely walled and was surrounded by strong new earthworks with 24-pounder guns. With the Territorial commander on the spot there could be no indecision over orders. At the time of the Confederate approach it was the strongest post in New Mexico, and Canby was determined to hold it.

By mid-February the Texans were within two miles of Craig. They had marched along the west bank of the Rio Grande, the side on which Fort Craig was located. The Texans met no opposition. Once they met a small Federal advance guard, which retreated without a fight.

Below Fort Craig the countryside is often like a washboard: furrowed into hundreds of shallow washes down which cloudbursts drain into the river. Here and there the washes are deep enough to be called canyons, Just below Fort Craig there is a bit of plain, level enough for a battle. Here the Texans drew their formations, hoping to draw Canby's men out of the fort and into a traditional style of combat — line facing line.

Canby did not take the bait. He was sensible enough to realize his fort was strong walled, well stocked, and heavily armed. Let the Texans attack if they would.

Sibley had equal sense. He had been a Federal officer within Fort Craig and knew its strength. When the Union troops would not come out to fight, he decided to bypass the fort.

To do this he planned to drop back downriver a few miles to a good ford at the village of Paraje, cross there to the east bank, and go up past Fort Craig to a good ford at Valverde. There he would cross back to the west bank and follow the road north to Albuquerque.

Sibley had to wait two days because winds blew up sand and heavy dust. When the weather cleared, the Texans went back to Paraje, crossed the Rio Grande and headed north.

Canby knew every move that Sibley made but didn't understand until too late that Sibley was bypassing Craig. Instead he thought that Sibley was going to occupy some high ground directly across the river from Fort Craig and would attack the fort from there.

To appreciate what happened in the next two days, and especially during the Battle of Valverde on the second day, it is essential to understand that Valverde was no classic battle between two facing, massed armies. Except for what happened in the last few hours it was almost a running battle: Sibley's troops were strung out along the eastern bank; Canby kept hitting them wherever they appeared. The result was steady confusion, with troops from both sides moving to any point of conflict.

During the night before the big battle, Paddy Graydon went to Canby with an unorthodox idea. He asked for a dozen heavy-howitzer shells, packed six to a wooden box. Each of these twenty-four pound shells contained its own explosive charge, ignited by a fuse. Paddy's plan was to take a couple of wornout mules across the river, tie a box of shells to each animal, light the fuses, and drive the beasts into the Confederate camp. Canby approved.

Everything went as planned, up to a point. Paddy and his men got the mules within a hundred and fifty yards of the Confederate camp, lit the fuses, whacked the mules and ran.

Looking back, Paddy saw the faithful mules following *him!* The Union men just had time to hit the dirt before the shells went off. At least it kept the jittery Texans alert for the rest of the night.

The next morning Sibley was half sick but able to mount into his saddle. Some said later that he was tipsy, but the general — while not unfriendly to a bottle — had not been well for several days.

To tell the story of the Battle of Valverde as simply as possible, this record will mention only the larger units and will identify them by the names of their commanders.

The first Confederates to head north toward the Valverde ford were Scurry's men, with Pyron's battalion on the left between Scurry and the Rio Grande. While those forces headed north, other Texan units under Green, Sutton, and Teel headed for the river bank directly opposite Fort Craig, to give the appearance of a straight-on attack.

They all mounted and rode out about 8:00 A.M. It was a fine day, a little cold, and with the clouds that are so common in the sky of New Mexico. Pyron's troopers rode to where a great black mesa loomed in their path. On the left this mesa dropped to the river's edge, so Pyron went around its right, or eastern, flank. Reaching the northern end of the mesa, the Texans saw that the river once flowed through an old channel, now dry. The curve of the dry channel opposed the curve of the flowing stream in a way that resembled a pair of elliptical buggy springs or like the upper and lower lids of a girl's eyes. Within this ellipse the Battle of Valverde opened, with the Texans based along the old channel and the Union troops with their backs along the flowing river. This meant that all of Canby's men had to ford the stream to reach their position, while Sibley's men had to come up single file past the black mesa.

Canby was watching from west of the river. He saw Green's men and those of Sutton and Teel appear in what seemed to be a direct attack. Some of Selden's men were sent to block that approach.

Then the Union commander saw the Texans led by Scurry and Pyron appear in the flat, elliptical plain north of the mesa. Canby sent Colonel Roberts up to take command of the crossing and stop the Texans from outflanking the fort. For the next few hours Roberts guided the Union attack. Under his command were companies led by Duncan and Pino, together with the artillery batteries of McRae and Hall.

The Union men reached the ford before the Texans did. Roberts sent Duncan's men and some others across to the east bank and ordered the batteries into position on the west side. By now it was 9:00 A.M.

Pyron's men rode up to meet Duncan's and the fighting started without any preliminaries. Scurry's men rushed up to aid Pyron; Roberts sent more troops across the river to help Duncan, and the Union batteries went into action. In a short while the Texans brought up their own heaviest guns, the battery commanded by Trevanion T. Teel.

Both Canby and Sibley withdrew some of the men involved in the feint attack directly across from the fort. Sibley sent Green's men up to aid Scurry, with orders for Green to take field command as the senior officer.

When Selden's Union men came back across the Rio Grande, Canby sent them up to help Roberts. With Selden went a Colorado regiment, under Dodd, that had marched on foot from the north to serve at Fort Craig; along with them went other large units under Colonel Kit Carson and Captain Benjamin Wingate.

The names of four of these Union men: Carson, McRae, Wingate, and Selden would later be honored as the names of four frontier forts. One of the men would die this day.

It was now almost noon. The battle lines were becoming stabilized; firing was constant. The Texans fell back to good positions along the old dry river bed. Sibley was feeling worse and had to lie down in an ambulance; Green took full command.

McRae's and Hall's Union batteries crossed to the east bank.

In the early afternoon the fatigue increased for both forces. They had been fighting almost five hours; now there was a slight lull. Both sides took advantage of it to eat as best they could and to refill their cartridge boxes.

The lineup of forces at this time was approximately what it would be for the rest of the battle. Along the Union line, McRae's battery was on the far left; troops under Dodd, Selden, Carson, and Duncan were in that order across the center; on the Union right was Hall's battery at the foot of the black mesa. Behind them flowed the Rio Grande.

Facing them was Sibley's Army of New Mexico. On its own left, at the foot of the mesa and facing Hall's battery, were Raguet's cavalry. In the center were the men under Scurry, Green, Pyron, and Hardeman. On the Texan right was Teel's battery, facing McRae's.

The whole line was about a half mile long.

The Union troops fought with energy and professional discipline, moving swiftly and decisively. The only wavering was among some of the raw militia.

The Texans fought with the dashing boldness that characterized them on every field of the Civil War. Sometimes their brashness led to calamity, as it did once during this battle: Captain Willis L. Lang led forty Texas lancers — yes, *lancers* — in a reckless charge against the Union left, where Dodd's men from Colorado waited. The Coloradans held their fire until the last possible minute, then in one crashing volley emptied more Texas saddles than any other Confederate unit suffered in a single action. It was the end of the lance as an army weapon in the West.

The afternoon continued without a letup in the fight. Both commanders began to plan their closing tactics. Canby, who had come down to the battlefield about three o'clock to the cheers of his men, decided to force the Texans out of their strong position along the dry river bed. To do this, he would hold his left flank anchored on McRae's battery. The rest of his front would swing in a wide arc, like a giant scythe reaping the Texans in the river bed.

Scurry's plan was just the opposite: he planned to smash the Union men where they stood, in a direct, full frontal assault.

Canby's plan was good but Scurry moved first, in two unforgettable charges. The first was by Raguet's cavalry, about two hundred men arrayed in a single rank over on the Confederate left. All hell broke loose on signal: rebel yells, small arms fire, and all available artillery. Raguet's men rode hard and fast on a short diagonal toward the Union right.

The charge was met at eighty yards by a withering fire from Carson's regiment, by shells from Hall's battery, and by every Union infantryman within range. Raguet looked back and saw a tangle of dying horses and men behind him. At least twenty percent of his troopers were down. This charge had failed just as the lancers had failed, and Raguet's men tore back to the safety of the old river bed.

Then the Union troops lost some of their coolness and began to chase after Raguet's men. This left a hole in the Union line — a hole that opened just when Green's Texans were starting the second forward push.

"Up, boys, and at them!" was the Texas battle cry.

Scurry's main sections headed for the Union left, where McRae's battery was anchored. The distance was about 450 yards, across open ground and straight into massed Union gunfire. By now the Texans knew a trick or two. Whenever McRae's guns flashed, the Confederates dropped to the ground, aimed, and fired. Then they were back on their feet, reloading and advancing. McRae was puzzled by the surprising recovery of the "casualties" after each salvo but kept on firing.

The Texans came on in a mad rush, pouring in a constant fire from revolvers and double-barreled shotguns, and at this moment a legend was born: the story of Alexander McRae.

He had been born in a distinguished North Carolina family. McRaes had served with honor in the War of 1812, two generations before. Young Alexander graduated from West Point in 1851. He had served in minor actions in the West, but this would be the young captain's first big battle.

When the Civil War opened, he resisted the appeals of his Southern relatives and stayed with the Union Army. His family opposed him. Now he stood alone, his gunners cut down. McRae slumped to sit on the tail of a quiet gun. His right arm hung limp, shattered by a Texas bullet; his left hand rested on the round cascabel at the end of the cannon, and he still had his revolver. Leading the charge against him was Major Sam Lockridge, of Tom Green's Fifth Regiment. Lockridge came up, placed one hand on the muzzle of the cannon and panted, "Surrender, McRae! We don't want to kill you!"

"I'll never forsake my guns," McRae replied. An instant later both men died as a hail of buckshot and pistol fire hit the battery.

George Pettis, a soldier with the Union troops from California who reached New Mexico months after Valverde, liked to write about how Lockridge and McRae fired at the same time in a battlefield duel. Trevanion T. Teel, who inspected McRae's body just after the fighting stopped, said this could not have happened. McRae's revolver was still fully loaded when he died.

McRae was the only soldier cited by commanders of both sides in their reports of that day. Canby wrote that McRae had a "loyalty that was deaf to the seductions of family and friends." Colonel Thomas Green, CSA, reported that "the gallant McRae fell at his guns."

His body was buried at Fort Craig. During the next five years, which included the first years of peace, there was neither wreath nor letter from his family. In 1867 the body was exhumed, taken to

Albuquerque and escorted through the town in a solemn march of hundreds. This was repeated at Santa Fe and at Fort Union, and then his remains were carried over the Santa Fe Trail to West Point, where they were buried with honors. From 1863 to 1876 there was an Indian-fighting fort named in his honor: Fort McRae, not many miles from where he fell.

McRae's death was not the turning point; in the confusion it was only an incident. The tide changed when the Texans seized McRae's guns and turned them on the Union men, first on those closest and then at those across the field.

Canby saw that sheer force would not carry the day for him, and in this melee there was no chance for organized tactics. He had no choice but to retreat, so retreat the Union men did, all the way to Fort Craig, fighting as they went.

Scurry went after them with five companies of Texans. When he got to the west bank of the river he was recalled by his commander. A white flag was being brought from the fort. Surrender? No, only a request that firing cease while the dead and wounded were removed. Agreed. The battle of Valverde was over.

Casualties? For the Texans: 36 killed, 150 wounded, and one missing — roughly one man in twelve. These were high losses for a force operating so far from home. For the Union: 68 killed, 160 wounded, and 35 missing or deserted.

Sibley's men were wild with joy at the victory but frustrated at not being able to get the Union men out of the fort. The Texans had hoped to replenish their supplies at Craig. All they got were the captured weapons, but these were good ones. Canby's regulars had the latest improved arms: the infantry carried the Springfield rifled musket, .58 caliber; the cavalry had the Harper's Ferry rifle, Colt's Navy pistol, Sharps' and Maynard's carbines, and a few Colt's revolving rifles for experiment. The Union volunteer militia carried rifled muskets, .69 caliber; Harper's Ferry rifle, calibers .54 and .58; and some companies had the smooth-bore musket, caliber .69, and the cavalry musketoon and carbine pistol.

Sibley decided to move on north to Albuquerque, where his men would find ample supplies and less opposition. Ten days later they were in New Mexico's central town, a cluster of earth-colored adobe buildings around a quiet plaza dominated by a Spanish church more than a century and a half old. The Texans rested there for a fortnight, fattening on the Union supplies found in warehouses.

Up north the territorial officials hurriedly left Santa Fe on March 4. Governor Connelly moved his capital to Las Vegas, New Mexico. His escort went on to Fort Union, less than a good day's ride beyond.

Now a new and decisive factor entered the game; the Colorado troops started moving south in earnest. Above all, it was perhaps the character of these Colorado men that helped decide the next and final battle. In many ways they were like the Texans: rough individuals who had gone west for gold and adventure, fine specimens of men, accustomed to initiative, danger, and with a relish for man-to-man fighting. Taken altogether they were unlike the plodding regulars and half-hearted rustics that Canby sometimes had to use as a fighting force.

Most of the Colorado men came from the East; some came from the South. To them the war between the states was not a faraway thing; their home folks were in it, and they knew the stakes.

On the day after Valverde's guns fell silent the Colorado troops started south. No telegraph brought the news of Canby's defeat — that came by a fast rider, and it reached the Coloradans on the march, spurring them into a herculean march of seventy-two miles in a single day.

By March 10 they were at Fort Union. Three days later Sibley's advance units entered Santa Fe. Now the two sides were less than a hundred miles apart. Nothing now lay between the Texans and the gold of Colorado except Fort Union, a star shaped set of earthworks astraddle the Santa Fe Trail where the plains meet the mountains. Sibley had once commanded there. Now the ranking officer was Colonel John P. Slough, an ex-attorney in command of the Colorado men. One of Slough's battle-ready officers was a fighting Methodist church elder named John M. Chivington.

There was only one path they could take between Santa Fe and Fort Union. Today men build superhighways where they will. In those earlier days the shape of the land dictated the trace to follow. In northeastern New Mexico the Sangre de Cristo mountains plunge down from the north. Then there is a slight break before a great escarpment begins, heading on southeast before it dwindles at the edge of the Texas Panhandle. Only in this slight break could wagon trains get through. The cut is known as Glorieta Pass, widening slightly halfway through its length, before the funnel closes again into Apache Canyon. West of that there are only a few rolling hills before the old Trail ends at Santa Fe.

The forces moved out: Pyron's Texans rode east from Santa Fe toward the pass; Scurry's Confederates headed northeast from Albuquerque to join up with Pyron at the west end of the pass. Between Scurry and Pyron together they had about eleven hundred men, but only seven hundred were fit for duty. Sibley stayed behind in Albuquerque, keeping an eye open for Canby, bottled up down at Fort Craig. Slough started west out of Fort Union with thirteen hundred men.

The weather in late March was cold enough to be thoroughly uncomfortable. In Glorieta Pass and in Apache Canyon there was still enough shade in early morning and late afternoon to keep big patches of snow on the ground. The cold white powder slid across the horses' pasterns as they walked, the scrub cedar, pinyon, and juniper trees still had a holiday decoration of snow.

Slough and the Coloradans halted east of the pass, while Chivington took a few hundred men and probed ahead.

Scurry had not yet come up with Pyron, who was waiting at Johnson's Ranch, an old stage station at the far west end of Apache Canyon. Pyron sent scouts out ahead, but Chivington caught them at Pigeon's Ranch, another stage stop located in the middle of Glorieta Pass. Alerted, the Coloradans moved ahead warily. With no word from their scouts, Pyron's troops were moving into Apache Canyon, at the end of the pass.

Chivington's men turned a sharp bend and saw the Texans only five hundred yards ahead. The Battle of Apache Canyon began at once.

Pyron's reflexes were fast. His men unlimbered two howitzers while the infantry formed skirmish lines at right and left. The first shells from the little guns were an unwelcome baptism to the Colorado men, who had never known battle.

Chivington ducked a howitzer shell and looked at the sloping sides of the canyon. He ordered two companies to climb the left-hand slope; a third company took off up the right. Soon the ex-miners were picking off the Texas gunners, forcing Pyron to fall back a mile and a half. There he set up his guns in a narrow defile where

Chivington's cavalry could not operate. This time Pyron had his own men up on the slopes.

Ordinarily, Chivington's cavalry would have followed Pyron's retreat, but the horses were more nervous than the men in their first roaring combat. Now the horsemen re-formed and moved in pursuit. When the Colorado major saw Pyron's new, strong position he ordered all cavalry to dismount, except one company held in reserve. This troop was to charge Pyron if he tried to pull back his guns a second time.

Chivington again sent his men up the canyon slopes, where they ran into Pyron's skirmishers. The Texans had never before faced their match. This was nothing like the walkaway at Fort Fillmore; nothing like the formal battle lines of hesitant militia at Valverde. The Colorado men fought like, well — Texans. The Union men yelled like wild Indians, leaped from rock to crag and then behind a tree, firing all the time with cool aim. Nothing stopped them.

Pyron told his guns to fall back. The instant their carriages turned, Chivington's reserve cavalry charged full tilt, their horses leaping a small arroyo. The guns got away, but the Battle of Apache Canyon was, for the moment, a Union victory.

Darkness was falling and Chivington suspected there might be too many Texans up ahead, so he called it a day and fell back toward the main Union force under Slough.

Both sides moved up reinforcements during the night. Scurry was nearing Apache Canyon when he received Pyron's urgent call for help. By midnight Scurry and Pyron were joined.

The next day was quiet, each side waiting for the other to move first. The night passed, and on the morning of March 28 Scurry — now commanding the combined Texas forces — moved toward the middle of Glorieta Pass. He left his supply train back at Johnson's ranch. A fatal mistake.

From the eastern end, Slough moved west into the pass and joined up with Chivington. The Union troops marched cautiously, and soon Chivington took four hundred men and cut off to the south on a flanking operation, about which more was heard later.

Slough continued straight ahead; so did Scurry. The two columns met head-on at Pigeon's Ranch. The old ranch house is still there, now a museum.

Scurry began with the traditional opening moves: artillery on a convenient rise of ground slightly off to the right and a skirmish line extended across the canyon floor, widest at this point.

The Texans went into action first, and Slough had to fight a defensive battle for the rest of the day.

The Colorado men repeated their previous tactics: climb the canyon slopes and pour fire down upon the enemy. The Texans did the same, and each side concentrated on the opposing artillery. Soon the guns on both sides lost their full effectiveness; the battle was fought on with rifle, revolver, and shotgun fire. It was charge and counter-charge for the rest of the day, with positions changing from hour to hour. The Union position centered around Pigeon's Ranch, whose owner said, "Zey foight six hour by my vatch, and my vatch was slow."

After one last desperate charge the Texans pushed back the Union men, but they were too exhausted to pursue and the Colorado men were too exhausted to recover. Darkness was coming, and the two sides withdrew. Each was confident it had won what seemed to be only the first day of the battle.

Scurry sent a message of victory to his men. It was premature.

Glorieta Pass, remember, was about seven miles long, with a high, flat-topped mesa along its southern side. Chivington planned to get on top of the mesa, traverse its length, and see what damage he could do in the rear of the Texans. This was why he had left the main column that morning.

One of Chivington's guides was Lieutenant Colonel Manuel Chavez, who had fought honorably with a New Mexico unit at Valverde.

Chavez guided Chivington's four hundred over one of the few trails to the top of Glorieta Mesa. They rode cautiously across it, threading their way around rocks and through juniper and pinyon woods, with patches of snow still in the hollows of the ground. For five hours they rode, hearing the gunfire off to their right. About one-thirty they came to the edge of the mesa. Some of the men advanced to peer over the brim.

"You are on top of them," Chavez said softly.

And indeed Chivington was — more than he had ever hoped. Down below was the entire Confederate supply train, sixty to eighty wagons, scattered around the few buildings of Johnson's Ranch. Off to the right was one Texas howitzer on a small hill, the muzzle aimed into Apache Canyon. A few rearguard Confederates strolled about, and perhaps two hundred more sick and wounded Texans were resting.

Chivington sent Captain William Lewis and most of the men down a steep path to the right. The Texans heard them coming, but the odds were too great. In less than an hour the wagons had been set on fire, the gun spiked, and the camp scattered. Only one Union man and three Confederates were killed in this little skirmish, but what happened at Johnson's Ranch changed the history of the West.

When Scurry found the charred heaps at Johnson's Ranch, there was nothing to do but fall back to Santa Fe.

Slough took the Coloradans back to Fort Union to rest and re-equip.

Sibley came up to Santa Fe from Albuquerque and held a council of war. The shortage of ammunition, now less than forty rounds per man, was a vital factor but what really tipped the scale was news that Canby had left his lair at Fort Craig and was marching north. The Texans might face one army; they could never outfight two with their supplies so low.

There was nothing to do but retreat, so they left Santa Fe and marched south. They missed Canby's main force but had minor battles at Albuquerque and Peralta. Farther south, the Texans left the Rio Grande and made a wide detour to the west, bypassing Fort Craig. Early in May they were back in El Paso, and there on May 14 Sibley read a message congratulating his men for their valor.

The Civil War still had three years to go, and before it ended the men who had fought at Fillmore, Valverde, and Glorieta would continue to fight in the Sibley Brigade at Galveston and in Louisiana.

From the Rio Grande to the Mississippi. No other Southern command anywhere rode so far for a fight.

6

Black Day for the Navy

TEXANS are said to be braggarts. While they enjoy a tall tale, it is debatable whether they brag more or less than anyone else. But they do know that a man who brags may be underestimated, and if you underestimate a man you may be in for a surprise. So it was a surprise to the Union navy and army when four gunboats, a hundred and eighty picked marksmen, and nearly five thousand troops were soundly beaten by forty-three Texas Irishmen at Sabine Pass during the Civil War.

Texas Irish? There were such. Today Texans are almost a nationality unto themselves, but there were many groups of foreign origin who came to the early Southwest. Texas had colonies of Germans, Czechs, Wends, French, and — on the San Patricio grant (naturally) and in Houston — Irish. And one of those Irish was Richard W. Dowling, who came as a lad of ten from Galway in Ireland to New Orleans in America. He went on to Houston, and when he was nineteen he married and opened a saloon, but not necessarily in that order.

The saloon was a good one and it was called the Shades, because of the fine trees along the street. Dick's wife was a good choice, too: the daughter of Ben Odlum from County Kildare. Odlum had already been in Texas more than twenty years, and he was a man of property, substance, and family. Dick and Anne were married in 1857, and no man at the charivari would have bet the next drink that Dowling had only ten years left to him, rich years every one.

The Shades was a favorite spot for the Irish stevedores who manhandled the incoming flood of cargo off the steamers that came up the bayou to Houston, or the cargoes of baled cotton that went out. When the Irish decided to follow the example of their countrymen in New York's Bowery and organize a volunteer fire company, Dowling joined and took an active part. Houston's Hook & Ladder Company No. 1 served its members as lodge, lounge, fraternal order, sports club, and benefit society all in one.

Social, too, but with a bit more show, were the Davis Guards, a new militia unit that Dowling joined in 1860. Anne's uncle was the commanding officer, but Dick did not join for purely family reasons. Lincoln was campaigning in the north, and secession was a new word being heard in the shade of the magnolias. It was heard, too, along the bar at Dick's new saloon: the Bank of Bacchus. He announced himself as president and cashier, "for the purpose of dealing in the exchange of liquors for gold, silver and bank notes." He was not only the president of an unusual bank, he was a first lieutenant in the Davis Guards, a naturalized citizen, and a father. He was only twenty-two.

When the Civil War began, the Davis Guards found, not entirely to their displeasure, that a militia oath was not an empty pledge. Along with six other similar units, the "Davies" became part of a regiment under John Salmon "Rip" Ford, the same Rip Ford who, a few months later, sent another contingent of Texas soldiers west to seize New Mexico.

Ford's own regiment was detailed to move to the mouth of the Rio Grande, to take over any Federal forts in that area. He failed to consult the Davis Guards. Their Irish independence frothed over, and they said the Guards had decided not to go. But they found they were in the army, indeed, and so they went south — to engage in such a series of brawls and disorders that their company actually was disbanded for a while. It wasn't mutiny, just high spirits, explained their commander Odlum. So they were shipped back to Houston, transferred to a second regiment and finally to a third; Cook's Regiment, Heavy Artillery.

Officially they were known as Company F, but they were still popularly known as the Davis Guards. During the rest of 1862 they learned to handle artillery and manned a succession of small forts along the coast below Houston. Colonel Joseph J. Cook, in command of their regiment, was a graduate of the U. S. Naval Academy. He made them into good artillerymen, with the limited ordnance they had. During all of 1862 they saw only one engagement, a small one from which they had to retreat when their single ten-pounder pop-gun was disabled.

On New Year's Day, 1863, the Davis Guards went with several other outfits to recapture Galveston. The battle was brief and triumphant. Dowling's men fought beside the Sibley Brigade, recently back from New Mexico.

Later that January, Dowling took part in a small campaign to drive off some Union gunboats that had been blockading the entrance to the Sabine River. That river was a strategic waterway dividing Texas from Louisiana and was an important route for shipping.

Cook's regiment, along with Pyron's regiment that had returned from Valverde and Glorieta, went to the village of Orange, Texas. There they boarded two Confederate gunboats, the *Josiah H. Bell* and the *Uncle Ben.*

Dowling found himself in charge of a gun crew responsible for a cannon that was indeed the grandfather of all guns: a sixty-four pounder and rifled as well. It was of absolutely no consequence to Dick that the gun was mounted forward in a completely exposed position.

The two Confederate gunboats sighted a pair of Union blockaders, the sloop *Morning Light* and the schooner *Velocity*. The blockade vessels fled; although they were well armed their guns were no match for Dowling's long-range sixty-four pounder on the *Bell.* The *Bell* captured the *Morning Light;* the *Uncle Ben* seized the *Velocity.* The Confederates took their contraband into the mouth of the Sabine. *Velocity* became a Confederate vessel. *Morning Light* was burned to prevent it from falling into the hands of a new fleet of blockaders that hurried to counter the Confederate menace.

The Davis Guards then settled down to long months of the dullest possible duty around Sabine Pass. The river, flowing south, widened into a lake about six miles above the Gulf of Mexico, the lake appearing on the map like a sweet potato dangling at the bottom of a stem. Below Sabine Lake was a six-mile channel known as Sabine Pass.

At the lower end of the lake was Sabine City, ambitiously named. Until the blockaders twisted their tourniquet on river traffic, Sabine

City had been a busy supply port for the Confederacy, shipping cotton out and supplies in.

There had been a small fort there a year before, in the summer of 1862. Major Getulius Kellersberger, a Confederate engineer, went over for an inspection tour and pronounced it inadequate. The major was a Swiss who had emigrated to California in the gold rush of '49 and had worked there for a time as an engineer. His opinion of the little fort was correct; in September, 1862, it was pulverized by three Federal vessels. The Texans spiked the guns and fled; the Union ships stood off beyond range and fired leisurely.

The task set for Dowling's men was to build a new fort between the old emplacement and the village. The new earthwork was sometimes called Fort Sabine but more often was mentioned as Fort Griffin, although it had no connection with another Fort Griffin that was built later over in the buffalo country of the Texas Panhandle.

The fort, if you could really call it that, was a rectangle of low dirt walls surrounding an area about the size of a modern city block. It stood on a point of land, a sort of elbow, on a slight rise of earth. In that part of Texas, thirty feet above sea level is considered altitude. A road ran off northwest across the sand about a mile to Sabine City, and across the road near the fort stood a small hotel.

The Texans did the best with what they had, and when it came to design they had a good man available. Colonel Valery Sulakowski was one of the few long-time professional fighters in Texas, and his skill was invaluable. Born in Poland, he had been in command of a Louisiana regiment during the early months of the Civil War. While he was designing the fort on Sabine Pass he was also engaged in some string-pulling on another project that is worthy of an entire book. General Magruder, commanding in Texas, had proposed to Lieutenant General E. Kirby Smith, Magruder's own superior, that Sulakowski be allowed to carry out an ingenious plan.

The plan was bold. Sulakowski knew that there were two thousand bales of cotton not far up the Brazos River, balked by the blockade. The colonel proposed to find a schooner or any similar vessel, load it with cotton, and make a dash for Havana. After the cotton was sold there, a small steamer would be bought, one that was sturdy enough to cross the Atlantic but also with a draught shallow enough to allow it to go back up the Brazos for the rest of the cotton.

Once in Europe, Sulakowski would be put in touch with John Slidell, the Confederate commissioner. Armed with proper credentials, the colonel was then to proceed to Poland and recruit a small legion. Kirby Smith agreed to payment of $80 (in cotton) for every new recruit, sworn in and fully equipped. And Smith also promised to make Sulakowski a brigadier general if he came back with at least two regiments. The Polish soldiers were to be allowed to elect their own officers, and if they served their full enlistment they would automatically become naturalized citizens of the Confederacy, entitled to all soldiers' bounties and benefits. A grand plan, but it was never carried out.

Colonel Sulakowski laid the basic design for Fort Griffin, and Maj. Kellersberger supervised the work. Dowling's Irish supplied the muscle.

The fort faced southeast, down Sabine Pass. Its two strongest sides were the front and the southwest wall, because the latter might be crucial in defending the place against an infantry attack by land. The walls were mounds of earth about four feet high, reinforced slightly inside by using a few timbers salvaged from the wreck of the burned blockader, *Morning Light.* Across the back was a redoubt, not unlike the players' dugout in a modern ball park, where men could get some shelter during a bombardment. There were no outer defenses, no rows of pointed stakes or twisting ditches. The front stared down the Pass, and its southwestern side looked across a plain dotted with mesquite.

Kellersberger dug up and repaired the two thirty-two pounders that had been spiked and abandoned when the Federals attacked the older fort a year before. They also brought in two twenty-four pounders and two thirty-two-pound field howitzers. The later four guns might have been part of those surrendered by Union forts in Texas in the opening days of the war. All six guns were smoothbores. The howitzers were mounted fully exposed on the walls, or *en barbette.* If the fort followed the usual arrangement of its day, the other four guns probably were wheeled cannon, each on a simple floor of planks laid on the hard earth.

During late August the gun crews went through gun drill again, again, and again, sometimes practicing with live ammunition, firing at poles set up in the channel. Probably they had not yet received

Gorgas' new *Ordnance Manual for the Use of Officers of the Confederate States Army,* but they followed the general procedures of standard gun drill.

At the moment of firing, each gun was in its forward position known as "in battery." The next movement was that of moving the piece back until its muzzle was at least a yard inside the parapet wall, so it could be reloaded.

This movement was not done by a twist of the wrist. A thirty-two pounder weighed about a ton and a half. Its fourteen-spoked wheel came up to a tall man's shoulder; the massive hub was beside his waist.

Two cannoneers stood beside each wheel, holding handspikes: stout oaken crowbars about six feet long. In addition to these four men were two more who stood at the rear of the piece, their handspikes jammed into the end of the trail where it touched the ground, so they could guide the gun as it moved.

The front man at each wheel stuck the outer end of his handspike beneath the thick rim of the wheel, touching the earth, and ready to lever the wheel backward. The outer cannoneer at each wheel thrust his handspike through the spokes near the rim, with the end of the handspike under the gun carriage. When he pressed down, his handspike levered down on a spoke. All men worked together on the command of *Heave!* Even so, a thirty-two pounder seldom went back on a single heave.

When the piece was moved back, the cannoneers leaned their handspikes against the parapet and began loading the cannon, each man moving through the motions assigned to his number.

Number 1 seized the long-handled, woolly-ended sponge and plunged it into the muzzle, Number 2 helping him to push it to the deep end of the bore. Without this precaution, any bit of smoldering cartridge paper or other spark might ignite the new powder charge prematurely. When the sponge had been driven home the two men turned it, three times counterclockwise and three clockwise. The sponge was then pulled.

Meanwhile, Number 3 had picked up the rammer and Number 4 had come forward with the next cartridge of powder.

Number 1 leaned the sponge against the parapet or on a special stand and took the rammer from Number 3. Number 2 took the cartridge from Number 4, pushed it in the muzzle, and helped Number 1 force it home. When they felt it hit bottom, they pulled the rammer out about two feet and rammed it in hard.

By now Number 4 was back with a ball and a wad (if the gun required a wad). This, too, was jammed home and the rammer withdrew.

The gunner, or seventh man of the crew, stuck a small pick down the vent-hole to break the powder bag.

Then the piece was heaved forward into "in battery" position and the gunner sighted his piece. He spun a wheel below the rear of the barrel to raise or lower the muzzle, tapping on either the left or right side as a signal to the cannoneer on that side to heave the gun by inches for a lateral aim.

His aim completed, the gunner stepped aside. Number 3 put a primer in the vent and, holding a lanyard, stepped back. A quick jerk on the lanyard operated the primer. The heavy piece recoiled, but Numbers 1 and 2 were ready with chocks to steady its backward thrust. Then they picked up their handspikes and made ready to go through the entire procedure again.

Thus the whole maneuver was repeated, with the successive commands of: *From battery! Heave! Load! Sponge! Ram! In battery! Heave! Point! Ready! Fire!*

A good thirty-two pounder, with its barrel elevated five degrees, could hurl its thirty- two-pound shot 1,922 yards, or a little more than a mile.

When the action finally opened, Dowling had forty men with him, plus a surgeon and an Army engineer who happened to be there at the moment. It can be seen that he barely had enough men to provide standard crews for six guns.

While Dowling's men were busy with their own routines that summer of 1863, their future was being debated by Union commanders in Louisiana and Washington. It was the midpoint of the Civil War. Vicksburg had fallen and Union gunboats controlled the full length of the Mississippi. The Battle of Gettysburg had been fought in July. New Orleans had been occupied, and the blockade along the Texas coast was as tight as ever.

A new menace had developed. In Mexico, French troops had occupied the capital and Maximilian was soon to be made emperor. President Lincoln, busy as he was with campaigns in the East, did not overlook what was happening in the Southwest. Mexico might still have designs on Texas; it was only fifteen years since the treaty had been signed to end the war with Mexico.

And so it was considered necessary to make some show of force in Texas. Lincoln believed it would be enough to land troops at the far southern tip of that state, to keep any Mexican units from venturing above the Rio Grande.

Lincoln's officers did not all agree. There were those who felt that Texas should not be merely sealed off but should be entered and occupied. Some proposed to strike in from the northeast corner of the state, up around Arkansas. A plan by Major General Nathaniel Banks was finally accepted; land at Sabine Pass in southeast Texas and strike inland toward Houston.

Dick Dowling's little company would soon face an Irish Thermopylae.

The little fort was not yet complete. It was far from being what Colonel Sulakowski wanted. On September 4 he sent a message to Major Kellersberger to speed its completion.

At the top level, the operation was planned to be an Army venture under the command of General Banks. Because troops would have to be moved by sea, the Navy was involved, under Commodore David Farragut. Neither of these officers felt that such a minor campaign required their personal attendance. The job of preparation was left to two officers in the New Orleans area: Major General William B. Franklin for the Army and Commodore H. H. Bell for the Navy.

The Commodore sat in his cabin on the U.S.S. *Pensacola* off New Orleans, studying the list of vessels that might be used. For the fighting escort, there was little choice. The sluggish waters of the Sabine were only six feet deep in most places where the gunboats must go. This ruled out the really effective ships, those in his West Gulf Blockading Squadron, except as they might lend support by standing off the entrance to the Pass.

The transports were no particular problem for Bell. There would be four or five thousand troops; that probably meant some wagons, of course, and some mules, artillery, and other gear. A seagoing livery stable! Well, that could be handled by using fifteen or twenty of the shallow-draft Mississippi River steamboats now in the Navy's possession. A couple of tugboats might be sent along, in case the cranky riverboats had trouble.

But there was no simple answer to the fighting part of the problem. Gunboats would have to be used; there was no ironclad that could operate in only six feet of water. And there were only three gunboats with such a shallow draft: *Sachem, Clifton,* and *Arizona.* The *Granite City* was added to the list; technically it drew seven and a half feet, but if it steamed in with coal bunkers partly empty, and if the pilots were good and the engines held, it might get past the worst places.

Bell was not fired with enthusiasm as he regarded the list. All four gunboats had seen hard service. They were old, with decayed frames and weak machinery. Even on routine patrol duty, they were always in need of repairs. Altogether they mounted twenty-seven guns: howitzers, smoothbores, a few good Parrott rifled cannon. And twenty-seven guns should be able to win over the six or eight that spies reported were in the Confederate earthworks on the Sabine.

One other tactic was planned: use of sharpshooters. Bell had no marines available, but the Army could supply picked riflemen. They would have to fire from the deck; gunboats had no fighting tops. As the gunboats closed in toward shore, within three hundred yards, the marksmen could pick off Confederate gun crews in the low fort. The riflemen would be handy, too, if the Rebs brought up any field artillery along the shore.

This was an old trick, but effective. The buccaneers had used it two hundred years earlier, picking off Spanish gunners on the galleons. It had even been used in the Crimean War in 1855 by both sides until they designed screens of heavy rope to protect the gun crews.

And so the orders went out to assemble the little fleet. The flagship was the steamer *Clifton,* eight guns, with Acting Volunteer Lieutenant Frederick Crocker in command. *Clifton* had several blacks among its crew, all experienced in handling a riverboat. Crocker had mounted all of his rifled guns along the starboard side and his smoothbores on the port side. Ordinarily this enabled him to choose either battery for maximum effect according to the target, simply by turning one side or the other to the enemy. (Once up Sabine Pass he would regret this arrangement.) In the bow was Crocker's favorite gun: a nine-inch pivot gun with an improved firing mechanism.

The steam gunboat *Sachem* had a propeller instead of paddle wheels. Among its five guns was a Parrott, one of the best. There were some good fighting Irish in the crew, men such as Toomey, McNerney, Ryan, Sullivan. (Gael would meet Gael at Sabine.) Its commander was Acting Volunteer Lieutenant Amos Johnson. Hardly Annapolis stuff, but these volunteers all had done good work on the big river.

Then there was the *Arizona*, first Navy vessel of that name. Not an ironclad, but at least she had an iron hull. Among its armament were one thirty-two pounder mounted above the focs'l and another forward on the gun deck. She was at anchor near Bell's flagship. Bell wrote an order to *Arizona's* commander, Acting Master Howard Tibbits, telling him to move over to the big transport *Catawba* nearby and take on board a hundred and fifty sharpshooters. Tibbits was then to steam to the rendezvous where the marksmen were to be divided among the other gunboats.

Commodore Bell chose the gunboat *Granite City* as the last of the four combat vessels. It was iron-hulled but was armed only with light howitzers. Still, at close range the howitzers could be effective anti-personnel weapons after the other boats' heavy guns had done their damage.

Granite City was under Acting Master C. W. Lamson. It was also ready at hand below New Orleans, taking on coal in preparation for a patrol into Berwick Bay along the Louisiana coast. Bell ordered Lamson to forget the Berwick Bay orders, halt the coaling work, pick up thirty sharpshooters, and leave to join the others.

While the Commodore was writing his orders, Major General William B. Franklin was gathering the troops he had assigned, from the Nineteenth Army Corps, and was hustling them on board the river steamboats that were to be used as transports. Franklin would board the *Suffolk* and make it his command post. Others would be the *St. Charles, J. C. Landis, Exact, Laurel Hill, Thomas,* and *General Banks.* (These seven would finally move into Sabine Pass.) There was also the *Belvedere,* the *Crescent,* and others including tugs to bring the entire fleet of transports, tugs, and gunboats to twenty-seven vessels.

The whole idea had started as a military venture. Banks planned to have the troops landed as quickly as possible and aid the gunboats in crushing the Confederate fort at Sabine Pass. The Navy's task force would merely handle transport and provide cover for the landing force.

Commodore Bell gave energetic support to this plan, but when he wrote to Farragut in Washington, describing what he had arranged, Farragut saw everything in a different light. He hurried to Gideon Welles, Lincoln's Secretary of the Navy, and read the dispatches to him. Laying down the papers, Farragut said, "The expedition will be a failure. The army officers have an impression that naval vessels can do anything; this call is made for boats to accompany an army expedition; it is expected the Navy will capture the batteries, and, the army being there in force with a general in command, they will take the credit.

"But there will be no credit in this case, and you may expect to hear of disaster. These boats which Bell has given them cannot encounter batteries; they might co-operate with and assist the army, but that is evidently not the object. The soldiers should land and attack in the rear, and the vessels aid them in the front. The soldiers are not to land until the Navy has done an impossibility, with such boats. Therefore there will be disaster."

The admiral's words were prophetic.

The *Official Records of the Union and Confederate Navies* carry the reports on which all writers, from the devoted Frances Sackett to the excellent Frank Tolbert and Dr. Andrew Forest Muir, have relied. They record that after stumbling past the mouth of the Sabine River in the dark, the flotilla ultimately gathered offshore at the assigned location.

Off the mouth of Sabine Pass lay the first obstacle, a bar of sand, oyster shell, and mud. There the water was only eight feet deep. The gunboats were to cross this, followed by as many transports as could operate in such shallow water. The other transports would wait until their troops could be ferried ashore in relays. Once past the outer bar there was a mile-wide expanse of twelve-foot depth. Beyond that lay Sabine Pass itself, perhaps six miles long, a thousand yards wide, and averaging about six feet in depth.

The Federals had hoped for surprise but there was none. Even while the fleet was gathering below New Orleans, word had traveled swiftly to General John Magruder in Texas.

The Texans did not know exactly where the Union Forces would attack. The little fort was certain to be hit, but it was probably to be only part of a broader operation. Troops were held in readiness at various points.

The Battle of Sabine Pass was fought on September 8, 1863. Dowling had seen signal lights moving offshore before dawn the day before. He roused his men and sent a warning back to his superiors. The gunboats and transports were not gathered at the rendezvous until late on September 7.

In an offshore battle, Union ships might have destroyed the fort with ease, steaming in line past the earthworks. But river fighting was dirty business. In a shallow channel lined with mudflats on both sides there was no chance to maneuver, no chance to stay out of range.

At five in the morning of September 8, *Clifton* got under way. With James G. Taylor, an experienced pilot, at the wheel the gunboat crossed the outer bar and then churned across the mile of deeper water and into the shallows of the Pass.

This was a reconnaissance, a probing mission to test the defenses and to survey the channel. By six-thirty *Clifton* was within two thousand yards of the fort. The gunboat opened fire with its nine-inch pivot gun, and during the next hour threw twenty-six shells at the fort.

There was no reply. Dowling's men waited calmly in their bomb-proof shelters, husbanding their ammunition until the real targets arrived.

One shot from *Clifton* hit a parapet of the fort, on the southeast angle of the walls. Another landed inside the emplacements but did only negligible damage. The other shells whistled over or plopped short.

On *Clifton*, Lieutenant Crocker watched the fort for any response. The earthworks appeared to be solid and strong. He could count six guns, some of them heavy. Were they all real, he wondered, or might some of them be dummy "Quaker" guns? There was no real sign of life; now and then a few figures moved inside the fort. Off to the north, up in Sabine Lake, he saw the smoke of a Confederate boat of some sort, possibly a gunboat or a ram, probably a cotton-clad with its crew safe behind the heavy bales.

Crocker saw no signs of other fortifications, no indications of any troops maneuvering across the flat land. He noted one significant fact: the aim and elevation of all of the pieces in the fort showed that they were aimed at one particular spot in the channel. The Rebels knew these waters well, and probably were ready to wait until a Yankee vessel came to that precise spot. A suicidal bearing for any gunboat, Crocker decided, and he made a mental note of the approximate location.

The gunboat commander studied the Pass. Mudflats were a menace along both sides. Along the western bank a sluggish little bayou meandered through the mud and filtered into the Sabine. Off to the southeast was a small lighthouse back on solid ground. Just opposite the fort itself, the channel was a little wider and in its middle was a long bar of oyster shell, where according to his charts the water was only four feet deep. This bar divided the river into two channels: the Texas channel on the west, near the fort, and another channel over by the Louisiana bank. At best, Crocker decided, only two gunboats could move abreast up the main channel, and they would have to separate to pass the oyster-shell bar.

Crocker signalled back to the offshore vessels and they began to move toward the mouth of the pass. The gunboats came in first, *Granite City* forcing itself through the silt. Then came seven transports, led by *Suffolk*. On the transports were two field batteries, with a total of twelve guns, together with fifty wagons. *Laurel Hill* carried two hundred mules.

Lieutenant Crocker ordered *Clifton* to move downstream and lie near *Suffolk*, so he could go on board and consult with General Franklin.

Crocker told Franklin that the fort could not be taken by gunboats alone. *Clifton* was the only one with heavy guns; the other three had less effective armament and their boilers and machinery were exposed and vulnerable. The attack needed army support, on land, as originally planned.

Generals Franklin and Weitzel agreed, but they wanted a closer look at the shoreline. Crocker called for his small boats and took the two generals along the shore, shortly after one o'clock.

In the fort, Dowling's men were relaxing with a good lunch of beef, sweet potatoes, and coffee, dining safely behind the parapets.

The small boats ventured inshore toward the mouth of the little bayou, about three-quarters of a mile below the forts. They grounded in mud a hundred feet from the bank. General Franklin watched the boat crews wading ashore, sinking to their knees in the silt.

Franklin judged that an infantryman with full pack, rations, and a musket would sink to his waist. And beyond the mudflat there seemed to be a marsh, with sand beyond that. Impractical.

But there was one spot where men might land; on the west bank, below the fort, perhaps within range of the fort's guns but still far enough that it would require skilled gunlaying. At this point there was a bend in the river bank, an elbow just sharp enough to stimulate a little current and make the bank drop off steeply with no mudflat. There and only there might one transport get in close to shore. That would be the *General Banks*, with three hundred men.

The generals discussed tactics with Lieutenant Crocker. It was agreed that two gunboats, *Clifton* and *Sachem* would move upstream in the lead. When they came to the reef of oyster shell in mid-channel, *Sachem* would swing to starboard and move up the Louisiana channel, steaming to be ahead of *Clifton* going up the western channel.

This would make it necessary for all guns in the fort to be aimed at a new point. Crocker had spotted poles in the Louisiana channel and suspected that the Confederates had also been practicing their aim at the far channel. It would be no great maneuver to change the lay of the guns at the fort, and *Sachem* would be in serious danger, but the maneuver would gain a few minutes for *Clifton*.

While the fort's gunners were concentrating on *Sachem*, the *Clifton* could move up the western channel under forced draft, hitting the fort with every shot that could be sent home. And while this was going on, the third gunboat, *Granite City*, could follow *Clifton* and screen the landing of troops from the *General Banks* where the channel bank was steep. The troops then would storm the fort. It was a good idea; too bad it didn't work.

At three-thirty in the afternoon, Dowling's men saw the surge of smoke from every stack in the fleet downstream and his gunners hurried to their posts.

Clifton and *Sachem* approached. *Clifton* halted to fire several rounds of short-fuse shells at the fort. The only damage was done by one shot that hit the elevating wheel of a gun. *Sachem* moved up the eastern channel. As it neared the markers placed for practice firing, Dowling's men waited for the moment when they could aim at the wheelhouse. A good hit there might cut a tiller rope and make the gunboat a sitting duck, out of control.

Sachem came within exact range. Dowling's first round fell short — the approved technique, because only by a test shot that fell short could a gunner know how much to change the elevation.

Then the battle was truly opened. Dowling's Irish gunners were in a frenzy of action, firing at will, each gun crew on its own. One of the howitzers recoiled off its platform. The other five guns continued without letup.

They aimed first at *Sachem* in the far channel, and one of the Confederate twenty-four pounders put a shell through the dome of *Sachem's* exposed steam boiler. Sharpshooters on the deck fled like scalded cats; the steam billowed across the water. Her guns went silent, and soon a white flag went up.

Dowling then turned his guns on *Clifton*. One shot cut the tiller ropes and the gunboat slewed around out of control. On *Clifton*, Crocker could bring only three of his guns to bear on the fort. There was a jolt as *Clifton* went aground. Another shot from the fort hit Crocker's best gun on its firing mechanism. The gun crew kept it in action by hitting the firing primer with a boat's hatchet. The young commander saw his executive officer fall with a mortal wound. Twice the crew paused to put out small fires.

A few minutes later another shot from the fort went through *Clifton's* boiler. The sharpshooters ran from the deck or jumped overboard. Crocker saw ruin facing him. Someone on *Clifton* hauled down its colors.

And what of the other boats? *Granite City* should have been moving up behind *Clifton*, sheltering the transport *General Banks*. Both *Granite City* and *Banks* were lingering, hesitant, downstream.

The gunboat *Arizona* was moving up the far side of the Pass, toward *Sachem*. *Sachem's* commander called to *Arizona*, begging to be taken in tow; *Arizona* instead went about and retreated down the Pass, followed by *Granite City* and the *General Banks*.

Until the gunboats struck their colors, Dowling's gunners never ceased. At the height of the firing, four officers rode in from Sabine City. Other Confederate troops had been on the move toward the fort since morning but arrived too late.

Altogether the firing lasted only thirty-five minutes, and in that time the guns of the fort fired a hundred and thirty-seven shots. Not one man in the fort was hurt. The gunners wore heavy fingerstalls to guard against heat as they aimed the guns. Two of Dowling's gunners had their fingerstalls burned away and their thumbs badly seared.

Dowling saw men in the water, wading ashore from *Clifton* just below the fort. He thought at first they were a landing force until he saw they moved with arms raised. Then he ran down to meet them.

Seeing an officer on shore, *Clifton's* commander hailed him and asked for a surgeon. Dowling replied that he had no boat. One came ashore from the vessel to take Dick and his surgeon aboard.

On *Clifton*, Crocker offered his sword. Dowling refused it and went below to inspect the powder magazine, while the fort's surgeon aided the wounded.

Next the surgeon went over to *Sachem*, where he found a screaming group of badly scalded men. The doctor was the first Confederate aboard the disabled gunboat. He found a good supply of flour and used it as a makeshift dressing for burns. Finally all men aboard the two gunboats were taken ashore; the Union lost about three hundred men as prisoners or killed.

The other gunboats and transports headed south out of the Pass, across the bar, and on into the Gulf. *Crescent* dumped 200,000 rations overboard; *Laurel Hill* jettisoned two hundred mules by pushing the hobbled animals over the side.

It was the last Federal attempt to enter Sabine Pass during the war. Criticism was hot in Washington while crowds went wild in Houston. There were harsh remarks in Navy hearings. In the East, the Battle of Chickamauga was fought on September 19-20, and lack of a clearcut Union victory there, combined with the fiasco at Sabine Pass, caused United States credit to drop abroad. The price of gold in dollars went up five per cent in Europe.

When peace came, Dowling went back to his saloon in Houston, and his men went back to a medal and speeches. In 1867 Dowling died during a yellow fever epidemic.

But in the four years that imediately followed the battle, Dowling remembered what the signal officer of the *Sachem* had said at the surrender:

"How many men and guns did you have?" the Yankee asked Dick.

"We had four thirty-two pounders, two twenty-four pounders, and forty-three men."

"And do you realize what you have done, sir?" asked the gunboat officer.

"No, I don't understand it at all."

"Well, sir, you and your forty-three men, in your miserable little mud fort in the rushes, have captured two Yankee gunboats, many stands of small arms and plenty of good ammunition, and all that you have done with six popguns and two smart 'Quakers.' And that is not the worst of your boyish trick. You have sent three Yankee gunboats, six thousand troops and a general out to sea in the dark. You ought to be ashamed of yourself!"

7

Confederate Victory—
After Appomattox

FIVE WEEKS after Robert E. Lee surrendered to Ulysses S. Grant at Appomattox, the last battle of the Civil War was fought in the deep Southwest. Perhaps the combatants did not know the war was over, or wouldn't agree that it was, or it might have been a politician's last grasp for glory on the battlefield.

At the southern tip of Texas, a few miles upstream from where the Rio Grande enters the Gulf of Mexico, stands an historical marker with the words: "The last battle of the Civil War, known as Palmito Hill, was fought by Confederate Troops under Colonel John S. (Rip) Ford and Union Forces on May 13, 1865, 34 days after Lee's surrender at Appomattox." The marker is about fourteen miles east of the center of Brownsville on State Road 4 in Cameron county.

Battles have a way of happening at the least likely places. Sometimes they also run late — in the War of 1812 the Battle of New Orleans was fought two weeks after the peace treaty had been signed.

Few military experts would ever have bet that the last guns of the War Between the States would be fired by men running through chaparral; yet there was a familiar ring in the memories of older officers in Washington when the delayed news arrived from Texas. Some of the leading commanders had fought in the same region as young men during the war with Mexico almost twenty years before.

The lower Rio Grande swings in a wide curve and is moving almost due east by the time it reaches the sea. Off the river's mouth are two islands, one small and one long, almost like an exclamation point, parallel to the Texas coast.

The dot of the ! is Brazos Island; the long upper part is Padre Island, and the channel between the two is Brazos Santiago Pass. Between the ! and the Texas mainland lies the shallow Laguna Madre, perhaps three to five miles wide. Between Brazos Island and a point of the mainland is a small channel called the Boca Chica, "little mouth," so shallow it is little more than a nuisance.

Padre Island runs about a hundred and ten miles north from the Rio Grande to Corpus Christi. The low, sandy island was famous for treasure tales before Texas was born, and the legends have grown every year since. For example, John V. Singer (whose brother made a fortune in the sewing machine business) was a wealthy Union sympathizer who reportedly buried a fortune in coins on the island before he fled when the Civil War started.

The mouth of the Rio Grande was not the best channel in the world for navigation. Only a few steamboats managed to get past its shallows and into the more navigable waters above. Less than thirty miles upstream was the Mexican town of Matamoros. Across on the United States' side the countryside was flat, covered with sand dunes, mesquite, and chaparral. Here and there meandered the *resacas*, the dry and dead channels through which the Rio Grande once had flowed. In one of those, the Resaca de la Palma, U.S. and Mexican armies fought in an early battle of the war between their two countries in 1846. An equally important battle was fought a day earlier at nearby Palo Alto.

To establish a strong point, the American troops in 1846 built a fort across form Matamoros; it became known as Fort Brown, surrounded by the few buildings that were the start of Brownsville.

Large *ranchos* developed along the northern bank of the river between Brownsville and the sea: Rancho San Martin, White's ranch, Palmito ranch, and Cobb's ranch. A dusty road ran east from Brownsville along the northern bank of the Rio Grande, connecting the ranches and wandering on to Boca Chica. It was along a few miles of that dirt road that a running battle was fought between Yank and Reb on a May afternoon.

The battle site is usually called Palmito Ranch. The Spanish word *palmito*, "little palm," translates as palmetto in English. Perhaps the purists would say either Rancho del Palmito or Palmetto Ranch; the name used most often is crossbred: Palmito Ranch — or Palmito Hill to identify the exact spot where fighting started.

Brownsville had a military importance far greater than its size, even though its population was a respectable 30,000. When the Union navy blockaded the Atlantic and Gulf Coast ports of the Confederacy, the only port of entry still open was Brownsville. A flood-tide of military supplies: percussion caps, medicines, wagons, and all of the essentials for an army, was gathered at the Mexican town of Matamoros then sent across the river to Brownsville. There was no blockade of Central America; ships heavy with cargo left New York harbor and other ports of the world, destined for Mexico. From Matamoros-Brownsville the freight wagons rolled north into central Texas and on to Louisiana and Arkansas. They returned south with cotton. At one time, a five hundred-pound bale of cotton was worth two hundred and fifty dollars in gold. Also at one time there were more than fifteen hundred bales lined up at Brownsville. It was obvious why the Confederates guarded Brownsville and why the Federal forces wanted the town.

When the Civil War began, the Texans controlled Brownsville. When the Union forces set out in 1863 to retake Texas, the Federal troops first tried to make a landing in the northeastern part of the state. There they had the door slammed in their faces by Dick Dowling's Irish gunners. The Yankees then went down to Brownsville with a sizable army and retook Fort Brown.

A year later the Texans under Colonel John S. "Rip" Ford came back, and the fort again changed hands. The Confederates held it until the end of the war.

Ford was a remarkable individual, a superb cavalryman who — if he had served in the Virginia sector of the war — might have become the "Murat of the Confederacy." More recent military students have compared his dashing tactics to those of General George Patton, also a cavalryman, who had started his career in the Southwest with "Black Jack" Pershing in the chase after Pancho Villa in 1916.

Toward the end of the war, Ford's immediate superior was Brigadier General James E. Slaughter. There was no love lost between the two, and Ford had little respect for Slaughter as a tactician.

Rip was a Tennesseean who arrived in Texas soon after the decisive battle at San Jacinto in 1836. Ten years later he served in the Mexican War as adjutant of a Texas Ranger regiment under John C. "Jack" Hays. One of Ford's duties then was to write a report on each soldier killed, and he usually ended each document with the words "Rest in Peace." As casualties increased and his work load grew, he used the abbreviation "R.I.P." and gained a nickname.

Most of Ford's troopers did not wear official Confederate gray but favored the costume of the region: black felt hat, a scarf at the neck, spurs in Spanish style with big wheel rowels, a six-shooter, one or two bandoleers of cartridges, and a carbine; otherwise ordinary shirt, pants, and boots.

About two months before the war ended in Virginia, Lew Wallace, a Union general, came to Brazos Island on a peace mission. By then it was no secret that the war had become a dragged-out affair. Wallace (who later was territorial governor of New Mexico during the days of Billy, the Kid, and became famous as the author of *Ben Hur*) sent a message to Slaughter and Ford. An informal conference was proposed. After some delay it was arranged and the three had a long talk.

Wallace pointed out that a major battle in the lower Rio Grande valley would not affect the outcome of the war. That could be decided only by events in Virginia. A death-grapple in the far Southwest would bring only needless killing. Ford and Slaughter agreed. Wallace returned to the North.

As Ford saw the outcome of that talk, it meant that the two forces would no longer seek each other out like tomcats in spring but would continue their respective military rounds in a sort of peaceful coexistence. There had been a drouth in the Brownsville area the year before, a bad one, and forage was poor. Ford and Slaughter had about thirteen hundred Confederate troops altogether, and the informal truce allowed units to be scattered around the district to places where forage, wood, and water were available. Many of the men felt that the war was ended and simply walked off to head homeward. Ford held about three hundred men at or near old Fort Brown.

For about three months after Wallace left lower Texas there was no serious fighting in that area. Up north, the fighting ended with Lee's surrender at Appomattox, but that did not mean an automatic cease-fire everywhere. There were those in the Confederacy who felt that somehow the war might be continued west of the Mississippi, and it was some time before General Kirby Smith, CSA, agreed to a capitulation in the West. Even after that, orders had to be sent through military channels, with a directive first to the Department of Texas and then on down to the unit commanders. As far as Ford was concerned, the war was still on until he received official orders to the contrary.

The surrender at Appomattox was on April 9. Exactly when the news reached both sides in the faraway Rio Grande valley is not known. One story said that Ford learned of it only after the fight on May 13, from a Union prisoner. Another tale was that around the first of May — or two weeks before the final battle — a small steamboat was moving upriver toward Brownsville when a passenger tossed some newspapers to Confederate soldiers at Palmito ranch. Among the papers was a copy of a New Orleans journal containing news of Lee's surrender.

Just before the action started, Ford could muster quickly only the small force in or close to Brownsville. The Union forces were a larger, mixed group, without a single unit of the Regular Army; all were volunteers. The largest outfit was the 62nd U. S. Colored Infantry Regiment, commanded by Colonel Theodore H. Barrett. He bore the brevet or temporary rank of brigadier general and was in command of all units on Brazos Island. His lieutenant colonel was David Branson. With the black troops was the 34th Indiana Veteran Volunteer Infantry Regiment, known as the "Morton Rifles," under Lieutenant Colonel Robert G. Morrison. In addition there was part of a New York volunteer regiment and one company of the 2nd Texas (Federal) Cavalry, under Lieutenant James Hancock.

The 2nd Texas was an unusual outfit. During the course of the war, two regiments of pro-Union Texans had been formed at Matamoros, under Colonel Edmund J. Davis and Colonel John L. Haynes. The Confederates labeled these regiments as gangs of deserters, although there was no proof that they were other than pro-Union men from the beginning. The 1st and 2nd Texas (Federal) Cavalry had seen most of their action in the Louisiana sector before the 2nd was sent to Brazos Island. Colonel Haynes was a Brownsville man.

It was said in some newspaper accounts printed after the end of the war that General Barrett, the ranking commander on Brazos Island, was a politically appointed New Yorker who hoped for his own political career after the war. There is no record that he had seen any action previously during the war, and there was some indication that he wanted to go home with a few battle laurels that could help his political campaigning.

At any rate, Barrett wrote to his immediate superior, Brigadier General E. B. Brown, asking for permission to engage Ford's Texans. Permission was refused. Barrett may have decided to move against Ford to gain a reputation before the last chance was gone. Or he may simply have known that the war was over and assumed it was his duty to march into Brownsville and accept the town's surrender. Either way, it was Barrett who took the initiative.

On May 10, Barrett ordered Lieutenant Colonel Branson to be ready to march the next morning with two hundred and fifty men of the 62nd Colored Infantry. Each man was to take a hundred rounds of ammunition and rations for seven days. A steamer would ferry the men from Brazos Island to the mainland.

Branson and his men reported at 4:00 A.M. the next morning, ready to go. It was the old army game of hurry up and wait. The steamer's machinery had broken down, so the men stood around all day. During the day the order was changed regarding rations; each man was told to carry only five days' supply. Barrett also increased the force by adding fifty men of the 2nd Texas (Federal) Cavalry under Lieutenants Hancock and James. The cavalrymen were to march dismounted, as infantry. Two six-mule teams with wagons were sent along to haul extra ammunition and supplies.

Late in the afternoon the men were told to move out on foot and cross the shallow Boca Chica channel. A spring rain was falling; the men had a miserable time crossing the Boca Chica, but by 9:30 they were all on the mainland, heading along the dirt road toward Brownsville.

About two in the morning they came to White's ranch and moved up cautiously. Scouts had reported a day or so earlier that a Confederate outpost of perhaps sixty-five men was at the ranch. Branson's men found the place deserted. All signs indicated that no one had been there for at least a day.

Branson took the men west for another mile and a half and then had them bivouac for the night in a thicket along the river bank on their left. It was a fairly safe shelter. Rebel scouts would check the White ranch carefully if they rode by on patrol, but they might overlook the thicket.

The night passed without alarm; the Confederates were still unaware that a Union force was advancing. This advantage was lost the next morning when the men were spotted in the thicket by a patrol of Mexican soldiers on the south bank of the river. They were men of the Imperial Mexican Army, not unfriendly to the Confederates.

Branson gave the order to march and the command continued west toward Palmito ranch. Along the way there was occasional firing as they encountered pickets sent out by the Confederates. Around noon the Federals reached the ranch, fourteen miles from Brownsville and roughly halfway to their objective. They stopped there on Palmito Hill to eat, rest, and feed the mules. At the ranch they captured three of Ford's men and a couple of horses.

During the afternoon they met their first real resistance when they clashed with a hundred and ninety men of Giddings' regiment of Texans, under Captain William N. Robinson. (Col. George H. Giddings, who took no part in the battle, was a noted stage line operator whose coaches made the run from San Antonio to San Diego, before the war.)

The Texans' fire was hot enough to drive the Union men back to White's ranch for the night. One Union soldier was wounded. Before they left Palmito Ranch the Federals burned or destroyed the supplies they had seized that morning.

Branson sent a courier back to Brazos Island with a report to Barrett. Around 10:00 P.M. Robinson sent a similar messenger to Ford in Brownsville.

After the war was over, Branson said that battle plans had been laid and forces set into action when he knew that Lee had surrendered. Branson said he tried to send the news to the Texans but that they refused to honor a flag of truce from any unit containing black troops. This statement was never confirmed by any records of the Confederates. Branson stated that he finally found a Texan who got through to the Confederate lines with word that the war was over, but that the battle started anyway; this report also was not confirmed.

In Brownsville, Ford was meeting with General Slaughter when the messenger from Robinson arrived late at night, reporting the first skirmish. Ford asked Slaughter what he intended to do. Slaughter said he had already secured a carriage and planned to leave the town. There was a hot exchange between the two officers, ending with Ford's declaration, "You can retreat and go to hell if you wish. These are my men, and I am going to fight."

Slaughter then decided against retreat. Messengers were sent out to all outlying Confederate units scattered across the countryside, telling the men to rally at Fort Brown.

During the next morning, May 13, the day of the battle, Ford waited until the first units had gathered. He also had four twelve-pounder guns in two sections, under Captain V. G. Jones. Another pair of guns was borrowed from the Imperialist army at Matamoros; the gunners were French but they knew how to handle their pieces. (This was during the French-supported regime of Emperor Maximilian in Mexico.)

Late in the forenoon Ford rode out with his men, all mounted and moving at a gallop — even the artillery. Slaughter stayed behind, waiting for more men to gather. After Ford had left, Slaughter was told that a Mexican rebel leader named Juan Cortina, leading a force in opposition to the Imperialists and thus favoring the Union cause, might try to attack Brownsville as part of a concerted plan with the Federal forces. Slaughter delayed still longer until this rumor proved to be untrue. When he finally rode out to follow Ford he was so late that he missed most of the fighting.

While Ford was gathering his men in Brownsville that morning, reinforcements were also moving up to aid the Union men. Barrett had received the news the night before, when Branson's courier rode in. Before dawn Barrett left Brazos Island with two hundred men of the 34th Indiana Veteran Volunteers Infantry. They joined Branson at White's ranch early in the morning. The Union force then totaled about five hundred men. Barrett took personal command.

The Federals moved forward at once. By 8:00 A.M. they were back at Palmito ranch, still held by the Texans who had stayed there during the night. Ford's reinforcements had not yet reached the scene.

The Union men soon drove the Texans back from the ranch. Then the Federals destroyed not only the new supplies they seized but also burned some of the ranch buildings the Texans had used as barracks.

There was a brief pause, and Barrett sent a detachment back to Brazos Island with the prisoners and wounded. The action had consumed most of the forenoon. Early in the afternoon there was

a short, sharp counterattack in the chaparral. The Yanks stood their
ground and eventually pushed the Texans back across a small open
prairie and out of sight beyond some rising ground. A short distance
to the Union rear, the 34th Indiana had taken its position on a hill
about a mile west of Palmito ranch, and Branson's advanced units
withdrew to rest with the Indiana men. They were at that point
when Ford arrived to hit them with his full Confederate command
in the middle of the afternoon.

The Texans, who had been pushed back beyond some rising
ground, continued their heavy skirmishing fire against the Union
men. They were engaged in this action when Ford's men rode up in
haste from Brownsville, past San Martin ranch, and up to join
Robinson's troops.

Ford studied the situation facing him. The Union troops were
spread out in a line about three-quarters of a mile wide, across the
road, with their left flank near the Rio Grande.

There was no opportunity for much maneuvering. Ford ordered
Robinson's men to move out to the Texans' left and attack the Union
right flank. To bolster Robinson's tired men, Ford sent along two
fresh companies under Lieutenants Cocke and Wilson. He also sent
along one section (two guns) of artillery under Lieutenant Gregory.
The cannon could move under partial shelter of the chaparral and
some hills.

Ford himself held the center with the main portion of his forces
and one battery of guns. The two French pieces were moved out in
front and told to wait limbered up and ready to move.

The opposing lines were about a half mile apart. Ford's own two
guns unlimbered and made ready to fire; the French guns out in
front were still limbered. When Ford was ready to start the action,
he shouted to those around him, "Men, we have whipped the enemy
in all our previous fights! We can do it again!" (Ford later said he
was not optimistic about his chances for victory but was determined
to try.)

The men cheered. Ford shouted, "Forward! Charge!"

The artillery opened with a crashing fire; every musket blazed,
and the wild Rebel yell echoed across the mesquite. Immediately
the Union leaders saw that they were at a disadvantage with no
artillery of their own, and the noise seemed to indicate an enemy
force possibly larger than their own. Barrett at once ordered a

retreat. A hundred and forty men of the 62nd Colored Infantry were told to act as a rear guard, with the rest of the 62nd in support.

Ford saw the retreat begin and continued his charge. His own section of artillery limbered up and followed. As Ford rode forward he passed the pair of French guns, waiting limbered up and ready to go. Ford shouted at them to follow him. Knowing no English, they misunderstood him, and after Ford had ridden a short distance he looked back to see with surprise that the French gunners were unlimbering their pieces and making ready to fire. He rode back and shouted, "*Allons!*" Then they understood and quickly limbered up to follow him, but precious minutes had been lost.

To add to the confusion, a river steamboat owned by the King and Kenedy firm came up river while the fighting was in progress. The Texans did not recognize the vessel at once and were doubtful which flag it flew, so Ford's artillery officer had one gun fire a couple of rounds at the boat. The shots missed, and the Texans realized almost at once that the boat was friendly.

Meanwhile, the Texans who had been sent to outflank the Union right were gaining a partial success and were pushing the Federals back. Barrett saw their intentions and had the 34th Indiana and the 2nd Texas (Federal) form an oblique line with their backs to the river, their left anchored at the center of battle, and their right flung out to halt the Texans. The right wing was kept moving in a fast retreat, so the Texans were never able to get around the Union men — no matter how fast Ford's men moved, they always found themselves facing Federal soldiers who had the river at their backs.

The Texans held the initiative and kept moving forward. Part of the 34th Indiana was retreating at double-quick time and moved right through a portion of the 62nd Colored Infantry who were moving at only quick time. There were a few moments of confusion until the 34th Indiana got through. Forty-eight men of the 34th Indiana were cut off and surrendered to Ford's men.

For the rest of the afternoon the Texans drove the Union men back in a start-and-stop action. At times the guns would limber up and move forward to a new position. Then the Federals would halt to put up a strong delaying fire. More Union skirmishers were taken prisoner by the Confederates in these brief encounters. In spite of the heavy firing on both sides, the action was so mobile that there were relatively few casualties in relation to the amount of firing.

The classic strategy would have been for Ford to swing still far-ther out to his left and get between the Yanks and their base at Brazos Island. He did not have enough men to do that easily, and he knew there were more troops back at the island. They would have realized from the sound of artillery that a battle was in progress. If more Federals came from the island a strategy of encirclement would have been reversed, with Ford's own men caught between two fires.

So the Texans continued to hammer the Union troops back, past White's ranch and on toward Boca Chica. Somewhere along there, between Cobb's ranch and the Boca Chica, one part of the 62nd Colored Infantry halted long enough to fire the last organized volley of the Civil War. After that there was only scattered fire. The Union troops were perhaps a mile from the water crossing at Boca Chica.

The old reports say that on that particular afternoon the tide was in and Boca Chica was a marshy slough with shallow salt water. Off at one side was a levee or causeway providing a narrow road to Brazos Island. The Federal troops crowded across this levee; some splashed through the water. A color sergeant of the 34th Indiana wrapped a battle flag around himself and tried to cross through the water. He was shot by a Texan, and the Confederates pulled the body ashore and took the flag. (Rip Ford later flew it in front of his house in Matamoros.)

The first Union men across the causeway formed into a firing line among the sand hills on the far bank, to give a covering fire for those who were still in retreat.

At that moment, Brigadier General Slaughter arrived for the first time during the battle. With him rode Cater's Texas battalion.

The new battalion was ordered to head for the levee and cut off the retreating Union men. They could not get there in time. The last Federal troops crossed to safety.

In his exasperation, Slaughter waded into the water and emptied his revolver at the Union troops, far out of pistol range on the opposite bank, three hundreds yards away.

Then the firing on both sides dropped to a sputter, continuing for almost another hour before it ended. Dusk was falling, but the

Texans could see that new Union men had come forward from the interior of the island and the far bank was lined with a force that greatly outnumbered the Confederates.

As the shooting stopped, Ford said, "Boys, we have done finely. We will let well enough alone and retire."

The Union men began to disappear in the distance. Off the island, in the river, was the Union gunboat *Isabella*. In the twilight a single shell came from the Federal side; in the falling shadows it was hard to see whether it had come from the *Isabella* or from a field piece on the island.

It was the last Union shot of the war.

Among the Confederates was a young soldier, only seventeen. He was as exasperated as his general had been. The youth raised his Enfield and fired one futile shot at the place where the shell had exploded. A Texan officer described later that the youngster used "a very profane expletive for so small a boy, causing a hearty laugh from a half-score of his comrades."

The last Confederate weapon of the war had been fired. It was the evening of May 13, 1865.

Ford ordered the Texans to herd the prisoners together, bury the dead, and pick up any discarded weapons.

Some of the Union men who had fled into the chaparral earlier in the fighting were cut off from any chance to cross the levee to Brazos Island. While Ford's men were picking up scattered muskets, a young officer rode up to report that some of the Federals in the brush had taken refuge in a bend of the Rio Grande near Palmito Ranch.

Sergeant R. S. Caperton was told to take a squad of dismounted troopers and capture the Union men at the river bend. About twenty were taken, including Lieutenant Hancock of the 2nd Texas (Federal). Some of the Federals tried to escape by swimming across the Rio Grande. When they reached the opposite bank they were shot by Mexicans — either bandits or Imperialist soldiers — and their bodies were stripped and thrown back into the stream.

The last battle of the war was, in fact, over, but neither Ford nor Slaughter was certain of it at that moment. Ford believed that the Union forces on the island might be as many as three or four thousand. (There were not that many, but they did outnumber the

Texans.) He thought it possible that there might be a counter-attack during the night.

Slaughter wanted to press on in pursuit, but Ford — who had been on the field during the entire action — knew his men were exhausted. Some of the artillery horses were in such bad condition that they had to be unhitched from the guns, and there were no immediate replacements handy. Many of the cavalry mounts were in no shape to continue.

When Slaughter realized that further pursuit was not possible, he said to Ford, "You are going to camp here, are you not?"

"No, sir," replied Ford.

"I have ordered down several wagons loaded with subsistence and forage," returned Slaughter.

"I am not going to stop here in reach of infantry forces at Brazos Island and allow them a chance to gobble me up before daylight," Ford retorted.

"But remember the prisoners," said Slaughter.

"I do, sir, but if we Confederates were their prisoners, we would be compelled to march to a place of safety from attack by the Confederates," Ford replied firmly. That settled it; the Texans rode back to Lake Horn, a strong position about eight miles from Brownsville, and camped there for the night. There was no pursuit by Union forces.

Five days after the battle, Lieutenant Colonel Branson wrote his formal report and sent it to the acting assistant adjutant general of the U.S. forces at Brazos Santiago. Brigadier General Barrett didn't send in his report until August 10.

There are no official Confederate reports in the known records. Captain Carrington, an officer under Slaughter, wrote a good account about eighteen years after the war and had it checked by Ford before publication. Ford also wrote a short account some years after the fight, and other brief accounts appeared from time to time.

Reports of casualties were varied and conflicting. Each side, traditionally, claimed low losses for itself and high losses for the enemy. The Union loss was perhaps thirty killed and wounded, with about a hundred and thirteen lost as prisoners. The Confederates said they had only five wounded and no dead, but one Texan officer mentioned "burying our dead" so there may have been some.

The stories told by veterans also differed on the subject of prisoners. One said that no black prisoners were taken; another said that no blacks would allow themselves to be captured; and a third version said that some blacks were taken who admitted they expected to be shot or returned to slavery but instead were paroled.

There were similar variations in accounts of what happened to the Texans who fought on the side of the Union, in the 2nd Texas (Federal) Cavalry. One version told how the Confederates allowed those men to slip away during the march back to Brownsville, because the Texans didn't want to see their "own" men tried as deserters. Some of the Union men, watching from the island in the last hour of the battle, said they saw Confederates deliberately shoot blacks and captured Texans; the Confederate version was that such men fought to the death to avoid capture.

In any event, it appeared that all of the prisoners whom Ford took back to Brownsville were soon paroled. He had no men to guard them nor supplies to feed them.

Ford himself did not consider the war ended, because he had received no official orders to that effect. He realized that the chance for final victory was gone but preserved all appearances, except for disbanding nearly all of his men.

Slaughter returned the pair of borrowed French guns and sold the four Texas cannon for $20,000. One report alleged that he intended to keep the money. Ford was said to have arrested Slaughter, seized the funds, and distributed the money as partial back pay to his men and to himself — less than was due in every case. Slaughter fled to Mexico; he had always sympathized with the cause of Emperor Maximilian there. He never claimed for himself the credit for leading the last Confederate onslaught of the war.

A few days after the battle, Lieutenant Colonel Branson and a few other Union officers rode to Brownsville. They were not repulsed. Rip Ford agreed to meet the small group as long as the meeting did not involve the formality of a surrender. He treated them all to a round of eggnog and posed for a tintype with Branson. Then he took them on a tour of Matamoros across the river, to the astonishment of the Imperialist military forces there.

Not long afterward, Ford moved with his family to Matamoros. The town was emptying rapidly as dealers in military supplies left, their bonanza ended. Ford found a home without any great search, and he hung the captured Indiana flag over his doorway as a warning to the Mexican factions who still warred with each other in their own country.

On May 28, the ranking Union commander in the area, General Brown, came to Brazos Island and marched with a large command moving in a leisurely two-day jaunt into Brownsville. They found the place deserted by Confederate troops, but they managed to seize about five hundred bales of cotton. A thousand more bales had been hustled across the river in the few days preceding his arrival. Brown was told that on the day of the battle a body of Imperial cavalry had crossed the river to Brownsville and waited there in reserve, in case Ford needed help. That rumor was never confirmed.

Eventually the Confederates surrendered throughout Texas. General Magruder surrendered to Union General E. R. S. Canby, who had commanded at Fort Craig in New Mexico when the Texans fought there three and a half years before.

There was one remaining Texan unit that stayed in combat status after the Battle at Palmito Ranch, although the unit saw no action. It was a detachment of about two hundred Confederates who had been sent west of Austin into the San Saba and Concho country, where they were cut off from all communication. Their commander, Major Brown, had been assigned the task of rounding up deserters, thieves, and bushwhackers. He had about thirty such prisoners when his unit rode back into Fredericksburg, Texas, late in May. There he learned that the war was over. He disbanded all of his force except a small detachment to guard the prisoners and rode with them the eighty miles on to Austin. When he reached the capital he found the place in chaos, with the governor fled. Brown had no choice but to let the prisoners free, on their word that they would return home. He stayed in authority until May 30.

On June 2, Rip Ford received the long-expected orders that the war was at an end. He was told to arrange for paroles for all of his men and did so.

The last echo of the last battle.

8

Comancheros of the Staked Plains

SOUTHWESTERN LORE holds few figures more intriguing — or elusive — than the *Comancheros*. Those were the men who moved back and forth across the border between Texas and New Mexico, trading with the Comanche Indians. Their occupation lasted more than a hundred years. They started as small peddlers and ended as cattle rustlers on a grand scale.

Some were licensed, some were smugglers. At different times they dealt in guns, slaves, horses, cattle, and buffalo hides; they also rescued captives and served as intelligence agents.

Lack of organized records made it easy until recently for any fictioneer to write as he wished about the Comancheros, without contradiction. The evidence is there but scattered: in old letters from Spanish governors to their viceroys, in the tales of Santa Fe traders, in reports to Washington from official Indian agents and army officers, and — toward the end of the era — in court records, depositions of witnesses, and in memoirs of ranchers who were victimized.

There are also the oral records of folk-say, with their bits of truth twisted and magnified through a hundred years of retelling, waiting to be proved or disproved. These tales have fanciful descriptions of as many as six hundred "renegades" of all nationalities who rode by night; who painted their faces to appear as Indians, and massacred immigrants; who never appeared in towns; whose leaders had no names — and who also never appeared in even a passing mention in any acceptable historical document.

And yet there was a germ of truth in all the folklore.

135

The Comancheros were an inevitable development of their time and place; the result of definite geography, population, and way of life. The traders appeared because all of these factors existed when and where they did between A.D. 1700-1800. The Comancheros disappeared because there was a new geography, a new people, and a new way of life between 1800 and 1880.

Start by visualizing the map of Texas, which looks not unlike the pointed fist so favored by old signpainters: a finger pointing to the left, the clenched fingers suspended, downward, and a thumb uplifted. The fist itself is central Texas; at the far fingertip is El Paso; the uplifted thumb — fat and stubby in the case of Texas — is the Panhandle, because across its top runs the thin panhandle of Oklahoma.

Within the Panhandle lies a sea of grass, the Llano Estacado, or Staked Plains, where only a skilled land-pilot could guide the early travelers. And in the right angle formed by pointed finger and uplifted thumb lies New Mexico, a royal province of Spain until 1821, then a state of independent Mexico until 1848, and after that a frontier territory.

In the Panhandle, the Comanches appeared soon after 1700. They were a proud nation, soon on horseback with mounts of Spanish origin, a nomadic people who lived by the hunt instead of tilling the land. Their shields were their fortresses, their conical tepees were their towns, and the buffalo were their sustenance. They valued bravery above survival and courage above property. They warred to their unhappy end against two nations whose culture was based on acquisition, possession, and survival. And the war was not a pretty thing but was filled with primitive ways of killing.

But this is not the story of the Comanches; rather it is of the Comancheros who traded with them.

During the 1630's, about the time Roger Williams was starting the first settlements back east in Rhode Island, the Spanish had been in New Mexico almost a hundred years. Their population along the upper Rio Grande then was small; perhaps not more than two hundred and fifty men bore firearms.

They had already ventured eastward into the buffalo plains. One young captain named Alonso Baca led an expedition three hundred leagues, or roughly seven hundred and fifty miles, eastward across the plains in 1634. The Indians they met at that time were Plains

Apaches, soon to be pushed out by the Comanches who were moving down from the north.

A form of slavery was common in New Mexico, not identical with that practiced in the American South, but still a type of involuntary servitude. In the 1640's the trade for such captives had already started with the plains Indians; Matias Romero, who had been High Sheriff of Santa Fe, was accused of illicitly trading to secure captives for the Spanish governor.

Other traders went out on the plains to secure buffalo robes, and in 1660 one of those traders had a strange experience that landed him in deep trouble when he returned. He was Diego Romero, then thirty-seven. His father was either Dutch or Flemish, had been born in Brussels, and came to Santa Fe in 1619 as a skilled armorer. Diego was born in Santa Fe, and led an exuberant life, often with companions who were not fully approved by the padres.

In August, 1660, one of the local *dons* sent Diego and five companions out to trade for buffalo skins on the plains. The men rode until they came to a ranchería or village of the Indians. Diego explained, by sign language, that he had come to trade. Then he asked the Indians if they remembered his father, a ruddy-faced man who had once come also on a trading expedition. The father "had left a son with an Indian woman" and Diego then announced that he intended to leave another.

The Indians discussed this unusual news among themselves, agreed to the idea, and set about making elaborate ceremonial arrangements. About four o'clock in the afternoon they brought forward a tent of newly-tanned hides and set it up in the field. Then they brought two bundles of fine skins, one of antelope and the other of buffalo, which they placed near the tent.

Next they brought another new buffalo skin which they stretched on the ground and put Diego on top of it, lying on his back. They then began a ceremonial dance, which they indicated was a wedding dance. It was this dance, as much as the marital relations that followed, that got Diego into trouble when he returned home. It was a *catzina* or *kachina* dance, considered a heathen abomination by the Church fathers.

The dance continued for hours, with the Indians taking turns, singing, and raising Diego up and down by lifting the skin in accordance with the movements of the dance.

When the dance ended around nightfall, they picked up the buffalo hide by its corners, with Diego still lying on it, and carried him into the tent. Then they brought in an Indian maiden and left the two alone for the entire night.

When the morning dawned, the head men of the village came "to see if Don Diego had known the woman carnally." When they were satisfied that he had done so, they anointed his breast with the blood, put a feather in his hair, and proclaimed him a chief. They gave him the two bundles of skins and the tent.

Romero had been gone about a month when he and his men arrived back at the New Mexican frontier village of Galisteo. There one of the men in the group told the story to the father *guardián* at the convent. The padre wrote down the details and got some of the men to sign as witnesses.

Romero was arrested, charged with heresy, and all of his possessions were seized. The trial before the Inquisition moved slowly, but when it ended four years later he was sentenced to be brought forth in a public ceremony of the Inquisition, wearing an humble penitential garment, with a rope around his neck, and made to confess his sin. He was condemned not only to forfeit all his property but was taken away from New Mexico to serve four years at the oar in a Spanish galley.

When the first Comanches arrived on the plains, around 1705, the Spaniards had already developed their limited but regular trade with the plains Indians. They continued trading with the newcomers. Almost in the same year, competition was moving toward New Spain, for the French were starting outposts into what is now southern Illinois and near the mouth of the Mississippi. And from French traders the Comanches soon secured guns.

The Comanches also rapidly acquired Spanish horses, at first almost exclusively by raiding Spanish communities, such as Taos in 1716, from which they took new mounts by the hundreds. Before long there were wild mustangs on the plains. Their new mobility allowed the Indians to venture far afield; they met the French explorer Bourgmont in Kansas in 1724. The red plainsmen also rode east to trade with the Wichita Indians, and from them the Comanches obtained some of their first trade guns.

The Spaniards along the Rio Grande did what they could to retaliate against the Indian raids, partly to protect their own property and partly because they had promised protection to the Christianized Indians in the pueblos. But the rumors about French traders had worried the dons even since Villasur and Archibeque had hurried to their death in battle on the river Platte in 1720, where there were reports the French had stirred up the Pawnees When a party of traders from Louisiana, headed by the Mallet brothers, arrived in Taos in 1739, the Spanish knew the threat of French rivalry was real.

At first the Spanish tried to increase their military strength by enlisting Indian auxiliaries from the pueblos, in 1733.

Through the years the Spanish and the pueblo Indians had acquired slaves, by trade or conquest, from the nomadic tribes beyond the settlements. One such captive said he was from the Pawnees, "more than a thousand leagues away." Not all were Indians; in 1731 there was mention of a four-year-old girl ransomed from the Comanches; she was "very white and beautiful as though she had been a Flemish child."

The slaves were kept in servitude, their treatment varying with the nature of their masters. Some were assigned to hard labor; others were treated as members of the family, even to the point of adoption. Some captive children were baptized; adult slaves were given religious instruction by the priests. The non-pueblo Indians were called *genízaros*, a word derived from the Islamic *janissary*.

In 1740, the royal governor of New Mexico issued a proclamation that any slaves who felt they were being mistreated should report their case to him. The result was the establishment of the village of Tomé, a few miles south of Albuquerque, where forty *genízaro* families were assigned land. In return, they were to explore the country in pursuit of the enemy, "which they did with great zeal and obedience," according to the old parchments which added, "for experience has shown us that some nations are constantly hostile to others and cannot endure the sight of one another."

For about the next fifty years, until 1786, Spanish policy alternated between punitive raids and attempts at peace. It had become evident that the arid plains could be a buffer zone against the French, especially if the Comanches were neutralized through conquest or treaty. So while the punitive forays continued out onto the plains, the soldiers and their Indian auxiliaries were warned not to mistreat captured Comanche women and children. An order issued to that effect in 1741 provided a fine of three hundred pesos for the first offense, and for a later offense the same amount plus six months' exile if the offender was a Spanish soldier. If an Indian auxiliary committed a second offense he would receive two hundred lashes and six months in prison. It was noted that the order was loosely enforced.

In the early years the Comanches, also, alternated between war and peace. One of their first points of meeting with the pueblo Indians was at Taos, northernmost of the Rio Grande settlements. Sometimes the plains Indians raided Taos; on other occasions they rode in for peaceful trading.

Spanish officials suspected that the Taos Indians were keeping the Comanches posted on all troop movements. At a big festival in 1746, attended by many visiting chiefs, an order was issued that all Indians within New Mexico were to stay at home and have no talk with enemy tribes. No one was to venture more than two or three miles from his own pueblo without a travel permit. No permits were allowed if the purpose of the trip was to visit the Comanches, nor were any permits issued for such vague reasons as a search for strayed livestock. A few years later, in 1754, an edict was given that forbade any Spaniard to visit the Comanche villages, under penalty of fifty lashes.

The early settlers who ventured out on the plains to hunt buffalo or to trade with the Comanches were not described as Comancheros in the records of the time. That word was first used by Josiah Gregg in his book about the Santa Fe trade published in 1844. The word may have been in local use earlier.

In these days of easy touring it is difficult to appreciate the degree to which the Spaniards limited travel by their own people, not only to the plains but between villages and pueblos. For travel within the province, it was necessary to apply to an official, the *alcalde mayor*, for a permit. If a trip to the plains was planned it was necessary for the *alcalde* to pass the application on to the governor for approval. A few old and well-known settlers were exempt. To secure a license, the applicant had to be a citizen of good character and furnish references. When the *alcalde* delivered the permit, he also gave a brief lecture on the laws governing trade with the Indians. Any trader who went out without a license was subject to arrest on return. Villagers along the frontier were told to report on the movements of strangers. There was, of course, some illicit trade by small groups.

For many years after the Comanches arrived, the greatest amount of trading occurred at Taos Pueblo, in those years when the plains Indians preferred peace instead of war. Usually in July or August the Comanches rode in and set up their camp. The "Taos fair" was a thriving activity by 1748 and was repeated over many years; it is still the reason for a local fiesta. The Comanches came by the hundreds, bringing as many as a thousand horses, plus buffalo hides, captives, buffalo meat, and antelope skins. Few Indians surpassed the Comanches in skill at tanning, for they could cure skins with or without the hair, reducing the pelt to a supple fineness. They knew how to use fuller's earth or other clay to clean the skins to a rich ivory shade.

No money was used; everything was done by barter. Two or three items were given agreed values that established a basis for bargaining on everything else. One of the essential trade products of the Spanish was the *belduque*, a knife made of a single piece of iron. One good hide was worth two *belduques*. A good horse was worth twelve to fifteen hides. An Indian slave girl, aged twelve to twenty years, was worth two good horses. With these few ground rules, values of everything else could be determined. Male slaves were worth less than female. Meat was traded for flour.

In some years the Taos fair trading was wide open; in other years the governor and a few officials controlled it for their personal advantage. As the fair became more popular and crowds increased, the local *alcalde* could not maintain order and had to ask for a contingent of troops.

The fair was more than a simple exchange of necessities; to the Comanches it was also entertainment and almost a form of gambling. No sooner had they traded for something than they tried to parlay their gains by trading again for something else. In horse-swapping, a good race before the trade was an essential test. The Taos men, Indians and Spanish alike, were sharper traders, and the Comanches usually lost. Still, the visitors stayed at the fair until their interest waned or their possessions were reduced to a minimum.

After the fair, the Spanish merchants loaded their carts and wagons with hides for the long trek down the Rio Grande to Chihuahua, where the skins were exchanged for manufactured products.

The New Mexicans offered awls, vermillion, axes, bridles, *machetes,* and — most prized by the Comanches — oven-baked bread. Spanish laws forbade giving guns in trade, but the Comanches brought along a gun or two they had secured from a French or English trader east of the plains. The Comanches also brought a type of "yellow tin" (probably brass) cooking pot that was a staple trading commodity received from the French.

A few years of peaceful trading alternated with years of warfare. In 1751 after the Comanches had raided the Spanish frontier settlement at Galisteo, Governor Cachupín organized an expedition at Santa Fe and went after the plains Indians. He had a force of fifty-four regular soldiers, thirty citizen soldiers, and about eighty pueblo Indian auxiliaries. Those that had guns probably carried the old *escopeta,* a flintlock musket with the spring on the outside of the lock. Few of those early weapons remain; perhaps the only examples are the ones now in the Museum of New Mexico at Santa Fe.

Cachupín's men met and defeated the Comanches, killing more than a hundred and dividing their gear which included guns, lances, swords, and bows.

In that same period, an incident occurred that was a bizarre link with an earlier episode in Southwestern history. Juan Archibeque (Jean l'Archeveque), who had been with the men who assassinated La Salle and had later gone to New Mexico, had a son named Miguel. Miguel died in 1727, and his widow remarried, to José de Reaño. Their son, also named José, around 1759 fell off a horse and suffered a brain injury. He was kept in custody in the presidio at Santa Fe because of his dementia, but he escaped one midnight late in February, 1763. José took with him a young relative and four *genízaros,* all riding on stolen army horses. Five months later a plains Indian reported to the *alcalde* that he had found the remains of two *españoles* and three *genízaros* out on the bison plains. Arrowheads were found among the bones. A strange end of another branch of the Archibeque legend.

Peace of a sort finally came to the Spanish and Comanches when Governor Juan Bautista de Anza made a treaty with the Indians at the old pueblo of Pecos in 1786. After mutual agreement on the advantages of peace, the formalities of a treaty were observed. De Anza presented a sword and a banner to the Indians. They in turn

dug a small hole in the earth and ceremoniously refilled it, signify-
ing peace.

Then a great trading fair was held. De Anza had two parallel lines
marked on the ground. The Spanish stood back of one line and the
Comanches back of the other, each party with its trade goods. Trading was done in the space between the lines. The Comanches
brought six hundred hides to trade, along with fifteen horses, three
guns, and several packloads of dried buffalo meat.

The treaty did not ensure permanent peace, but it went a long
way toward stabilizing the border. It developed a more or less
friendly attitude on the part of the Comanches toward the Spanish,
as compared to relations with other white nations. The treaty also
developed still farther the idea of trade, which both sides found to
their advantage. A trail soon was blazed between Santa Fe, New
Mexico, and San Antonio, Texas, although it had little traffic.

The nineteenth century opened, and with it came a new era that
saw the Comanchero trade rise, change, and die. There probably
were no professional, full-time Comancheros in 1800. It was essentially a part-time, seasonal occupation, in which a man and a few
friends might spend a few weeks venturing on the plains to trade
for hides, horses, or mules. Their stock in trade was worth perhaps
twenty or twenty-five dollars, consisting of some trinkets, a bag of
bread loaves, and some hoop-iron for arrow points. They might, if
they were lucky, go home with a mule or two and some well-tanned
skins.

Other New Mexicans went toward the plains with lances to hunt
buffalo in June or October. Before long a definite route was followed, and there were cart trails and favored camp sites. After 1820
hardly a year passed without some American trapper, trader, or
explorer writing an account that mentioned the old trails.

The Comancheros still did not offer guns; in fact, they often
traded for weapons. After the defeat of the Gutiérrez-Magee expedition into Texas in 1813, some of the filibusters who went back to
the Red River country near Louisiana found it profitable to trade
guns to the Indians. Those Indians then traded guns to the Comanches for horses.

The Comanches raided deep into Texas for mounts and suffered
one of their major defeats at the Battle of Plum Creek when they

met a force of Texans hastily gathered under the leadership of General Felix Huston.

For a century the plains Indians had taken captives from other tribes and from Mexico. Many of those were traded or sold to the New Mexicans, but only a few of their victims' names were ever recorded. By 1836 the Comanches were seizing Anglo captives, and when such prisoners were freed they sometimes wrote entire books about their experiences.

Mrs. Sarah Ann Horn had gone to the American Southwest to settle in an Englishman's private colony on the Rio Grande. In 1836 she and her two sons, along with a Mrs. Harris and her child, were taken by Comanches. Their husbands were killed. From April of that year until September they roamed with the Indians. Once a trader named Holland Coffee tried to make a trade for Mrs. Horn, but the Indians refused. Finally the Comanches brought her alone to the New Mexico town of San Miguel, and there she was bought, for about eighty dollars' worth of trade goods, by a Comanchero who was working for Workman and Rowland, two trappers and businessmen of Taos.

Mrs. Rachel Plummer was another woman taken captive when Comanches raided a fortified family home known as Fort Parker in Texas, in 1836. She was finally ransomed by Comancheros who were agents for William Donaho, a New Mexican trader, when the Indians were within seventeen days' travel of Santa Fe. Another captive on the same raid was Cynthia Ann Parker, who was not returned for twenty-four years. In that time she had two Comanche sons, one of whom became the chief, Quanah Parker.

In the rescue of Sarah Horn and Rachel Plummer, the fact that they were ransomed by Comancheros working for men in Taos and Santa Fe indicates that trade on the plains was becoming organized on a business basis.

In every storied episode of the Southwest there seems to be at least one personality who played what is today called a "cameo" role: a transient bit that hints at an entire story in itself. One such man was Alexander LeGrand, who was sent by President Burnet of the Texas Republic in 1836 in an unsuccessful attempt to make a peace treaty with the Comanches.

He had a colorful background that gave rise to even more colorful tales. One wild version of his life was that he was a Frenchman who had been working for an English mining firm in New Mexico. There he fell at odds with the *alcalde* and was condemned to wear chains and work at street cleaning. The fiction then continued that he was released, joined the Comanches, lived with them for fifteen years, and became a chief — returning with a war party to kill the *alcalde* and nearly destroy the old palace.

The verifiable truth is that LeGrand was born in Maryland. He first appeared in records as captain or wagonmaster of the train of Becknell, Storrs, and Marmaduke, when they made their famous trip with wagons over the Santa Fe Trail in 1824. He went on to Mexico and became a trader there. He was said to have surveyed a large Southwestern land grant in 1827, but the verification of that is incomplete. He fought in the Texas Army in 1836. There are LeGrand documents in the Texas archives, with ample proof that he knew the Llano Estacado as well if not better than most men of his time.

The Comanches were difficult to deal with when it came to a treaty that involved their lands. The Spanish and Mexicans had sought only peace and trade, never cessions of territory. There are indications that the governors of the land along the upper Rio Grande also found it advantageous to sow suspicion in the Indians' minds against the encroaching Anglos.

New Mexico in 1840 had almost fifty-five thousand population. An outer fringe of settlements had been established between the Rio Grande and the buffalo plains, including such towns as Vegas de las Gallinas (Las Vegas), Vado (San Miguel del Vado), Tecolote, Anton Chico, Mora, and Sapello. When the Texan-Santa Fe Pioneers first reached New Mexico, they were met by Comancheros who took them to Anton Chico.

The Comanchero trails were becoming a definite part of the landscape by then, with the leading trail following down the Canadian River. A branch of that trail went along the Tierra Blanca, and there was another well-traveled route down the Pecos River to Bosque Grande, then eastward to the head of the Yellowhouse. Today such towns as Lubbock and Amarillo in Texas; and Portales, Fort Sumner, and Tucumcari in New Mexico; are on or near famous Comanchero campgrounds.

Over those trails the Mexicans traveled with homemade carts made entirely of wood: wooden wheels, wooden axles, wooden rack bodies. Wheels were heavy, often drilled off center. Oxen dragged the *carretas*, whose hubs complained in a soprano scream of agony at each revolution.

Then came the end of the war between the United States and Mexico, resulting in a new government at Santa Fe. As far as the Comancheros were concerned, the most bothersome new officials were the Indian agents whose job included regulation of all trade with the tribes on the plains. Both Texas and New Mexico were part of the United States when James Calhoun became the Indian agent at Santa Fe in 1849. His superior, the territorial military governor John Munroe, wrote to Washington that the extensive illicit trade with Indians was the region's greatest problem.

Calhoun at once issued a ruling that no one could trade without a license. License requirements were not unlike those of the Spanish and Mexican period: be a citizen, post a bond up to $5,000, pay a ten dollar license fee, produce character references, specify the tribes with whom the trader wished to deal, and agree not to deal in firearms.

Calhoun had a difficult case early in his new career when Indians, probably Apaches, carried off a Mrs. White after an attack on a wagon train along the western end of the Santa Fe Trail. Calhoun promptly realized the value of experienced Comancheros and traders as go-betweens in such cases, for he hired Encarnación García and Auguste Lacome to bring back Mrs. White. García learned she had been killed. He did bring back four other captives from his search, which ranged as far south as the Guadalupe mountains near the San Antonio-El Paso road.

The new agent learned, too, about the custom of peonage, when a twelve-year-old boy named Refugio Picaros, captured by the Comanches in Mexico, was sold to José Francisco Lucero at Mora in 1850 for four knives, four blankets, six yards of red cloth, some corn, and a plug of tobacco.

Calhoun became the territory's first civil governor in 1850 and at once tried to arrange a peace with the Comanches. The Indians at first doubted the ability of the new regime to preserve order. The trading post of Bent's Fort had been burned by its owners, there were few troops in New Mexico, and the plains were still unguarded.

Still, some of the Comanche chiefs came in for a parley after Calhoun granted a license to a trader named Latz, who was allowed to trade down toward Bosque Redondo and tell the Comanches that Calhoun wanted to talk peace.

Six chiefs, each with his wife, came to the frontier town of Anton Chico to meet with Calhoun. The negotiations started in the afternoon with the ransom of a Mexican child. That night the Comanches fled, leaving behind their robes, provisions (including twenty loaves of bread), kettles, and even a rifle.

Calhoun deputized several Comancheros and friendly Indians to find the vanished Comanches, reassure them, and return their goods. The pursuers caught up with one old Indian who could not keep pace with the others. From him it was learned that shortly before midnight someone had whispered to the Comanches that Calhoun planned to have them all killed before dawn.

One of the next Indian agents in the territory was John Ward, and he was also strict on licenses issued to Comancheros. A Mexican from San Miguel applied for a permit, but when his papers were not in order the license was denied. An Indian from Santa Clara pueblo was given a pass readily; so was a Santo Domingo pueblo Indian who wanted a pass for himself and eighteen tribesmen.

Ward was succeeded by John Greiner, who continued the same strict policy. Pueblo Indians were given passes and licenses freely; Mexican applicants received sterner investigation, but men such as Domingo Sanchez and Juan Lopez were given permits good for two weeks to three months — partly because these individuals always came back with reports on the location and disposition of the Comanches. If Greiner didn't like a man's credentials or his looks, he simply told the applicant that no more permits were being issued at the moment.

The trade in captives continued, with some of the territorial officials adopting the system of peonage as a solution to the servant problem. Comancheros continued to ransom prisoners from the Indians. One of these captives was Nelson Lee, who had been a Texas Ranger and was horse-trading near El Paso when he and three others were caught by the Comanches. Lee was an Indian's slave for three years before he killed his master and escaped. The Comancheros found him hiding in the mountains.

When authorities began to tighten up on licenses for those who traded with the Indians there were two results: those who secured licenses began to make it a full-scale operation instead of a seasonal activity, and those who could not get licenses often traded illicitly.

It became a risky business, too, as warfare increased on the southern plains. The army was small in the days before the Civil War, and when that conflict opened there was even less authority to control the tribes.

One man who worked valiantly during the 1850's to solve the Indian problem was an interesting Texan, Robert S. Neighbors. He was a Virginian in his early twenties when he served as acting quartermaster of the Texas Army. He had been a Ranger under Jack Hays and was in San Antonio when the Mexican General Woll seized the town. Neighbors was a Perote prisoner, and after his return home he became a Texas agent to control the Indians. He believed in going out to deal with the tribes around their own council fires, rather than make them come to the agency.

When Texas was annexed to the United States, Neighbors continued to serve as a U.S. Indian agent. In 1850 when Texas tried to set up its own counties in the eastern half of New Mexico, Neighbors was sent to do the organizing. He did establish El Paso county. With a fine knowledge of the plains, he served well with Army Lieutenant Randolph B. Marcy in laying out a road across the Panhandle. As Indian raids — and counter-raids by the whites — increased, Neighbors worked to reduce lawlessness by both sides. He was in the town of Fort Belknap in the autumn of 1859 when a stranger named Edward Cornett walked up to him and said he didn't like the way Neighbors proposed to deal with Indians. A short argument followed, and Cornett shot Neighbors. He was forty-three.

After the Confederates were defeated in New Mexico in 1862, the U.S. troops there turned their attention to the Indians. They rounded up most of the Navajo and herded them into a mass camp at Bosque Redondo, an old Comanchero campground. That camp, together with the military posts such as Fort Union, provided a good market for beef, and the Western cattle business got its first real start. It also started a rich new activity for the Comancheros: cattle stealing, which became especially profitable for the unlicensed traders.

While the soldiers at Fort Sumner were busy guarding the Navajo at Bosque Redondo, a new post named Fort Bascom was started in 1863 to control the plains Indians. At first it was a lonely station; liquor could not be sold within five miles of an army post, so the little town of Liberty was formed five miles west of Fort Bascom to provide the amenities. After the post was deactivated in 1870, Liberty continued until the turn of the century, when the railroad went through about eight miles south. Folks then moved down by the tracks, and Tucumcari, New Mexico, was born.

Comancheros on their well-worn trail passed Fort Bascom, and more than one officer at the post frequently gave the trader some small goods, asking him to bring back whatever it might bring. A pot or a length of cloth might bring a steer on the return trip.

The fort had its own herd of beef cattle, replenished from time to time by ranchers in the vicinity. In 1867 a peculiar incident showed that not all illicit dealing was done by unlicensed Comancheros.

One morning several cattle were missing from the post herd. Troopers rode off at once following a clear trail. After about forty miles they saw the steers ahead, being herded by two cowboys who fled as the soldiers approached.

A few of the cavalrymen rode after the cowboys, who headed straight to the ranch of a cattleman who held a government contract. The rancher was not at home; he had just left for the fort to give a lame explanation why he could not make delivery of beef promised for the next day according to his contract!

Captain George Letterman was in charge of Fort Bascom at that time, and he had his hands full dealing with the elusive unlicensed Comancheros. Six of them once tried to bypass the post, but news came to Letterman and he sent out the troopers. The traders, with six burros, were caught sixty miles east of the fort. When asked for their papers, the Comancheros said that the license was being carried by companions who had gone on ahead. That was an old trick. Letterman confiscated their goods: five hundred pounds of beans, forty butcher knives, and several pounds of lead and powder.

Letterman also seized cattle brought back by traders, if he had reason to believe the animals were stolen. At one time the post was holding eight hundred head of contraband, and on later occasions the impounded herd passed seven thousand.

The soldiers at Fort Bascom were sometimes a little slipshod in handling goods confiscated on the plains. Captain Letterman carefully spelled out his firm instructions: an accurate inventory was to

be made and turned in, listing all items confiscated. Each Comanchero was to be allowed to keep a pistol or rifle and thirty rounds
of ammunition.

During the last years of Fort Bascom's activity, 1870, Captain
Horace Jewett found the illicit traffic was becoming too much for
the post to handle. He asked in vain for the creation of a power of
citizens' arrest, by which anyone could arrest unlicensed traders or
those dealing in stolen cattle. Jewett also complained that some of
the wealthiest merchants in Santa Fe were back of some illegal trade.
Once Jewett's men caught some Comancheros and had them sent
to Santa Fe where they could be given "very close questioning" in
an effort to learn the names of their backers. The men were freed
instead, on the grounds that the charges against them were inadequate.

At one time all licenses were revoked in an effort to stop the trade.
Later the rule was relaxed enough to allow a few licenses, but the
men who obtained the permits subcontracted with other individuals
by the score. The trade soon was as big as it had ever been. In 1867
at least seven hundred traders visited the plains. An outbound party
of Comancheros might swell to a hundred men as it moved through
the villages along the Pecos River, from San Miguel, through La
Cuesta, Anton Chico, and Puerto de Luna. Operating under one or
two licenses, the individuals were grubstaked by other merchants
such as Adolphe at La Cuesta or Hughes and Church at Puerto de
Luna. On the return trip, those merchants got part of the cattle,
others went to the licensee, and each Comanchero had enough left
to make his trip worth while.

Even the trading was becoming systematized. Instead of wandering around like gypsy peddlers with a few trinkets, the Comancheros
headed directly for established campsites such as Mucha-que and
Quitaque, favorite spots for Comanches. At those sites, Comancheros
such as Polonio Ortíz from La Cuesta, or José Tafoya who traded
under a license issued to a man named Jennings, had semi-perma-
nent shelters for use on frequent trips. If the Indians had no cattle
when the traders arrived, the traders arranged details of the trade
in advance and waited until delivery was made. At times they even
let the Indians use guns on loan. In rare instances they delivered
the trade goods in advance, but if the merchandise consisted of

whiskey the kegs were buried secretly a distance from the camp, lest the Comanches try to seize the liquor before completing the trade.

Movie makers in recent years have coined whimsical plots involving white men painted to resemble Indians, to mislead those whom they raided. Comanchero records show no exact proof of this, but one known instance came close.

In the 1930's a letter turned up in the Texas adjutant-general's old records indicating that there had been an organization of white men operating near the Indian Territory (Oklahoma) line. The group was large and well knit; men in the lowest echelon would steal horses a short distance out from the reservation boundaries, making it appear that Indians had done the raiding. It was not indicated whether the men were in Indian costume or only left Indian "sign" of their presence. The stolen horses were passed north, through the gang's channels, to a ready market.

Guns and whiskey became major staples in the trade. One camp of Anglo traders in the northern Panhandle was stocked with four hundred gallons of liquor when it was seized by soldiers in 1873. (It is quite probable that the inventory as reported ran a little short, for a cavalryman's life was hard enough to entitle him to a little liquid reward.) As early as 1856, Robert Neighbors alleged that Jesse Chisholm had traded seventy-five rifles to the Comanches.

There was still a limited amount of the old-time trading, but prices had become inflated. In the 1870's a superior mule was worth a keg of whiskey; ten pounds of coffee brought a good packhorse; a very ordinary mule was traded for five pounds of tobacco.

But the real trade was in cattle. More livestock had moved onto the ranges as the plains were cleared by buffalo hunters, and for a few years the Comanches themselves found beef a substitute for bison. In the big Comanche trading camp at a place they called Quitaque, in the late summer of 1867, one trader saw 15,000 horses and "Texas cattle without number." A few years later one party of two hundred Comancheros was moving a herd of two thousand head about forty miles from John Chisum's ranch in New Mexico.

Some sub-licensed traders such as José Tafoya bought 2,500 steers at a time. José Medina, a Comanchero from San Miguel, saw 8,000 cattle in one place on a trading trip. Ranchers such as Charles Goodnight estimated that as many as 300,000 Texas cattle moved over the trails to New Mexico. Sometimes the Comancheros took their contraband direct to the final buyers; at other times they were taken over by unlicensed traders who were too timid to venture onto the plains.

In the days of the Spaniards, the term Comanchero was a proud name, denoting a man with courage enough to risk his life in trading trinkets for hides. By the late 1800's the word was akin to profanity.

As the nature of the trade changed, many Spanish-Americans in New Mexico frowned on the outlawry. Many leading *patrons* looked on the Comancheros as low thieves; Hilario Romero, a sheriff of San Miguel county in New Mexico, helped the *Tejanos* recover their stock but prevented them from taking more than they had lost. Often the Comancheros brought their herds to Spanish buyers in New Mexico, who then sold them to *Americanos* engaged in driving the herds north of Colorado or Kansas for resale at high profits.

Each group involved had its own moral values; no one felt he was doing wrong. The Comanches felt they were only repaying themselves for the loss of their buffalo herds. The Comancheros knew they were buying stolen cattle but felt that as long as they gave payment in goods the deal was honest enough.

But the Texans were naturally outraged. Charles Goodnight stormed into Las Vegas and took his case to court. He didn't win, but after more than thirty years' fighting up through various claims courts he finally was awarded partial payment.

In 1872, a Texas rancher named John Hittson took matters into his own hands. Modern historians Charles L. Kenner and J. Evetts Haley have unearthed the details of his raid. Hittson rallied his own posse of about ninety gunfighters, collected power of attorney from many fellow ranchers, and rode on a wide foray through New Mexico, seizing any cattle bearing the brands listed. He shot any *Hispano* or Anglo who resisted. He proved his point but later admitted that the costs equalled the value of the cattle reclaimed.

The federal government finally decided that the only permanent solution was a military campaign, striking with such force that it would drive the Comanches to their reservation. The field commanders, including Ranald Slidell Mackenzie, on the Texas plains were told to start a relentless push. It was 1871; the trade with the plains Indians had lived more than two hundred years; it would die in the next four summers.

And some of the Comancheros themselves would be not only the problem but the solution, for they became scouts with the cavalry.

When Mackenzie was gathering mounts and supplies for his campaign, his outriders accidentally brought in one of the best assets for a successful march: an experienced guide. A sergeant with a detail of the 4th Cavalry rode down on a small band of Comancheros, killed two men and captured a third. He was Polonio Ortíz, from the village of La Cuesta on the Pecos. Ortíz showed Mackenzie how to cross the "waterless" plain by a route that had sufficient but not excessive water.

Others among the Comancheros also changed allegiance. A man named Johnson, whose nationality had long been a question mark, guided Mackenzie to the Palo Duro fight that finished the plains trade. Some, like José Tafoya, revealed information only under physical pressure that was less than delicate.

Mackenzie had much of the Comanche spirit deep within himself and was a good match for his enemies. During the Civil War he rose from a second lieutenant at twenty-two to a brevet brigadier general at twenty-five. When he led his men to the last major Indian battle in Texas, at Palo Duro canyon in the fall of 1874, he was only thirty-four.

In four successive summers starting in 1871 the plains cavalry rode in great loops, following the ex-Comanchero guides along the old trails. The trade was almost at a standstill; sometimes the troopers rode a thousand miles without seeing a single Comanchero. Buyers of stolen cattle hesitated to equip new groups of traders; those who stayed home in those years nursed deep resentments against their former comrades who had switched allegiance, and their grievances lasted for a generation.

Now and then there was action when the soldiers encountered Indians. It is not unlikely that the Comanches in those final days had at least a few Winchester repeating rifles, obtained from northern traders. Some accounts also mentioned Spencers, Henrys, and Sharps' rifles. Only two years after the Palo Duro battle, other Indians far to the north reversed the story when they met Custer. In that battle at least a few hundred Indians were said to have had Winchesters.

As Mackenzie's men rode the plains they saw, and partially recognized, the force that finally defeated the Comanches: the buffalo hunters who were beginning to swarm into the Panhandle to kill off the Indians' basic livelihood.

After the last big surround at Palo Duro, there were only legends, left to be gathered by such historians as A. B. Thomas, Rupert Richardson, and Ernest Wallace. Westward in New Mexico settlers such as Herman Moncus remain today to tell visitors where they can find the old Comanchero campsites.

Once there had been a three-way economy that built a great venture: the Comanche, the buffalo, and the Comanchero. They were replaced by another trio: the rancher, the cattle thief, and the cavalryman. And two of those passed also. They left only the reality of the cattleman and the legend of the Comanchero.

Comanchero — a name that once stood as a definition for courage in many had ended by meaning dishonor for the last few.

9

Slaughter on the Plains

THERE ARE three famous kinds: the aurochs, the gaur, and the buffalo. All are bison. The aurochs roamed in Europe, the gaur in India, and the buffalo in America. And in America one of the greatest herds ended in Texas — ended as completely as if it had made one last stampede over the edge of the earth.

There were perhaps three million of them in the Southern Herd, a number that surprises people who believe that the buffalo lived only in the northern plains, hunted first by warbonneted Sioux and later by Buffalo Bill.

Yet it was a Texas buffalo that Cortez gazed upon, a shaggy beast in Montezuma's private zoo, ninety years before an Englishman first saw an American bison, near the river now called the Potomac.

Those who saw the animals first called them by odd names: cattle, the Mexican bull, the American behemoth, the crook-back oxen, and finally the buffle, buffelo, and buffalo. Scientists use the term *bison*, with many variations, and insist that the only true buffalo are the water buffalo of southeastern Asia and the buffalo of the African veldt. But common habit is a strong force, and if an automobile can be a car, a *Bos* (Bison) can be a buffalo.

In return, the buffalo left its name upon the land of Texas: on twelve different streams each called Buffalo Creek, and on a lake, a peak, a point, a bayou, two gaps, a draw, and two towns — one of them a ghost town. Not counting two villages called Buffalo Springs, of which one is also a ghost camp.

For fifteen generations the men who came after Cortez hunted

155

buffalo as a sport. Then in 1870 it became a business, and in less than ten years the business — and the immense Southern Herd — were ended. But before the end there were new names in the records: J. W. Mooar, Charlie Rath, Billy Dixon, Bat Masterson, Pat Garrett, Billy Tilghman, and John Poe, to name a few, all buffalo hunters in the Texas Panhandle and across the great Staked Plains. And the large-bore guns appeared: the Sharps Big Fifty, along with the Henry, designed solely for the buffalo kill.

The story of the great buffalo years in Texas follows a single cord, but that cord was plaited of strands from such strange sources as Queen Victoria, a teen-aged Chicago trolley conductor, a New England shirtmaker, a Comanche chief, and a Pennsylvania lawyer.

The great days of the fur trade and the mountain men had passed. The felt hat had replaced the beaver stovepipe. In their richest years of the 1830's and 1840's the fur companies had shipped thousands of robes down the Missouri to Saint Louis, but those had been Indian robes. A few hunters brought in buffalo hides to Missouri River ports in the years before the Civil War, but the trade was light. It was even less during the years of the War Between the States.

In those years, the Indians took advantage of the absence of troops on the western plains. The red men raided the few settlements in the Texas plains, and by the time Lee surrendered at Appomattox the northwestern border of Texas had been pushed back more than a hundred miles.

When the Civil War ended, the Army turned its attention to the plains again. By treaty and by force they drew the new boundaries of peace. In 1867 a treaty was signed at Medicine Lodge, Kansas. Among those on the whites' side of the council were Generals Sherman, Terry, and Harney. Facing them in solemn dignity were such chiefs as Satanta, Black Kettle, and Lone Wolf.

The Indians pointed out that already the Kansas settlers were pushing back the buffalo and had been doing so at the pace of ten miles a year. The Indians proposed that the red men would remain south of the Arkansas River and the buffalo hunters would stay north of the river. It was agreed.

It was a natural boundary, the Arkansas, a flowing landmark that coursed through Oklahoma, across the lower edge of Kansas, from headwaters in the Colorado mountains. There were no railroads then in the plains country, and the only cattle trails were far to the west, along the Pecos. The Arkansas was a line that everyone knew across the land.

But while the treaties were being made, a young Pennsylvania attorney was laying the groundwork for his new fortune in Kansas. He was Cyrus K. Holliday, and he intended to build a railroad: the Atchison, Topeka & Santa Fe. In late 1868 the first shovel of earth was turned at Topeka. The steel rails would divide the plains forever.

Forty years before the railroad was started, the old mountain men knew the joys of buffalo meat; their campfire cookery would rival the best by Escoffier, and as chefs they could easily have merited the *ruban bleu* in their specialty. They roasted the hump and the ribs, they ate the liver raw with a dash of gall to give it zest, they skewered bits of alternate lean and fat meat *en appolas,* and they ate and ate and ate — for it was peculiar that no one ever became ill from eating too much buffalo! Eight pounds a day was considered only a standard ration for one man.

The trappers loved best of all a delicacy called *boudin,* truly the *pate de foie gras* of the mountain men. This was made from the intestine closest to the stomach, filled with partly digested grass and acids into which the hunters sometimes added finely chopped meat before tieing the two ends and boiling it like a sausage or pudding. Others gathered wild cherries and pounded them into chopped dried meat to make pemmican. Another variation was produced by slicing chips off the underside of a fresh hide. These were placed in a bowl and boiling water was added to make a dish tasting not unlike boiled Irish potatoes.

When the big Texas Panhandle buffalo hunt began, hunters there preferred ordinary roast or broiled hump and ribs. Their next choice was a thin slice of meat dipped in batter and fried — exactly like today's "chicken fried steak."

The railroad construction gangs had no such delicacies. They wanted and got plain buffalo beef and plenty of it. Hired hunters, of whom Buffalo Bill was one, each day dropped as many animals as the commissary required. When hunted for meat, the buffalo often was skinned starting with a slit along the spine, so the hump and ribs could be reached easily. When hide-hunting became widespread, the skinners started along the belly.

By mid-1870 the railroad reached Emporia, Kansas. By the end of 1872 it had passed through Dodge City and was at the Kansas-Colorado line.

While the railroad was snaking westward across the plains, a hide dealer named W. C. Lobenstein in Fort Leavenworth was energetically seeking new markets for buffalo hides. He sent some to England, where the tanners found them of little value in making harness, belts, shoes, or similar articles for hard use. But the new hides turned out to be perfect for the leather accoutrements used by the army. And Queen Victoria's far-flung regiments needed more and more and more. Back in Leavenworth, Lobenstein spoke to Charlie Rath and Charlie Myers, two adventurous hunters who had been bringing in hides traded from Indians and trappers. Rath and Myers received Lobenstein's order for 500 hides to be delivered in the winter of 1870–71.

They hired other hunters to help them meet the quota, and one of these was Josiah Wright Mooar, a nineteen-year-old youth who had worked briefly in Chicago as a trolley motorman. J. Wright Mooar, who preferred to be called Wright, turned out to be a natural buffalo hunter. He not only knew how to hunt, but — more important — he could organize and run a businesslike outfit.

Mooar went to work as a hunter for Rath and Myers. At the end of the season he had several more hides than his employers wanted, so he shipped the balance to his brother in New York. There had been plenty of buffalo robes before but somehow the tanneries had never paid much attention to them until Mooar's hides were shipped east. After a few tests the tanners were enthusiastic, and the market was wide open for all the hides that could be shipped.

Now there was an unlimited market for buffalo hides and a new railroad to get them to that market. All that was needed was an army of hunters, and this was not long in coming.

In the summer of 1873 the Atchison, Topeka and Santa Fe reached the town of Granada, well into Colorado. A business recession was on, and the railroad decided to stop construction while it digested the vast chunk of land it had bitten off. Hundreds of men on the construction gangs found themselves out of jobs. But a new line of work was ready at hand: buffalo hunting. If a man had no special skill at hunting — and little skill was needed to kill buffalo in those early, rich days — he could sign on as a skinner at two-bits a hide or as a hustler and general helper at monthly wages that equalled or bettered railroad pay.

In the entire West at that time the buffalo generally were grouped into two vast herds: the Northern Herd and the Southern. The Southern Herd then comprised about three million head and was centered on Garden City, Kansas, smack on the railroad. From there it ranged west to the foot of Pike's Peak, southwest to the Pecos, once called the *Rio de las Vacas,* or River of the Cows for the many buffalo along its banks, and south to the site of modern San Angelo, Texas. There were buffalo out beyond all these boundaries, of course, but they were on the fringe of the Southern Herd.

The volunteer army of professional buffalo hunters had no standard-issue weapon. Each man laid hands on the best gun he could get and as soon as he had the cash he usually bought a better one.

They used all kinds: Spencers, Springfields, Sharps', Henrys. There were as many "favorite" rifles as there were models, with Sharps' having a slight edge on the Henrys. The Sharps name has vanished, but there is curious story about the Henry. This is where the New England shirtmaker entered the web of history. He was Oliver Winchester, a textile manufacturer who branched out into a business strange to him: he organized the New Haven Repeating Arms Company and bought out the assets of the bankrupt Volcanic Repeating Arms Company.

Three of the assets were priceless. They were a trio of employees named Smith, Wesson, and B. Tyler Henry. Henry had designed a good rim-fire metallic cartridge in the late 1850's and in 1860 secured a patent on the Henry rifle that used this cartridge.

The 1860 Henry was the father of the Winchester rifle, legally and physically. The first model was a brute of a gun, with a heavy octagonal barrel at least two feet long. The breechblock or housing at the rear of the barrel, containing the chamber and firing mechanism, was of thick, polished brass. The Indians later called it the "Big Yellow."

With metallic cartridges it was possible to devise a practical magazine that would make the gun a repeater. The Henry tubular magazine beneath the barrel carried fifteen cartridges. The trigger guard was long, with a fist-sized loop that was easy to grab. The guard lay back along the end of the stock. When the hunter pulled the lever down, a spent cartridge was ejected and a new one advanced into the chamber. At top speed, the Henry could fire all fifteen shots in half a minute.

A few of them were used during the Civil War. At least one of Sherman's regiments, and possibly two, carried Henrys on the famous march through Georgia.

There was more to a buffalo gun than a large bore, so not every large-caliber antique is a buffalo gun. Many of the Gold Rush forty-niners carried weapons with a caliber up to .60 inch.

Even the plainsman's Hawken rifle was .50 caliber, but its practical range was around 350 yards. Buffalo hunters wanted a gun with twice that range, three times if possible, and with a heavy slug. And in buffalo hunting a man did not object to a rifle weighing up to eighteen or nineteen pounds if necessary.

It had to be a breechloader, and this is where the Sharps' and the Henry were successful. Christian Sharps, whose guns had been called "Beecher's Bibles" in Kansas and had been carried by John Brown's men at Harper's Ferry, were single-shot weapons with a trigger-guard lever to open and close the breech. Some Sharps' had two triggers, fore and aft. After cocking the hammer with his thumb, the hunter pulled the rear trigger to set the front hair-trigger. This gave greater accuracy.

Both Sharps and Henry responded to the buffalo hunters' demands for special weapons. The first Sharps model for the new market was a .50-120-380 model, which means the bore was .50 inch, the powder charge was equal to 120 grains of wheat in weight, and the lead bullet weighed 380 grains.

Hunters found that the big bullet had a tendency to drift in strong wind. Sharps tried making a powerful .44 but the bore fouled too readily. He dropped down to a .40 caliber model but this was too weak for buffalo hunting. In the end the favorite was a .45-120-380, with a long cartridge. These sold new for $55 to $80.

Many of the .50 caliber guns were used by hunters who liked the Big Fifty best of all and would pay up to a hundred dollars for one, or the same for an equivalent Henry.

Buffalo Bill, who was primarily a meat hunter for the railroad and who killed 4,280 buffalo in eighteen months, liked a breech-loading, single-shot, .50 caliber Springfield. When J. Wright Mooar started he used this weapon, with a 70-grain center fire cartridge and a swedge-ring ball.

Hunters often carried two guns in their wagon, a heavy weapon and a lighter model. This gave them some choice according to the weather or the nature of the day's hunt. It also gave them a spare in case of an accident or loss. There is a record of one party that carried three Sharps' breech-loaders, one each of .40-90, .45-70, and .45-120.

In the last days of buffalo hunting, up in the northern tier of states in the 1880's a few hunters used a new .45 hammerless Sharps' with telescopic sights.

Buffalo hunters travelling in parties took along a good supply of ammunition, enough to last them through a winter's hunt. They carried lead, often known as "St. Louis shot tower" quality, in small bars packed in sacks holding twenty-five pounds. Their powder was usually black Dupont, packed in twenty-five-pound cans, with one six-pound can that could be refilled from the larger canisters. Powder sold for $2.50 to $5.00 a pound.

The hunters reloaded their own cartridges, sometimes adding a little more powder than standard. In the supply wagon was a reloading kit consisting of a bullet mold, primer extractor, swage or swedge, tamper, patch paper, and a lubricator. They often greased the cartridges with buffalo tallow but ordinarily did not grease the bullet, to reduce fouling.

With these portable cannon booming by the thousands, the plains of western Kansas and eastern Colorado were cleared of buffalo by 1873. Only a few fugitive bands remained. The hunters looked with longing eyes at the big herds south of the Arkansas River, south of the flowing boundary that had been drawn by the Comanches in the Medicine Lodge Treaty of 1867.

The strip of land between Kansas and Texas, below Dodge City and in the region now named the Oklahoma Panhandle, was then locally called "No Man's Land." Hunters began to drift down below the Arkansas and into this forbidden zone, where the herds were still big. In 1873 J. Wright Mooar decided to try his luck there, Comanches or not.

He and his brother John lined up eight hired hands. They had a successful hunt that winter, and the supply house of A. C. Myers in Dodge City offered to set up a supply base in the Texas Panhandle, still farther south, if the hunters would continue.

In the spring of 1874, Myers sent out a long train of freight wagons, south to a spot called Adobe Walls, about a mile from some old ruins in Hutchinson county, Texas

Those walls had seen fighting before. Around 1842-44, the fur trader William Bent had established a short-lived branch trading post there. It had adobe walls nine feet high around an eighty-foot square, with only one entrance. Bent found the roving Comanches and Kiowas would rather fight than trade, so he abandoned the post.

For almost twenty years the walls remained in peace, a crumbling but imposing landmark. In 1864, Kit Carson led a detachment of the 1st Cavalry, New Mexico Volunteers, out to discipline the Indians who had become active during the Civil War. With many frontier forts depleted when troops moved east, the Indians had found little opposition until Carson hit them hard at Adobe Walls. At the old ruins was fought one of the biggest battles between the whites and the plains Indians: about four hundred soldiers and Indian scouts against an Indian force variously estimated at between three and seven thousand. The soldiers moved back after two and a half days' hard fighting, and the First Battle of Adobe Walls was written into the records as a defeat for the Indians.

Ten years later, a second battle was about to begin. Charlie Myers set up a store there. So did Charles Rath, head of one of the most prominent firms involved in the buffalo-hunting supply business. Jim Hanrahan opened a saloon between the two stores. It was a small town, with perhaps twenty-eight men and one white woman. She and her husband had come down to open a restaurant. There was also a blacksmith's shop in the new community. Hunters came in with hides and went out with supplies; freight wagons trundled between the little town and Dodge City.

These developments did not go unnoticed by the Indians, especially by the Comanches, lords of the southern plains. The red men saw not only the violation of a treaty but the end of the buffalo — and that meant the finish for the tribes as well. They gathered in council and Chief Quanah Parker advised combined action by warriors from five tribes: the Comanches, the Kiowas, the Kiowa-Apaches, the Southern Cheyennes, and the Arapahoes. All agreed to fight when the proper moment arrived. It was soon in coming.

The Indians rode down upon Adobe Walls during the night of June 27, 1874.

The town was ready when they came. A lone hunter had come in with an advance warning, and the townsfolk grouped inside the three adobe buildings, barricading the doors. Eleven, including "Dutch Henry," were in Myers' store; seven were in Rath's. The others were in Hanrahan's saloon, and in this group was an experienced buffalo hunter and scout named Billy Dixon, along with an eighteen-year-old kid named "Bat" Masterson.

The Indians charged at dawn, to the sound of a bugle! One of the warriors, or perhaps a renegade with them, had a bugle and knew the proper calls for rally and charge. So did the whites inside the town, and the Indians galloped straight into the long-range fire of heavy buffalo guns. There were hundreds of Indians, perhaps a thousand, but their carbines were no match for the Big Fifties. One of the first to be hit was Quanah himself, who crawled inside a rotting buffalo carcass to hide. He survived.

For three days the Indians rode repeatedly against the town. When it was obvious that there would be no easy victory, the tribes began to quarrel among themselves. The besieged town's little garrison grew as more buffalo hunters managed to creep in during the night; soon there were almost a hundred men inside the buildings.

After a few more days of half-hearted attacks, the Indians rode away, taking along at least fifteen dead and many wounded.

If it was a victory for the hunters it was a bitter one. For months the Indians waited in scattered war parties, ready to plunge in attack on any small party of buffalo hunters or freighters who ventured onto the plains.

Bat Masterson made it back to Dodge City. Troops came down from Leavenworth, and General Nelson Miles came with them as far as Dodge City. Billy Dixon quit buffalo hunting and signed on as a scout under Miles, staying in his new work for almost nine years. Later he went back and homesteaded two sections of land that included the crumbled remains of Adobe Walls.

But in spite of the danger of Indians, the business of hunting went on, simply because the stakes were high. A man could easily make a thousand dollars in a good season, perhaps twice that amount.

After the battle at Adobe Walls in June, there was little hunting for a while. In the summer months the buffalos' hides grew mangy as they shed. By October the pelts would be rich again, and in December the hides would be of prime pelt quality.

During the winter of 1874-75, the Mooar brothers hunted along

Coldwater Creek and San Francisco Creek in the Panhandle. Winter in the Panhandle is never pleasant; the sudden winds called northers sweep down from Canada bringing sleet or snow. The sunlight is thin even at its best, but the air is clear. The herds could be seen from far away. When spring came it ended the second big season of buffalo hunting in the far northern Panhandle, and already there seemed to be fewer buffalo. In the first year everyone had said the kill was only keeping pace with the normal increase, but with more than a thousand men out with guns the end of the herd was in sight.

The more experienced hunters decided to join the crowd at Fort Griffin, down on the Clear Fork of the Brazos in Shackelford county.

Fort Griffin was becoming the center of the buffalo hunting industry. During the Civil War the Comanche raids had pushed back the outer ring of Texas settlements. When the war ended, a chain of border posts was established from Fort Richardson in the northeast to Fort Davis down by the Big Bend country. Fort Griffin was built in 1867 and garrisoned by Negro troops of the Tenth Cavalry. It was located dead-center in the heart of good buffalo country and squarely in the middle of a long distance from anything else. The closest railroad was two hundred miles away down at Calvert, Texas. Freight wagons could make it to Fort Worth, and other supply wagons could come from Fort Sumner, another two hundred miles distant in New Mexico.

But F. E. Conrad had a good supply store at Griffin, and the big Kansas hide firm, Lobenstein's, had a buyer named T. J. Hickey on the spot, ready to buy.

In 1875 Texas was trying to make up its mind about whether to preserve the buffalo or let it be wiped out. Lieutenant Colonel George P. Buell, then in charge of Fort Griffin, did not take kindly to buffalo hunters. He could not order them to stop hunting, but he tried everything he could to keep them from ranging more than twenty miles from the fort. Beyond that distance, he said, he would not be responsible for what the Indians might do to a party of hunters. The hunters paid no attention.

A bill came up in the Texas legislature in 1875, proposing restrictions on the buffalo slaughter. General Phil Sheridan was then in command of troops in Texas. He rode up to Austin from San Antonio to speak personally against the bill. Sheridan stated flatly that the only way to solve the Indian problem was to kill off all the buffalo; then the Indians would leave.

The bill did not pass. Three years later there was no need for a law.

The hunt became organized more efficiently than ever before. At Denison, Texas, or any of a half-dozen outfitting points, each party assembled its gear. This included from two to twelve wagons. A small group might head out with two wagons, each with a four-horse team. Among the supplies might be 550 pounds of lead, 50 pounds of powder, about 600 brass cartridge shells, four pieces of patch paper, a reloading outfit, four or five dozen skinning knives, a portable grindstone, and dutch ovens. They took along a spare gun or two and all of the old newspapers, magazines, and other reading matter they could buy or beg.

In setting up a camp, the ground would be cleared for about a hundred feet and two tents set up: one for cooking, one for sleeping. In a large party there would, of course, be proportionately more. Two posts were set in the ground a few inches apart and the grindstone mounted on top, with its crank at a convenient height.

Then forked saplings were set into the ground to mark a rectangle about five by fifteen feet, with another forked post in the middle of each long side. Long poles were laid into the forks and across these shorter sticks were placed, making a rack six or seven feet high. On this rack the buffalo tongues and an occasional hump were hung to dry. Bags of dried buffalo tongue could be marketed, along with the hides. The rest of the animal was left where it fell, except for the meat needed at camp.

The hunters themselves were no moccasined plainsmen in fur caps and fringed buckskin jackets, with powder horns and flintlocks. They preferred blue or red flannel shirts, a pair of overalls or work pants stuffed into top boots, a coarse jacket, and a brimmed hat. In addition to his rifle, the hunter carried a hundred cartridges in a double belt, enough for the day's hunt. Often a six-shooter and a bowie or other large knife was added. Many carried a rest stick or two to support the barrel of the Big Fifty. Altogether he carried perhaps thirty-six pounds of equipment.

If a man hunted alone, he might head out with a pocketful of cartridges, on a light scout. If he planned to do his own skinning or help others handle this task, he usually wore a curious, wide, flat leather scabbard from his belt. It was divided into three sections or sheaths for a ripping knife, a skinning knife, and a butcher's sharpening steel.

There were two major methods of buffalo hunting, plus four techniques that were used less in Texas than up north. The principal methods were the still hunt (with the hunter in a more or less fixed position) and the chase or running hunt. Other practices, once followed by Indians and hunters elsewhere, included driving the buffalo into pens to be killed, or surrounding a herd by using several hunters, or driving the herd over a cliff or into a bog, or hunting on snowshoes.

Some hunters left camp on horseback; many went on foot if they knew they were in good buffalo country. After tossing a handful of grass into the air to get the direction of the wind, the hunter set off. Unlike cattle, the buffalo grazed facing into any moving air.

If the hunter had average luck, he found a herd grazing or resting, perhaps three miles from camp. If the herd was moving, the hunter had to move fast to get around them.

In either case, as soon as he was within good range the hunter kept out of sight by moving through any gully or dip or by crawling. Then he gauged the distance, set his sights, and found or made a comfortable rest for his rifle. If one cow appeared to be older than the others, she probably was the leader and became the first target.

The first shot. If not a hit, the hunter paused a moment if the herd was still at rest. Any sudden sound startled the buffalo, but if they saw nothing happen they usually remained quiet. Another shot, that time perhaps a hit. A stricken buffalo rocked unsteadily and fell. The others milled around a little, as if puzzled. If any animal tried to move away, that one became the next target.

Slowly, steadily, that was the secret. Much depended on the fact that the buffalo was a stupid animal. At least it was when the herds were big; as their numbers grew smaller they panicked more readily. With a milling herd, the hunter fired rapidly to bring down animals on one side and thus turn the herd.

The critical target was a spot about the size of a man's hat, just back of the shoulder bone.

In a good stand, records were phenomenal. In the first days of organized buffalo hunting in Kansas, a still-hunter dropped a hundred and twelve buffalo in forty-five minutes, and they all fell in a semicircle of two hundred yards' radius.

It was a poor day when any hunter couldn't get from twenty to forty animals. The running chase was effective but the result was more subject to chance.

As soon as the shooting ceased the skinners came up to get at their work. In cold weather a carcass might freeze overnight; in warmer weather it might swell enough to tighten the hide. A fresh carcass was easier to skin. Wounded buffalo were finished off with a revolver shot.

The skinners each wore a triple scabbard and often carried a stick called a fritch or fritchell, pointed on one end with a heavy nail in the other. This was used to prop the buffalo into a convenient position.

When the skinner went into action, he removed a hide in five to eight minutes. With one deft circle of the ripping knife a cut was made on each leg at the hock or the knee. The head was circled, and the hide split full length along the belly from front to back.

Then the curved skinning knife was brought into use and the hide removed. The trick was to do it quickly, neatly, and not gash the hide carelessly and reduce its value.

This sounds easy, but how do you turn an animal over if he weighs anywhere from a half ton to a ton? Each skinner had his favorite method. One way was to work with the animal lying on a side, either side. The exposed upper side was skinned first, working from the belly up to the spine and as far beyond it as possible. The loose hide was then rolled or kicked under the spine and the animal turned over. If plain muscle and a fritch stick wouldn't do it, a rope or chain dragging from a wagon axle could be looped over a leg and the animal pulled over. Finishing the job was easy.

The wagon was then loaded and the hides hauled back to camp. Sometimes they were salted in the field. At the base camp, hides were taken to a level spot, unrolled, and stretched to their utmost. Every outfit carried bags of pegs, and the hides were pegged down, raw side up. The salting was completed, and the raw side was also covered with arsenic or some similar poison to prevent hide-bugs from attacking the skin and making it worthless.

A party might consist of two or three hunters, four to six skinners, and an old hustler or boy who did the chores around camp. These chores consisted of turning the hides — after the first three days and then every other day. The helpers were kept busy pegging hides, repegging, reloading cartridges, drying tongues on the rack, and baling hides.

When dried, the hides were about like a sheet of heavy plywood, except they were longer, wider, and heavier. They were as hard as flint and were, in fact, called flint hides.

When cured, they were sorted into piles: One for the best quality robes, one for standard grade bull hides, another for cows, and a fourth pile of "kips" or calf hides. Each pile was stacked loosely about six or seven feet high. Strips were then cut from a freshly-killed or green hide. The strips were run from peg-holes in the uppermost skin to peg-holes in the bottom skin. By using a makeshift arrangement of chains and saplings, or by plain manpower, the bale was compressed and tied.

Day after day the hunt went on. Buffalo hunters were rugged, dirty, violent men, intense in their work. Camp was a litter of boxes, hides, and gear of all kinds strewn with no regard for the simplest housekeeping.

Finally it came time to sell the hides. In the beginning the hunter had to haul his own skins to town. Then he began to find hide buyers at such field centers as Fort Griffin. Toward the end of the era the buyers were paying for hides on the ground. Good standard hides initially brought $1.75 to $3.00. By 1876, when the market was temporarily glutted, a robe sold on the Texas range, with the buyer doing the hauling at his own expense, brought from sixty-five cents to $1.15. Twelve years later, when hides were scarce, a skin of robe quality brought from fifteen to twenty times as much. Although the buffalo nickel didn't appear until 1913, in 1872 five cents bought five pounds of buffalo meat in some village butcher shops.

Wagon freighters operating between an army post such as Fort Griffin and a railhead such as Fort Worth made double money by hauling supplies out to the fort and carrying hides back.

The wagons used for the hide trade had big, flat beds similar to hay wagons. The hides were not loaded in bundles but were loose, overlapped, with about 200 fifty-pound hides lashed down to make a load on the lead wagon.

Behind the lead wagon was attached a trailing wagon, loaded with 100 to 150 hides. Six yokes of oxen pulled the two wagons, pulling the vehicles one at a time through rough places. As many as twenty-five such outfits might be seen at one time on the Panhandle plains during the busy season. This was not unreasonable, because a successful hunting party might end the season with two thousand hides, requiring six two-wagon outfits to haul the hides to market.

And in peak years there were estimated to be fifteen hundred hunters in the Panhandle. Together with their skinners and hustlers the total may have been five thousand men.

Hide centers such as Fort Worth were busy. At an auction in that city during the 1873-74 season, up to 200,000 hides changed hands in a single day.

And then, as spring came and the quality of hides dropped, the hunters left their camps and went back to what passed for civilization. If they went to Fort Griffin the quality of culture was dubious. About a mile from the orderly fort the disorderly "Flat" had developed. It had no civil law, and the Army shrugged and looked the other way. It was then Army policy to let the buffalo hunters sweep the plains clean.

Gunmen came to the Flat to learn or practice or perfect their trade. Dancehall girls and gamblers poured in. Red-haired Lottie Deno, Texas' poker queen, ran her game. The hide hunters carried plenty of money, and the Flat offered every known means of relieving the plainsmen of their burden.

The business of buffalo hunting — for it was a business and not a sport — reached its peak in Texas during the winter of 1877-78. At least a hundred thousand hides were taken in two months.

The following year there were only scattered herds; the Southern Herd that once included three million thundering, shaggy beasts, was down to a few thousand.

The hunters moved away, vanishing with the buffalo they had exterminated. Some went to hunt on the range of the Northern Herd, which had another five years to go. Others became miners in Colorado. Some settled down to business in Texas; many became ranchers on the land they had cleared of both buffalo and Comanche, for the Indian threat had vanished with the herds. For a year or two there was still a little hunting to be done. And there was a rich harvest to be made in bones. At first thought to be of little value, the bones were found to be useful in refining sugar, in making carbon, or for fertilizer. The horns were used for combs, buttons, and handles.

A wagon freighter named Kilfoile, who operated between Fort Worth, Sherman, and Mobeetie, hauled bones on his return trips. For years he had been the object of laughter as he gathered great piles of bones beside the outward trail and marked them with his sign. But when the railroad came to Fort Worth and Kilfoile sold his mountains of bone for six to eight dollars a ton, clearing at least $25,000, the laughter ended.

Storekeepers in villages on the plains took bones in trade, heaped them up, and sold them to bone buyers who came through on regular trips. Many a homesteader struggled through his first year on what he made by gathering the bones on his new land.

In 1880 buffalo hunting as a trade ended in Texas. The gamblers and the girls of the Flat had left Fort Griffin, and in 1881 even the fort closed.

There was one last big hunt in Texas, during the fall and winter of 1887-88, when a man named Lee Howard led a party out for the last fugitive herd. The hunters went into the region about a hundred miles north of Tascosa, up in the northwestern Panhandle not far from where Amarillo is today.

These men were more like sportsmen than professional hide hunters. There were perhaps two hundred buffalo left. and they were wary creatures. Howard's men split into two parties and managed to kill fifty-two animals. An old-time hunter would have declared this a good hour's work for one man.

Ten of the best specimens were skinned carefully so they could be mounted by taxidermists. The heads of the other forty-two were preserved entire, for mounting as trophies. The mountable complete skins with heads went for $50 to $150; the separate heads sold for $10 to $50; the robe skins brought about $20 each. One lot of twenty-eight prime robe skins was bought by the Hudson's Bay Company for a total price $350.

Yet the economy of Texas had been undergoing a change while the buffalo were vanishing — and partly because of their disappearance. Now the great cattle drives began.

Before the railroads came, there was no way to get big herds to market except by sea. There were no local markets, except a few forts, and to reach such posts as Fort Sumner in New Mexico it was necessary for cattlemen such as Charles Goodnight to drive his trail herds in a wide loop southwest to the Pecos and up that river. There was no other way to avoid the Indian menace. Even the buffalo caused trouble with a trail herd by stampeding into the cattle or otherwise diverting them. Now the herds could trail north to Abilene or to Dodge City across plains freed of any menace.

Then the great ranchers began, and a few of them such as Goodnight even tried experiments with buffalo. He had a herd of thirteen.

And so the buffalo passed into obscurity, with its story to be chronicled expertly by such men as William Hornaday, Frank Roe, and Wayne Gard. Bat Masterson became a lawman; so did Pat Garrett and John Poe. Charlie Rath became a prosperous merchant; J. Wright Mooar settled down to ranching. Lottie Deno went over to Deming, New Mexico, and became an upright citizen.

The buffalo hunting business in Texas went from nothing to nothing in less than ten years, with only five of them really good.

10

Log Jam – Texas Size

FOUR FAMOUS RIVERS drain the watersheds of Western history. In the north flows the great Missouri, route of the earliest fur trappers. Below that is the Arkansas, famed in the days of the Santa Fe Trail. Then comes the Red River, once the borderline of nations and then of states. Far to the southwest is the Rio Grande. And of these four, the most exasperating was the Red. It contained the most incredible log jam in American history. Twice the jam was cleared: once by a famous riverman and once by an obscure Army lieutenant, but the river always came back with more trouble. Of all major episodes in our Western history, the clearing of the great Red River Raft has perhaps remained the most obscure.

First Lieutenant Eugene Augustus Woodruff of the Army engineers was only six years out of West Point when, in 1872, he first saw the lower end of the immense tangle in the river. Before a year had passed he conquered the river, but while his report was being handset he died of illness. Woodruff had no chance to enjoy continued glory, as had riverboat captain Henry Shreve, who cleared the same river forty years earlier only to see it choke up again.

The Red River flows more than thirteen hundred miles from its sources in northwestern Texas down to where it joins the Mississippi below Natchez. It starts with four forks: the North Fork, Elm Fork, Prairie Dog Town Fork, and the Salt Fork. The first and third of these join to form the start of the Red River proper. Nearly half its length is in Texas or along the Texas boundary with Oklahoma and a bit of Arkansas.

In ancient times the Red did not flow into the Mississippi, but into the sluggish Atchafalaya River that parallels the Great River a short distance west. Near the juncture of the Red and the Atchafalaya, De Soto's men buried the body of their dead leader in secret — in the year after Coronado's soldiers first saw the land where the Red River rises.

The *Rio Roxo* was a boundary between the possession of France and Spain. After the Louisiana Purchase it became the southwestern boundary of the United States, between the states and Mexico. It was later a boundary of the Republic of Texas. It became the dividing line between Texas and Oklahoma, east of the Panhandle, but the Greer county dispute arose between the two states — based on a quarrel over whether the South Fork or the North Fork was the main channel.

But it was downstream that the real difficulty lay, near an outpost called Natchitoches. The French established that fort in 1714, four years before New Orleans began. A Spanish trail for commerce led out of Mexico, up through San Antonio, and on across the Sabine River to Natchitoches. The post was about four hundred miles up from the confluence of the Red and the Mississippi.

Above Natchitoches the Great Raft began. For a century and a half after the French started Natchitoches the raft frustrated boatmen, settlers, and plantation owners. Experts who can estimate such things believe it may have started two or three centuries before the French arrived.

The raft was, altogether, from 150 to 165 miles long. It was not a solid mass, but was really a chain of smaller rafts, varying in length from a hundred yards to a few miles. Some rose and fell with the current, which could be seen moving beneath. Others were packed solid to the bottom, even in a depth of twenty-five feet, and wedged so tightly bank to bank in places that a horseman might ride across unaware that he was passing over a river.

Other rivers of the Southwest had similar log jams, all called rafts, but none as great as that in the Red River. The Red had no significant rapids; its drop is slight and its current smooth as it flows through a valley rich with thick soil that once supported a heavy growth of timber.

When spring freshets came the Red might rise as much as thirty feet in as many hours, flooding its banks, spreading out twenty miles in some places, and uprooting trees large and small whose roots had no fierce grip in the soft soil.

Downriver the trees floated, rolled, and tumbled — cottonwoods especially, but also cedar, ash, and elm. In Louisiana great cypress trees grew in the river itself, rooted firmly to the bottom. Against such a tree or against any point of land in some sharp bend, a floating tree might become lodged. Soon other debris was lodged against the first, then more and more. As the freshet ended, jagged stumps and branches embedded themselves deep into the ooze, anchored firmly to catch more trees in the years and generations that followed.

Year after year the river trundled down new wreckage and a rich deposit of silt to fill the interstices, until the rafts became islands, either floating or firm, bearing on their top a crop of shrubs, weeds, and even full-grown willows. It was not all destruction, for the annual flooding produced rich bottomland, where the first Louisiana cotton was planted. By 1809 it was a chief cotton area.

In the soft earth, a swift, flood-time current could and did cut new channels. Along the lower half of the Red River lay a network of lakes, swamps, and bayous, large and small, through which the stream was diverted as new balks arose.

The Red became a river of history, divided by the Great Raft into "upper" and "lower." The upper reaches were crossing points for raiding parties of Comanches or for settlers from the United States moving in clandestine travel down into Spanish and later Mexican Texas. Fifty years later the upper river was a barrier to the great cattle drives moving north out of Texas. The Chisholm Trail forded it at Red River Station, from 1857 to 1876, when the herds moved up the Dodge Trail farther west. Doan's Crossing then became the major ford. It had a small settlement, at its peak consisting of perhaps a dozen buildings and a hotel known as the Bat's Cave. Six million longhorns waded and bellowed their way across the shallow Red at Doan's before the railroads ended the old trails.

In the lower Red River, pirogues, keelboats, and steamboats made their way from the Mississippi up to Natchitoches, where they were stopped by the Great Raft. Now and then explorers and trappers managed to filter through the network of bayous to reach the upper river.

Year after year the rafts grew on their upper end, perhaps as much as a mile a year. Their downstream end diminished as logs rotted or were torn loose, and thus the chain of rafts moved slowly upstream. By the early 1800's their lower end was four hundred miles from the Mississippi. Riverboats could go that far and no farther.

In 1825 the Arkansas legislature asked Congress to clear away the Great Raft so supply boats could reach the new post at Fort Towson, about three hundred miles above the lower end of the raft. What happened then was hilarious. No one in Washington knew much about the Great Raft. The request moved through routine channels to General Winfield Scott. Scott considered it a simple matter and wrote an order to Captain George Birch at Fort Jesup, Louisiana, telling Birch to take twenty-five men and clear up the rubbish.

Birch and his detachment went up the Red River by keelboat until they came to the raft. Then they had no choice but to continue on foot, and in the next two months they hiked along the river for almost a hundred miles, finding a chain of a hundred and sixty-eight rafts of various sizes. The only thing they cleared was a report.

Five years later, Army engineers were given a small appropriation and tried to clear away the raft. They worked for a year and ripped open fifty miles. Then their funds ran out and the river soon restored the jam. It would take Washington another fifty years to realize that it was not a one-time job but a continuing operation.

Everyone along the river had his own idea about how to remove the raft. One man proposed that a dam be built upstream, allowing the downriver section to go dry and then the logs could be destroyed by burning. Others felt that much could be gained simply by burning all logs exposed during the season of low water, which ran from late July to early December. Another proposed dams at bends where the stream might be forced to cut new channels around parts of the raft. None of these ideas worked.

Transportation costs were so high on overland freight from Natchitoches to Fort Towson that a small fortune awaited the man who could get supplies through by boat.

Colonel Benjamin R. Milam, of Long Prairie, Arkansas, decided to try the water route in 1831. He secured the services of the steamboat *Enterprise*, which would also tow two keelboats.

Supplies were loaded, and the steamboat left Natchitoches late in May, 1831. The water was lower than it had ever been at the season. For three weeks the *Enterprise* struggled through twisting side channels, cut-offs, and bayous. The boiler fires were stoked with green timber. The crew hacked at logs and hauled at snags. On rare occasions the boats passed a small settlement, where they were "saluted, toasted, and cheered." By mid-June the cargo was delivered. It was the start of river navigation on the upper Red, but everyone knew that no regular schedule was possible against such obstacles. Ben Milam was killed four and a half years later, fighting in San Antonio during the first stages of the battle that ended with the fall of the Alamo in 1836.

But what one riverboat could do, others could do if the Great Raft were cleared. An upsurge of demands to Washington resulted in a government contract for Henry Shreve in 1833. Shreve was to clear the river.

A better man could not have been found. River snags were nothing new to him. He had pioneered in clearing the Ohio and then the Mississippi of snags and had spent twenty years up and down those streams. He had designed special catamaran boats with double hulls, efficient at lifting sunken logs. One of the craft, the *Archimedes*, was his choice to lead the fleet that would clear the Red River Raft. Along with the *Archimedes* went three other snagboats, a hundred and sixty men, and supplies for three months — as a starter.

They started chewing their way into the Raft in April, 1833. By the end of the first year, he was seventy-miles into the log jam. The powerful boats smashed, pulled, lifted, and hauled the logs free. Then they were cut into sections and allowed to drift downstream. When the current was too sluggish to carry away the cut sections, they were piled on the banks, to be washed downstream by the spring floods. In the first year alone, savings on freight costs over the reduced land distance to Fort Towson were greater than Shreve's expenses.

Next year Congress gave him more money and he was back, and he came back every year for five years. To get public support, Shreve gave demonstrations at river towns, showing dramatically what his snagboats could do.

As he neared the upstream end of the Raft, he found his work was four times as difficult as it had been at the start. The lower end of the Raft was full of old, half-rotten logs; at the upstream end the timber was often green and tough.

Still, in 1838, he cut through the last of the raft and the river ran free. It ran so free, in fact, that its current picked up speed and in many places cut the channel ten feet deeper.

Shreve moved on to new accomplishments along the Mississippi, and within a year or so the Red was clogging up again.

By 1841 the rafts were re-forming. A year's hard work by one dredge made it more or less clear, but steamboats often had to tie up to the bank at night to avoid snags. Some boats were designed with watertight compartments or "snag rooms" in the bow. Other vessels were designed for very shallow draft. One of these, the *Glide*, drew only ten inches of water.

Plantations developed along the upper river, each with its own landing. Thirty villages started to grow. Shreveport itself was organized in 1837 by Henry Shreve and a group of associates. It became a flourishing river port.

Then came two years of heavy rains, washing down new debris and undercutting the banks. As flood levels subsided, the banks gave way and the valley echoed with the crash of great trees falling. Those who heard it then said the sound was like that of distant artillery. Between 1842 and 1844 the new raft became four miles long, not counting several smaller rafts and jams.

Upriver planters became desperate as their cotton bales piled high. Land speculators, who had laid out townsites, went bankrupt as buyers spurned villages that were river ports to nowhere. Some produce could be floated down to the upper end of the rafts, then hauled overland to Shreveport at the high cost of $1.50 a hundred pounds. Freighters made profits both ways by charging the same rates for the return loads.

The Senate investigated the matter, of course, but chiefly grumbled over the colossal expenditure of $425,800 on raft clearance between 1828 and 1841. Little was done, beyond a few half-hearted attempts financed by miserable appropriations.

By 1854 thirteen miles of the Red River were blocked to all traffic except pirogues. During the Civil War neither the North nor the South paid any attention to navigation on the river, except for a dramatic period in the spring of 1864 when Union forces under General Nathaniel Banks had to build dams in the stream. During this episode, known as the Red River Campaign, a fleet of ironclad Northern gunboats and heavy transports moved up the river to a point above Alexandria. This was well below Shreveport and still in the lower river where the water usually was deep enough for river traffic. The Union troops landed but met defeat in the Battle of Mansfield. Then the gunboats found themselves in difficulty during the retreat. The heavy gunboats needed seven feet of water. At the Alexandria Falls, a slight but important rapids, water had fallen to only three and a half feet.

Happily, the Union regiments included some from Maine, with many experienced lumberjacks in the ranks. These men built a dam of logs across the Red, and the gunboats were able to ride through on the artificial crest when the dams opened. Along their retreat the boats were attacked by Confederates on shore, including many men of the old Sibley Brigade that had fought in New Mexico. General Tom Green, who had been a Confederate leader at Valverde on the Rio Grande, died in the fighting along the Red River in Louisiana.

When the Civil War ended, it was apparent that clearing the Red River would be a major contribution to the economic development of the entire long valley.

In 1872, Lieutenant E. A. Woodruff was given the task, with enough funds to do the job. Woodruff was born in Connecticut and had been living in Iowa when he was appointed to West Point. He graduated from the Academy in 1866, seventh in his class, and was promoted from second lieutenant to first after a year in the Engineers.

The careful preparations and special equipment used by Henry Shreve were dwarfed by the massive preparations made by Woodruff. He did not intend to hack open a narrow channel for a single boat, but to clear a wide passage and deepen the channel as well.

His first job was to find a light-draught steamboat that was equipped for the special tasks ahead. Finding none in New Orleans, he searched among the boatyards at Louisville, Cincinnati, Pittsburgh, and Saint Louis, and he also wrote to other river towns. Finally, in Saint Louis, he found a wrecking boat named the *Aid,* which could be bought for $19,000.

The *Aid* was only three years old and had been built in Pittsburgh. She had two hulls, catamaran type, with double ends so the vessel could move easily in either direction. It was Henry Shreve's basic design, with forty years' improvements.

Each hull was 136 feet long, 15 feet across in beam, and with a gap of 14 feet between the hulls. She had three boilers, big ones, each 24 feet long and with two stacks. A recent inspection had approved a working pressure of 136 pounds of steam. A separate feed-pump, driven by a steam-powered donkey engine, supplied the boilers with water under pressure.

The *Aid* had been designed to lift heavy machinery from wrecked riverboats and had unusual gear for that purpose. Thirty-six feet back from the bows was a railroad rail running across both hulls. A similar rail lay across the hulls another thirty-two feet aft. Riding on these rails was a fore-and-aft carriage on which four heavy windlasses were mounted. The salvage boat could straddle a sunken wreck and roll the windlasses to any desired point for a powerful lift. By extension on the two railroad rails, the equipment could be projected over either side of the *Aid*.

Although the vessel was already well-equipped, young Woodruff added some improvements of his own. First the boat was dry-docked, caulked, and its planking inspected. More trusses and framing were built in. Then a sloping apron or sort of porch was added between the hulls in front, twenty-one feet long and edged with iron. This apron would slip beneath many snags, or men could stand on it to work with saws and axes.

Two large boom-cranes were added, with thirty-foot spars, each capable of lifting six tons. For comforts, Woodruff had some living quarters built for officers and crew.

As a final touch, Woodruff added a sort of fire-hose, adapted from the pumps used on steam fire engines and capable of spurting powerful streams through two hoses, each two and a half inches in diameter. These could wash the mud from snags and logs and help open a channel. He also devised some steam saws, forerunners of today's portable saws. They used cross-cut saws operated by steam at the end of a seven-foot beam.

Woodruff had started his search in mid-August; by late October the new equipment was installed. The young lieutenant wanted to be ready for work on the raft in early December, when the river began its seasonal rise. There was another reason for hurry: Saint Louis was having a smallpox epidemic. The *Aid* headed downstream in a hurry, but not soon enough. A suspected case developed and the boat was quarantined. They were released before the waters started to rise in the Red, so no useful time was lost.

On board was a picked party of seventeen experienced Michigan lumberjacks, all sturdy axemen.

The *Aid* went down to New Orleans, where it was joined by two crane boats. Each was 65 feet long, 20 feet wide, and with a hull three feet deep. On deck was a cabin to accommodate twelve. A heavy crane was mounted forward, with a 20-foot boom, using tackle with 4-sheave blocks and a hand-cranked, geared winch turned by six men. This rigging was powerful enough to pull the bow of a crane boat beneath water. Crews for the two auxiliary boats were enlisted at New Orleans and Shreveport.

The water was still low when the boats reached their first work station in the Red River. While waiting for the stream to rise, Woodruff put gangs to work along the banks. They girdled trees on shore and then boarded the jammed rafts in the river. There they cut down the growing trees, chopped away at exposed logs, then pulled out any embedded logs that would yield. To make work easier along the banks, two large flat scows were built.

The men tried to burn the dead wood on the rafts but without success. Sometimes logs could be burned if they were cut, split, and piled. It was easier to chop logs into small sections that could be floated downstream.

Rivermen had long known the risks of sunken logs and had even classified them by types. The worst were "snags," or logs that were buried in the river, concealed during high water. They were immovable and as firm as rocks. Most had jagged ends of heavy main branches sticking up; a few had only the trunk still remaining. A ragged trunk thirty inches in diameter and lurking only a foot or two beneath the surface could menace the biggest riverboat.

Almost as bad was the "sawyer." This was a large tree, uprooted during flood season. It floated downstream, until its heavy, rooted end sank and became anchored on a sandbar. The sawyer thus lay at an angle to the bottom, its upper end on the surface and pointed downstream. The river swept away all leaves, twigs, and small branches; passing debris snapped off the larger branches and left jagged points. For months or even years a bleached limb might point skyward above the rippling water, holding up a warning finger to the pilots. Other sawyers were submerged but still rose and fell slightly. Because the logs pointed downstream, a boat headed in that direction might glide over a sawyer with little damage. A steamer headed upstream, on the other hand, might ram itself on this dreaded spike. A river pilot's most terrifying experience was to be proceeding upstream over apparently placid waters and then see a sawyer rise directly ahead, lifted by the current as if it had been lying in wait like some water monster.

Everywhere the footing for Woodruff's men was treacherous. Some logs floated but were so nearly waterlogged that they sank under the weight of a man.

By January, 1873, the *Aid* was well at work in water deep enough for full efficiency. Three more work scows were built and two small steamers chartered to move the scows into position. In spite of this added expense, Woodruff completed his first year's work on schedule and at a cost that was ten per cent under the budget allowed.

The first task that faced the *Aid* was that of blasting open a channel for itself. A ton and a quarter of blasting powder had been brought from Saint Louis. There was also a small supply of dynamite, which proved to be worthless, either because it had deteriorated during shipment or was poor quality from the start.

Planting a charge of blasting powder was not easy. It had to be placed in the deepest logs, but these were often hard to reach because of other logs piled on top.

Holes were bored through sunken logs and the powder charges placed and set off electrically. After each blast, the hydraulic hose was used to wash away the mud; the nozzle was attached to a long pole so it could be played into any desired spot under water. Then steam winches went into operation to pull out the loosened trees.

Woodruff was pleasantly surprised to find that many sunken cottonwood logs, even those that had been submerged for twenty-eight years, often would float when the overlying mud and silt was washed away. In some cases the root ends were waterlogged and dragged the trees down, but when the stump was sawed off the trunk floated free.

It was slow work at the beginning, but the men became more expert as the *Aid* inched ahead. The king-pin or keystone logs were spotted more readily, and each log removed made the rest of the work easier.

The *Aid* moved ahead, cutting its own channel through each raft.

Other crews had to prod, cut, and blast to keep the downstream channel from clogging up again as new debris floated down.

To the workmen's delight, the river current was not strong enough to deflect a saw operating across the current. This made it possible to loosen a log and let the current hold the floating trunk parallel to the boat while saws cut the tree into sections, without lifting the timber from the water.

As the work became more systematized, the *Aid* worked at the head of its selfmade channel, pulling, prying, blasting, and tugging. Downstream behind the *Aid* were the work boats with saws, cutting up the logs set free by the *Aid*.

In addition to log jams, sawyers, and snags, Woodruff's men found their worst obstacle in the "planter," a tree that grew in the stream itself. Woodruff once encountered a cypress growing in twelve feet of water. Firmly rooted at the bottom, it had a trunk thirty inches in diameter, rising more than a hundred feet above the surface and with a full head of branches.

Such a tree would cease to be a menace if it were cut off six feet below the surface. Steamboats didn't draw six feet of water, but floating debris needed that much clearance. Otherwise the stump could form the anchor of a new jam.

To remove such obstacles, Woodruff decided to try a new product known as tri-nitro-glycerine. He had read of this remarkable explosive being used by a man named Mowbray in digging the Hoosac tunnel, up in Massachusetts. That was too far to haul TNT, so Woodruff arranged to have a hundred pounds of the stuff made in Saint Louis by C. D. Chase, a chemist. Chase had to have his chemicals shipped from Cincinnati and quoted the price of $1.50 a pound for the first test lot. It was agreed that if the new explosive worked well Chase would get a contract for five hundred pounds a month at $2.00 a pound.

The first shipment arrived in May, 1873, and Woodruff's men carefully poured five pounds into each cartridge. These were lowered on the upstream side of the giant cypress. The current held the cartridges against the trunk, about six inches from the bottom. A battery-powered exploder was used. When the charge was set off, the massive tree jumped ten feet above the river. Inspection showed the stump was cut off clean, with only a broomed surface that would soon be worn smooth.

Nitroglycerine became a favorite aid and large stocks were kept on shore in a special magazine. Where the crews formerly had spent a day or more struggling to pry loose a clutch of jammed logs, a charge of three to five pounds of the new explosive instantly loosed the tangle.

Stumps that were too irregular to be handled by the saws, or snags that resisted removal, were simply disintegrated by placing a small charge in a cartridge inserted in a hole bored by an auger.

Still, use of nitroglycerine was a slow operation. It was kept at a low temperature, although not absolutely frozen, during transportation. It was handled tenderly, and there were no mishaps. Woodruff had only one battery to set off charges and some time was lost moving this from place to place.

In late May he was nearing the end of the toughest section. A party of gentlemen from the Shreveport Chamber of Commerce rode out in carriages with their ladies to view the progress. The river steamer *R. T. Bryarly* puffed upstream with a full cargo, anxious to be the first boat through. When Woodruff cleared this section, steamers could go by a devious route. The *Bryarly* arrived on May 15; there were still a few heavy logs left to be pulled. Next morning the *Aid's* crew put in a good hour's work and then backed out of its narrow channel. With whistles blowing jubilantly, the *Bryarly* steamed through, the first riverboat in twenty-nine years to head for the upper reaches of the Red River. Upriver ten thousand bales of cotton waited on the river banks.

If there were benefits from removal of the Raft, to the town of Jefferson, Texas, the cleared river meant disaster. Jefferson, up in the far northeastern corner of the Lone Star state, was located on Big Cypress Bayou which drained into Caddo Lake and then into the Red. After Shreve first cleared the river in the 1830's, the village surged forward in commercial success as it became Texas' best river port on the Mississippi watershed. Steamers went down the bayou to the Red and thence down to the Mississippi and New Orleans.

By 1870 Jefferson was second only to Galveston as a port. It had been the first Texas town to have its streets lighted by artificial gas. According to folklore, the first brewery in Texas was in Jefferson, and it was the locale of one of the first commercial ice plants in America. Steamers brought rich furnishings for the homes. It had a lively newspaper intriguingly named the *Jimplicute*.

Jefferson was riding the crest of a wave, but when the Red River was cleared that wave subsided. Some citizens saw it coming and asked for help from the Corps of Engineers. To his regular work of clearing away the Raft, Lieutenant Woodruff was given the task of dredging a deeper channel up Big Cypress Bayou. He did it as well as he could, but he was gloomy — and correct — in his forecasts. When the Raft was cleared and the Red carried its full current, navigation was no longer possible on the lowered waters of the bayou.

Jefferson lost another chance for survival when it refused to grant a subsidy to the Texas & Pacific Railroad, then planning its route. The railroad went through the town of Marshall instead. Jefferson, which had a population of 4,190 in 1870 lost a fourth of its residents by 1890 and by 1930 was down to 2,329 inhabitants. It still has not regained its original size but remains one of the most charming places in Texas.

Woodruff wrote up a detailed report of his first year's work and sent it to the Chief of Engineers of the Army, who forwarded it to the Secretary of War. The Secretary included the document in his annual report to Congress in 1873. He did not print a large collection of photographs taken by Woodruff showing all of the vessels, the Raft with crews at work, and other remarkable views. Some years later this single set of pictures was withdrawn from the files and sent to a Congressional committee at its request. The gentlemen never returned the prints, and they have never been found. A visual treasure awaits either a devoted searcher or a casual discovery among some legislator's forgotten papers.

Before the official report was published, Woodruff died suddenly, on September 30, 1873.

There was much still to be done. All he had accomplished at the moment was to clear a narrow channel wide enough for one steamer. The next task was to widen this to a hundred and fifty feet, all the way, with special attention to those spots where new rafts might form. This took another three years. Not until 1876 was the work completed.

Yet even during the first year of Woodruff's work, other forces of progress were moving to make much of his labor go for nothing. The Missouri, Kansas & Texas Railroad (MKT) completed its line south into Denison, Texas, in December, 1872. There it linked up with the Houston & Texas Central, providing complete rail service from Saint Louis through Oklahoma and on to Galveston. Eventually this line carried much of the freight that otherwise would have gone down the Red River. But neither Henry Shreve, who died in 1851, nor Woodruff lived to see the end of the river steamboats. Each in his time did see the removal of the great Red River Raft, the obstacle that had appalled men for centuries, and whose clearance opened a great artery to the West.

11

The Peppery Little War over Salt

SALT ... sodium chloride ... NaCl ... rock salt ... halite ... hunger for which distinguishes farmer from nomad, because the hunter who eats meat raw or roasted retains its salts, while those who live on grains must add the precious mineral ... and in search of salt men traced their earliest trails, following primitive paths marked by ani-. mals whose instincts led them to the salt licks.

In New Spain the natives used *espumilla*, foam salt, cast up by tides or by salt springs, snow-white and pleasant for table use; or *sal piedra*, rock salt, evaporated in tidal basins or in salt ponds, stone hard, ready for the gathering and for trade.

How fortunate we are that the functions and the food most essential to life are pleasures in themselves! But salt was not only pleasant at the table, it was essential in curing meats, in tanning, and sometimes as a flux in working minerals.

In the New World, salt was there for the taking — until 1766 when José de Galvez was sent to America to inspect the sources of royal revenue. Henceforth no one gathered his own salt but bought his annual supply at a fixed price from a royal administrator. The price was kept high enough to yield a royal profit but also was kept low enough to let resentment simmer only at the grumbling point. Along the outer reaches of the empire in the New World, salt still was gathered and used for trade or to pay as part of the tax to support a mission. And through Texas and New Mexico there were salt lakes and ponds of Permian origin where salt was found. In 1590 the men of Castaño de Sosa's expedition were tracing the Pecos River northward, a river with water so brackish that it made them think of the legendary Rio Salado, the Salty River, tasting of brine because it was the long-sought link between two oceans. In October

187

of that year not far from where the village of Sheffield, Texas, now bakes in the sun just west of the ruins of Fort Lancaster, they saw "a salt bed, very big and very white, and with much salt, an unbelievable thing."

This was a region where salt had been laid down in the middle Permian time, when a vast, gently evaporating sea lay across what geologists today call the Delaware Basin, extending northwest of Pecos, Texas, over to where the steep cliffs of the Guadalupe mountains plunge down to meet the heat-shimmering flats along the Rio Grande valley. To the west lay the Orogrande Basin, where another sea spread across the Great White Sands and past the spot where the town of Tularosa would stand light-years later. When the oceans retreated there were deposits of salt so frequent that seldom did a man live more than a hundred miles from an ample supply. Ducks flying on their annual pilgrimages north and south learned that if they paused too long on these waters their plumage became so encrusted they could not fly. Fish in some streams today can survive only in the headwaters; the catfish finds it difficult to live and reproduce in the lower Pecos, so salty is its flow.

Salt was not so plentiful in Chihuahua, below the Rio Bravo that men later called the Rio Grande. There salt must be imported, especially from the town of El Paso del Norte that would in 1883 be named Juarez, or from Franklin across the stream on its northern bank — the village that would become El Paso.

Just when the salt lakes at the foot of Guadalupe Peak first were seen by the Spaniards is not known. When the Salt War began it was said by Padre Ramón Ortiz, who had lived in El Paso since 1838, that not long after the year 1656 the Spanish declared the "Guadalupe Salt Lakes" to be the common property of the towns along this part of the Rio Grande. A hundred years later José de Galvez made no mention of it when he set up the royal salt monopolies. No record has been found in the Mexican archives, although a survivor of the Salt War said he once saw a document with many seals but, being illiterate, could not read it.

If the early settlers used the lakes at all it probably was after 1682, when the village of Ysleta — the oldest continuing settlement in Texas — was founded. Around 1824 a more convenient source was found: the San Andres salt springs, north of El Paso, lying between the Great White Sands and the eastern slope of the San

Andres mountains. Carretas could go there with less chance of en-
countering Apaches, and there were a few springs of fresh water
along the way. The road to Guadalupe was a killer — two to four
days without water.

Padre Ortiz also said that in 1824 the San Andres salt springs were
officially set apart for the use of all people. James Magoffin, a trader
over the Santa Fe Trail from Missouri into Chihuahua, settled on
the site of present El Paso in 1849, after the war with Mexico had
ended. In 1852 he acquired a legal right to control the San Andres
salt spring, and in 1854 — along with his brother Samuel, Bigfoot
Wallace, and about two dozen others — he fought off a caravan
from Mesilla attempting to take salt without paying. This was "Magoffin's Salt War," a prelude to the larger conflict that later developed at the Guadalupe Lakes. Families from El Paso continued to
go the ninety miles to San Andres spring for their salt.

The Guadalupe Lakes were almost forgotten until 1862, when
they were noticed by Americans on two different occasions. A man
named C. B. Miller, of San Elizario, wandered up toward the peak
and saw several lakes scattered over a wide area, with one spring
of fresh water in their midst. He took some crystals back to the
village, where the people expressed surprise over the quality of the
salt. Miller said he saw no tracks around the lakes except those of
deer and other game. This was no real proof that he was first; if the
Spanish had used these lakes before discovering the San Andres
springs in 1824, the tracks of their horses would have vanished in
the forty-year interval.

Late in 1862 the California Volunteers of the Union army stationed a company at Pine Springs, near the base of Guadalupe Peak,
about twenty-five miles east of the lakes. Their job was to keep a
weather eye open for Confederate forces. With this unit was Albert
J. Fountain, later to play an important role in El Paso affairs. On a
casual scouting trip he saw the salt lakes. One of his Mexican scouts,
Gregorio Garcia, told him that this salt was of better quality than
what his people along the Rio Grande had been getting from San
Andres. Fountain later said that he saw no wagon tracks or other
traces of traffic from the villages to the Guadalupe Lakes.

By 1863 the people of the valley thought they had a practical
answer to the problem of reaching the lakes: follow the Overland

stage road east to Fort Quitman, then build a public road north from the fort to the lakes. The money was raised and the road built.

Carts began rumbling over the new trail for loads of salt. It became quite a business. One caravan used sixty work oxen and sixteen carts, coming back with 800 bushels. Usually it was measured by the *fanega*, a dry measure that varied in size according to the locality but was usually about two and a half bushels. Back in the villages, the salt sold for $1.75 to $2.00 per fanega, and in a good year perhaps 2,000 fanegas of salt were taken from the lakes. The supply seemed inexhaustible. All one had to do was shovel it into the cart; brine drained into the hole and in a few days the hole was refilled. Usually a thin shimmer of water, perhaps an inch or so deep, lay over the lakes.

It was common knowledge that under *Americano* law a private individual might some day claim this land. Samuel Magoffin had done it at San Andres. Other Anglos had claimed El Sal del Rey on what is today the King Ranch. They had also claimed La Sal Vieja, the Ancient Salt, some fifteen miles east of El Sal del Rey.

So there was no great surprise when Samuel A. Maverick staked a formal claim to some of the Guadalupe lakes in 1866. Maverick, who lived in San Antonio, was a notable Texan. He had been a prisoner at Castle Perote during the troubles between the Texas Republic and the Mexicans. His half-wild, unbranded cattle were those first to be called "mavericks." His grandson was Congressman Maury Maverick.

Maverick had acquired some certificates for railroad lands (although there was as yet no railroad through the region), and he asked A. J. Fountain, then in charge of the land district around El Paso, to have the land surveyed and the title entered. The Texas constitution had just been changed to permit such claims, so Fountain sent his assistant out to mark the boundaries.

Not much came of this first move. Maverick sent an agent to collect the charge for salt. Some of the people paid for a while, until they saw that there were plenty of other salt ponds in the vicinity lying outside the Maverick claim. Then they simply went to these other lakes.

For another ten years nothing happened, although all the time events were moving inevitably toward a break somewhere, over something.

It is easy, too easy, to dismiss the El Paso Salt War of 1877 as simply the result of rivalry between a pair of politicians, Charles Howard and Louis Cardis, or even to say that it was fought only over salt. That sort of thinking seeks the simple explanation. It accepts the surface disturbance — the incident — and rejects a more fundamental and complex underlying cause. It blames the symptom and not the disease. In this case the basic problem was a cultural conflict between Mexican and Anglo.

For years this was a touchy subject in Texas. Today it concerns the whole Southwest, from the mouth of the Rio Grande to the fields of California. We understand it a little better now; in 1877 few even tried to understand it.

This conflict began when Stephen Austin's first settlers went into Texas. Then as now the Anglo believed in the importance of hard work, energy, drive, financial success, and material progress as the greatest values in life. He saw nothing wrong in the scattering of a family as some went off to distant places. He regarded land as a commodity to be bought and sold whenever it was advantageous. Any action was honest as long as it was legal.

The Mexican — whether he was called Mexican-American, Spanish-American, Hispano, or Chicano — had quite different values in life. He regarded the Anglo passion for hard work as inhuman and soul-killing. It was far better to enjoy life. He looked with horror upon the dispersal of the family, and felt that the Anglos were always destroying each other with horrible, selfish frauds. Land was the realization of a dream, to be cherished, and kept in the family even after the family moved elsewhere; a Mexican would as soon sell his child as sell his land.

Each side had the perfectly natural group attitude that its ways were right and superior, and that any other way was wrong and inferior.

Around El Paso in the middle of the nineteenth century there were good men on both sides, but in general neither group then in the valley represented entirely the best of their respective nations. Many Anglos were men of low repute, seeking the anonymity of the frontier. A Mexican official who had toured the borderlands in 1828 wrote back to Mexico City that the Hispanos there "comprise what in all countries is called the lowest class — the very poor and very ignorant."

The close association of Mexicans with Anglos did not always create difficulty. In the war for Texas' independence, the 2nd Regiment of Texas Volunteers was an all-Mexican outfit that fought beside Travis. Perhaps one-third of those who fought against Santa Anna were Mexicans.

Serious difficulties started when land titles came under American jurisdiction, following the admission of Texas into the Union and after the Treaty of Guadalupe Hidalgo that ended the war with Mexico. Old land grants were to be respected, as long as proper evidence was brought forth. A time limit was set for this. Court cases cost hard money. The documents were not always available. Around El Paso, the story circulated that some of Doniphan's American soldiers in 1847 had stolen land papers from the archives and destroyed them. A fictitious tale, still current upriver along the Rio Grande, is that a territorial governor of New Mexico also destroyed land papers. And far downriver at Brownsville a Mexican named Juan Nepomuceno "Cheno" Cortina led a rough little border war in 1859-60, partly because his mother had been cheated in a land deal.

Several individual grants were confirmed and recognized under the American regime, but this recognition did not extend to plots of land used by all, such as grazing lands and salt deposits.

Around El Paso there were few if any disputes over land claims before the salt lake question arose. True, the Mexicans could not always understand the Anglo position in regard to the Rio Grande as a boundary. The river often changed its course. When it looped farther to the south, the Anglos claimed the newly encircled land as American. When it looped back to the north, the Anglos claimed that the boundary was where the river had originally been. Finally the Mexicans suspected any new Anglo move as a trick of some sort. They muttered that when the American used the word *good* he really meant *goods*.

Another irritation was the law passed in 1871, requiring all children to attend schools — schools in which there would be no religious instruction. Even more objectionable was the ruling that both boys and girls must attend classes together.

Nor could the Anglo understand the Mexicans' attitude toward their *patron*. A hundred years later the scholars would write books about this idea and call it *caciquismo*. The *patron* was not necessarily an employer nor a political boss nor a tribal patriarch nor the owner of a barony, but he might be a little of all of these ideas and a great deal of any one. Around the villages on the north bank of the Rio Grande near El Paso, this leader in 1877 was an Italian immigrant named Louis Cardis.

Cardis spoke the language of the Mexicans and understood their customs. He advised them, helped them in difficulties, stood up for them in disputes. He married a Mexican girl and was godfather to a neighbor's children. The result was a group loyalty to Cardis that was incomprehensible to an Anglo.

The deep-seated differences between the two cultures, exemplified in this loyalty to Cardis, was the underlying cause of the Salt War — not the salt itself. But if you believe that wars begin with simple incidents, then you might as well choose the incident of Charles W. Howard's arrival in El Paso in 1872. He had barely five years left when he came to the border town.

Today's leading chronicler of the El Paso Salt War, Dr. C. L. Sonnichsen, has traced Howard's background: a Missouri lawyer, Confederate lieutenant, one of the best pistol shots in Texas, a teetotaller, built low and heavy like a bulldog, utterly fearless, and a Democrat.

A man who drank only water was slightly out of place in El Paso. A Democrat was more so, because El Paso county was the last Republican county in Texas.

Howard formed a working arrangement with Louis Cardis, and in 1874 Howard helped Cardis win election to the state legislature. In that same year, Howard was named district judge. In 1876 he married the daughter of George B. Zimpleman, an Austin banker, and took his bride back to El Paso.

There is every indication that Louisa Zimpleman did not like El Paso. It was not much as a town. There were really four towns strung along the American bank of the river: El Paso (sometimes called Franklin in those days), Ysleta, Socorro, and San Elizario. People of all four villages knew each other, traded with each other, and married with each other. The total population of all four was around five thousand. Only one man in sixty was an Anglo, and most of these were notorious.

Louisa Zimpleman Howard fell sick in the summer of 1877 and died. During her last days her father came to the border town, and before he left he enlisted the aid of his son-in-law in what seemed to be a good venture: claiming all of the Guadalupe Salt Lakes.

Back in Austin, Zimpleman had a batch of Memphis and El Paso Railroad certificates, good for land. He had them approved at the state land office and took legal claim to three square sections below Guadalupe Peak. This was nearly two thousand acres. It took in all of the old Maverick land plus all of the other salt beds — one big lake and three small ones — plus the only spring of fresh water in the area.

In the July heat Judge Howard rode out to the lakes with his surveyor, Ward Blanchard. With them rode John E. McBride, who would be in charge of the salt operations. Three blacks and three Mexicans also went along, but the Mexicans dropped out after they had gone part of the way. They feared reprisals. The others went on, staked the claim, posted legal notices, and went back to post other notices in the towns.

The fee for taking salt would be seventy-five cents per fanega.

Some people paid the fee. Others asked questions. Postmaster John P. Clark in San Elizario told those who asked that they should pay the fee and then try to get their money back if it could be proved legally that the salt lakes did not belong to Howard.

Padre Antonio Borajo advised them to do just the opposite. Historical writers have been hesitant in dealing with the role of Borajo, lest they be accused of an anti-Catholic bias. However, two leading churchmen of the Southwest had troubles with the padre, so there is no bias involved in stating that Borajo was one of the small group of frontier priests who saw their power diminished with the coming of the Anglos and did what they could to retain influence through politics.

Father Borajo had been the priest at San Elizario and Socorro. He had difficulties with his colleague, Reverend Pierre Bourgade at El Paso, who later would be the archbishop at Santa Fe. And in 1877 Borajo unsuccessfully opposed Bishop Salpointe when that individual came to oversee Borajo's move to a newly-assigned post in a village on the Mexican side of the river.

More than once Borajo had become involved in the salt controversy. In 1870, when Albert Fountain was the newly-elected state senator from El Paso, Borajo proposed an arrangement by which Fountain would claim the lakes in his own name and divide the income. In return, the priest would urge public acceptance of the salt fee. Fountain refused. Borajo later tried to make a similar arrangement with Cardis, with no better success. Now the padre was urging opposition to Howard's claim.

Down in Chihuahua that September 16 — the equivalent of our July 4th — orators were speaking broadly of the Guadalupe salt lakes, claiming them for Mexico and promising the recapture of the land at least as far as the Pecos.

And Louis Cardis was rock-firm in his opposition to private ownership of the salt lakes in general and ownership by Howard in particular.

There was no action Judge Howard could take against words. He waited for some overt deed. John E. McBride was collecting salt fees now and then and was paying a few men to haul occasional loads of salt at $1.25 a fanega, laid down in the river villages. At last two men announced their intention to go after salt without paying for it. They were Macedonio Gandara of San Elizario and José María Juárez from south of the river.

This was a good opportunity for legal maneuvering such as any judge could devise. Howard had the two arrested on the grounds that they were planning mischief. He demanded that they be placed under a peace bond to guarantee that they would not steal salt. On September 29, 1877, they were brought before County Judge G. N. Garcia. He released Gandara but ordered Juárez to put up bond. When Juárez could not make the bond, Judge Garcia turned the prisoner over to Sheriff Charles Kerber for jailing.

This sort of legal tactic was new to people along the Rio Grande. They gathered in a *junta* to discuss it, and decided that it should work both ways. So a crowd gathered and proceeded to Judge Garcia. They asked for a warrant against Charles Howard and demanded that he, too, be placed under a peace bond. The judge tried to explain that there had to be some overt act, some formal complaint, some specific charge, before he could issue a warrant or order a bond.

The crowd, now approaching the attitude of a mob, decided they would have to handle the situation their own way and left.

During the night and the next day, the crowd "arrested" County Judge Garcia and his brother, who was a justice of the peace. They also arrested Charles Howard and his agent McBride, interning the four men in the home of Doña Apolonia Lujan. There they stayed for three tense days, while three or four hundred armed men milled around outside.

It was a standoff. The crowd demanded that the county judge and his brother the justice of the peace resign their offices; they did so and were freed. Howard began to fear for the lives of all Anglos in the vicinity. The Mexicans wanted Howard to give up all claims to the salt lakes, to leave the county and never return, and to post a bond of $12,000 that he would be true to these promises. Howard agreed. Among the four men who signed to underwrite his bond were the merchants John G. Atkinson and Charles E. Ellis. They would regret their signatures.

Both Cardis and Howard came to fear each other. Cardis was told that if any harm came to Howard, he (Cardis) would be killed by American friends of Howard. In his turn, Howard was told that if he escaped from the mob without meeting their demands he would be shot by four gunmen hired below the river.

Howard left, going to Mesilla, a few miles up the Rio Grande in New Mexico. A little more than a week later, he was back in El Paso, riding in with a small detachment of troops, sent down from Fort Bayard, N.M. Howard took a room in a hotel.

Wesley Owens, late a soldier in Company D, Tenth Cavalry, and at the time of these events a servant to Howard, had often heard the judge say that he would have to kill Cardis. Once when they were riding out from San Elizario headed for Fort Davis, Howard blurted out, "Wesley, when I get back from Fort Davis, if Cardis don't let me alone I'm going to kill him. I'm going to kill him anyway, he's been bothering me long enough."

On this particular Wednesday afternoon, October 10, Howard said to Owens, "Wesley, I feel restless, and I must have my revenge." The judge then left the hotel.

Sometimes between two and three o'clock that afternoon, Cardis had gone to the store of S. Schutz & Co., merchants at El Paso. The Schutz firm was an agent for the Overland stage line, and among Cardis' various interests he was the subcontractor for this company on the stretch running between El Paso and Fort Davis, carrying the mail. Cardis wanted to write a letter to send down to San Elizario and asked the firm's bookkeeper, A. Krakauer, to write the letter.

Jesús Gonzales, a laborer, was also in the store at the time, as was Leopold Sender, a salesman. Joseph Schutz, one of the store owners, was at a small desk in the office.

Cardis sat down in a rocking chair, with his back to the street entrance, and began to dictate the letter. Absorbed in his writing, Krakauer did not see Judge Howard enter. Schutz saw him. Howard had not been in the shop for nine months, but Schutz knew the talk around town — and the double-barreled shotgun Howard was carrying told still more.

Schutz left his desk and went forward to meet Howard. "How do you do, Judge Howard," he said loudly.

Cardis caught the tip-off. He got up from the rocker and walked around behind a high desk, one of those old desks bookkeepers favored, with high legs. However, behind it, Cardis' body was exposed from the waist down as he sat on an iron safe that served as a chair.

Howard asked for gun-wads. Schutz looked toward the rear of the store and saw Krakauer still completely absorbed in writing, still near Cardis and within range if any gunplay began.

"Krakauer, come away from there!" cried Schutz.

The clerk looked up, saw the menace at once and edged out the front door in a hurry. As he passed Howard and the store owner, he heard Schutz plead, "Don't shoot here, Judge. Respect my house and my family."

"I won't, if he gets away from there," said Howard, but instantly fired his first barrel. Howard at the moment was standing behind a showcase, about forty feet from Cardis. The heavy charge of buckshot went beneath the table and tore into Cardis' abdomen. He staggered up and took the second charge in his chest, the shot piercing a diary in his coat pocket. Cardis fell to the floor between the desk and the safe, lying on his left side and face, with his left hand under his head and the right hand, partly clenched, resting on the floor in front of him. His legs were cramped, his knees drawn up with the pain.

The total time, starting with Howard's entrance, could not have been more than two minutes. After the second shot, Howard shouldered his shotgun and walked out the front door.

Wesley Owens, at a nearby residence, heard the shots. He sensed at once what they probably meant and started out the door. The judge was coming across a small bridge and called out to Owens to fetch his (Howard's) gun. Wesley knew what weapon was meant: a sixteen-shot repeating rifle. By the time Howard arrived back at the hotel, Owens was there with the rifle. Howard handed him the shotgun in exchange, and Owens noticed that both barrels had been fired.

Cardis was not yet dead. He spoke no word, although he was still breathing. But not for long.

Edmond Stine, a local committeeman concerned with maintaining order during the unrest, was at his home in El Paso when he heard the shots. Shortly afterward a neighbor woman came to the Stine house and told his wife that Judge Howard had killed Don Louis Cardis.

Stine overheard the talk and ran out, heading for the Schutz store. He met Schutz in front of the place. The storekeeper confirmed the news.

Stine went inside. Cardis was still breathing but was near death. No doctor was available in the town.

A few minutes later, perhaps five or ten minutes after the shots, Deputy Sheriff H. H. Harvey (who also ran a saloon in El Paso) reached the Schutz store. He started over to feel the pulse of Cardis, who was now lying in a pool of blood.

"Don't touch him!" someone cried. "No one must touch him until an officer comes."

"There's been somebody here," replied Harvey, "for here's the tracks in the blood going around the desk."

Then it was evident that Cardis was dead.

Schutz wanted the body removed at once. Stine objected, saying they should wait for a coroner or a doctor or someone in authority. A half hour passed and when no official came they agreed that Cardis' body should be taken to his own home.

Several bystanders offered to help. Someone brought a length of plank, and Stine and Gabriel Valdes turned Cardis' body on its back, ready to be placed on the plank. As they did this they noticed that Cardis was wearing a gun belt with two holsters — the left one empty; the revolver in the right one was at half-cock. Stine asked Valdes to remove the gun carefully, and he did so. Then they carried Cardis' body home.

Cardis had known he was in danger. The last words in his buckshot-pierced pocket diary, entered three days before, were "Captain

Courtney advised me to be on my lookout, for Howard is making 'desperate threats at my life.'"

The letter Cardis had been writing was addressed to a man in San Elizario, discussing a move toward peace. Now there would be a move, but scarcely toward peace.

Schutz dispatched a hasty message to General Hatch, stating that "Don Louis Cardis was killed this moment by Chas. Howard, and we are expecting a terrible catastrophe in the country, as threats have been made that every American would be killed if harm came to Cardis. Can you not send us immediate help, for God's sake. — S. Schutz and Bro., and all Citizens of Franklin, Texas."

Schutz gave the message to H. H. Harvey, the deputy sheriff. Harvey sent it off by a Mexican, but the note never reached the general. The messenger was concerned about his own safety, so he waited about three weeks and returned the undelivered message to Harvey.

Howard returned to Mesilla unmolested. The half-expected uprising in El Paso did not occur. The valley was shocked, and there were deep undercurrents of resentment, but no mob appeared on the streets.

It did occur to some of the Mexicans that Howard had broken his promise not to come back to the river towns. That meant his $12,000 bond was forfeit, and a mass meeting was held in November to discuss how the money could be collected.

By this time the head of the Texas Rangers appeared in El Paso. This unique police organization, whose colorful history had been interrupted by the war years, had been reorganized in 1874 and was known officially as the Frontier Battalion. It consisted of six companies, A to F, and the top commander was Major John B. Jones. Jones stood an unimpressive five feet eight, weighed a hundred and thirty-five pounds, and was neat, tactful — and an excellent commander.

When the call came for Rangers at El Paso, there were no units within five hundred miles — and even those were up to their mustaches in their own troubles. So Jones went alone.

He talked to the men who excitedly wanted Howard's $12,000 bond forfeited, and when Jones finished talking they agreed to wait a while. His next move was to organize a Ranger unit, to be known as a special detachment of Company C of the Frontier Battalion.

In El Paso there were no men of genuine Ranger caliber, at least not in the full tradition of that force. But it was to be only a temporary organization, so Jones did the best he could. He recruited John B. Tays, the brother of a local minister, as the lieutenant to head the detachment. Tays was honest and sincere, but lacked the Ranger rawhide. The men he managed to get, about twenty in all, were no better than they should be. They used their own weapons at first; it wasn't until a month after the trouble was over that they received their first consignment of Winchester carbines.

The Rangers naturally were not regarded with the warmest friendship; the Mexicans quieted their children then — and for generations later — with the threat that "the *rinches* will get you."

Tays' men took up quarters in an adobe building in San Elizario. It stood alone, not linked to adjoining buildings, and it had its own corral and cistern.

On November 17, a small detachment of soldiers, a little more than a dozen men, rode down from Fort Bayard, New Mexico, under the command of Captain Thomas Blair. Howard rode in with them, arriving quietly at night. He surrendered himself to the authorities, was arraigned for killing Cardis, posted a bond of $4,000, and returned to Mesilla. The soldiers were quartered in El Paso; Fort Bliss had been inactivated some time prior to the Salt War.

About three weeks later, word was sent to Judge Howard that a large contingent of carts and wagons had gone to the salt lakes. Howard realized that he would have to "put up or shut up," so he decided to return to the river towns and be at San Elizario for a showdown when the wagons returned.

He went to El Paso and sent word to Lieutenant Tays in San Elizario asking for protection by the Rangers. Tays sent a small group of men into El Paso, to ride back with Howard.

Around 2:20 P.M. on the afternoon of Wednesday, December 12, 1877, Judge Howard rode out of El Paso toward San Elizario. The Salt War approached the shooting stage.

Tays had stayed back in San Elizario but decided to ride out to meet Howard. On the way he saw an armed, well-organized small band of men who appeared to have come from the Mexican side of the river. Tays had instructions to send for Captain Blair if it appeared that the affair might have international complications; only under such conditions was Blair authorized to bring in the soldiers. So, on sighting this group, Tays sent a messenger to the captain.

At El Paso, Blair was ready with a detachment of eighteen mounted U.S. troops, together with Lieut. Payne and his junior officer. Two hours after Howard and the Rangers rode out, the word came from Tays. Within another hour Blair was on a fast march, moving rapidly enough to outdistance his supply sergeant and two men with a pack mule carrying three days' rations.

Judge Howard, together with Lieutenant Tays and the Rangers, rode into San Elizario. When they reached the main part of town, they saw they were surrounded by many groups of armed men, with pickets on all roads. They stopped at Charley Ellis' store, but Tays soon ordered everyone into Ranger headquarters. Doors and windows were barricaded, and some men started to cut port-holes through the walls.

Blair and his men were coming up fast, but this was the middle of December, when the nights are the winter's longest. Darkness came early while the troopers were still riding. There was a fairly good moon, but the night was cloudy. Blair ordered his men to load their pieces but not to fire unless ordered.

About two miles out of San Elizario an armed man in the road challenged the captain. As the officer rode closer he saw a second man dart into the roadside bushes. When Blair asked the challenger to explain himself, the man mumbled something about "guarding animals against Indians." Blair and his men rode on.

When the detachment was well into the town, perhaps three hundred yards from the plaza, it was challenged again — this time by a dozen voices shouting almost at the same time and from as many different directions. Blair again rode forward to demand why they were being halted and by whose authority. The reply to Blair was that it was none of his business, that the guards had been posted by their "captain" with order not to permit anyone to enter the town.

Blair surveyed the surroundings. Not the best situation. Along one side of the lane was an adobe wall; along the other side was a close brush-hedge fence. Between him and the plaza were the armed opposition.

He told his challengers to send for their leader, at once. Several minutes passed and no one appeared. Blair then repeated his demand that the officer be brought, adding that if he were not on hand within five minutes, Blair's men would ride in and get him.

The men in the roadway said they would prevent the troops from entering. Blair said if they presumed to try this they would regret it. Just then their captain came up, and Blair again demanded to know by what authority they were stopping an officer of the U.S. Army. The captain said it was an affair of their own, with which the Army had no business. They were going to get Judge Howard, and if Blair tried to enter he would be met by their whole force.

Blair said he had no personal concern with Judge Howard but was there on official matters, and the mob would regret having stopped him. The rebel captain shrugged his shoulders and said firmly that they wanted Howard and would have him, and if the soldiers entered they would be fired upon; he further told Blair that all men in the mob were residents of El Paso—a statement Blair later learned was untrue.

Blair was, as they say in Texas, "between a rock and a hard spot." While the parley had been going on, more armed men were surrounding him. By now there were perhaps 120 to 150 men, all well armed, lining both sides of the narrow street. In several places ahead of him rawhide ropes had been stretched across the street. He was now outnumbered nearly ten to one.

Still, as he reported later to his superiors, "As far as I could judge, the condition of affairs contemplated in instructions to me from headquarters Department of Missouri, authorizing me to interfere, had not arrived. Had I believed my instructions required or even authorized me to interfere, I should have done so, notwithstanding the odds against me."

The fact was that Blair did not know whom to believe, and he had no wish to gamble the lives of his small force on the wild and conflicting reports he was getting from both sides. Those opposing him said they were all from the American side of the river, and that they wanted only Judge Howard. Their attitude, at least at the moment of confrontation, was quiet, serious, and menacing.

On the other hand, wild stories had been relayed to him in fragmentary form from El Paso officials and other Anglos — saying that the Rangers' building was mined and about to be blown up; that water from irrigation ditches had been diverted to undermine the adobe walls of the makeshift fortress; that the Rangers were already out of food and ammunition; and that the bodies of four dead Rangers had been seen on the roof of their little Alamo. These were all obviously untrue. Then what was true?

Behind their commanding officer, Blair's men under Lieutenant Payne had quietly posted themselves behind an adobe wall. Blair ordered Payne to retreat with the soldiers, and they moved out. Blair himself tried to move toward the plaza among the rebels, or even to get them to take him prisoner. He wanted to see what was happening in the plaza. The mob was quietly firm in denying him any choice. They led him back to his men, and the troops moved out, riding back to Ysleta for the night. Many on both sides said afterward that if Blair had pushed forcibly into San Elizario that evening the whole affair would have crumpled. But by the next morning the determination of the townspeople was too strong.

In San Elizario, Anglos began to make their way to Ranger headquarters for protection. One of the first to arrive was John G. Atkinson. Although unpopular in town he had operated a successful store. After the killing of Cardis and the arrival of the Rangers he saw that the climate was no longer friendly, so he sold his business to Charley Ellis and showed up at the Rangers' building with between ten and eleven thousand dollars, some of it in greenbacks and some in silver coin sacked in twenty-five pound shot bags.

Charley Ellis ran a flour mill and store in the town, and it was a favorite spot for the Rangers. A can of sardines made a good snack when a man was off duty. Charley was married to a woman named Theodora, and his chief employee was an Anglo named I. F. Campbell.

After Howard and the Rangers visited his store that night, Ellis began to wonder about what was going on in the dark, noisy streets. He stuffed a pistol into one of his boots and went out to look around. Noticing the crowd at Leon Granillo's house, he went over to talk to them.

"What does this mean, *muchachos?*" he asked.

They told him they wanted Howard.

"Don't act foolishly," advised Ellis, and for a while they talked. Suddenly Granillo shouted, "*Ahora es tiempo!* (Now is the time!)"

Eutemio Chaves rode up on horseback and threw a lasso over Ellis, starting off on a run dragging the storekeeper. Some distance away Ellis was killed. They found his body two days later, out in the sand hills. His scalp, eyebrows, and beard had been cut off; his throat was cut, and he had been stabbed twice.

When Ellis didn't return to the store, his wife hired Gregorio Garcia and five men to guard the store and mill. They held out for two days.

When Thursday morning dawned, Atkinson, McBride, and a Ranger named McDaniels left their quarters and crossed the street to the postoffice, where they climbed to the roof to speak to the crowd. Atkinson asked what they wanted.

"We want Howard," was the reply.

"If you want him, come and get him," replied Atkinson. The three men remained on the roof for some time, talking with the crowd, and then they climbed down to return to the Rangers' building. All at once the port-holes were completed in the small fortress — apparently Atkinson's speech had been only a diversion to attract the crowd's attention.

A shot came from a house down the street, answered by a volley from the Rangers. All day Thursday the firing continued, off and on. By now the crowd was reaching its peak; estimates ranged from two hundred to fifteen hundred, with three or four hundred being the accepted number.

And where was Captain Blair? By Thursday morning he was back in El Paso with his soldiers — except the supply sergeant and his two men. They never caught up with Blair the night before but wandered around on the wrong roads, lost the horse and supply mule during a flurry of gunfire in the darkness, and finally made it back to their base. The troops remained at El Paso from then on.

Sheriff Kerber wired an appeal for help to the Texas capital. The governor wired back authorizing him to "raise a hundred men." Kerber telegraphed in reply that he could not find even ten suitable men in El Paso, but that he would try to get help from New Mexico. The sheriff sent word up to Silver City.

In San Elizario, Lieutenant Tays was apprehensive over the unexpected efficiency of those attacking his Rangers. He wrote later, "I found that our quarters were surrounded by three lines of pickets, who had stretched rawhide ropes ... so that it was impossible for us to charge them. On the outside of the lines they had squads of cavalry stationed about two hundred yards apart, numbering about twenty men in each."

There was no doubt, then or later, that many — if not a majority — of the attackers had come from the Mexican side of the river, that they had come armed, and that they moved under a discipline that resembled a military unit rather than a mob. Many testified that a former Mexican army officer had indeed given some men a little military training. But there was no proof that the Mexican government, at either a local or national level, had given any help or encouragement to the crowd gathered in San Elizario. Still, Tays felt that nothing so well-organized could be spontaneous.

The Anglos, except for a few who knew the border people well, simply did not understand the strong family ties between the Mexican people in the valley. Barely thirty years earlier this stretch of the Rio Grande had not been an international boundary; to many Mexicans it still was no boundary at all. Brothers lived on opposite sides of the stream that almost always was easy to cross on foot. Neighbors across the line were joined by marriage or by the ritual of baptism, in which the godfather of a child became the *compadre* of its parents, obligated to help the family in any time of need. It was a kin-based society unequalled in the Anglo world. The trouble of one was the trouble of all.

Now the score stood: Cardis dead and Ellis dead. It was Thursday. The next man to die was a Ranger named Mortimer, the only Ranger killed during the entire conflict. He was a newcomer to the valley and from all indications would have lived if he had been less of a tavern bravo. He left the Rangers' building and went over to Ellis' store, then to the corner of Atkinson's house. The account says he knew the people were watching him and that he made "an insulting gesture," repeating it a second time with his back turned but he "had no sooner removed his hand than a bullet struck."

Tays ran out under fire and brought Mortimer into the Rangers' quarters, but he died soon afterward. Number three.

There were no other fatalities that day. On Friday the shooting continued — noisy but ineffective. During these days the houses and stores of all Anglos in San Elizario were looted to the bare walls. Most of the plunder was carried across the river. Yet while all of this was going on, a wagon train passing through to the Schultz' store in El Paso was allowed to proceed with no more interference than disarming its American drivers. Another Anglo, J. P. Hague, was allowed to pass through the vicinity without harm.

On Friday night, the mob attacked Ellis' store in force, where Gregorio Garcia was on guard until the ammunition was gone. His son, Miguel, was killed in this skirmish. Number four. (There may have been other local Spanish-Americans killed, but their deaths were not reported.)

On Saturday and Sunday the siege continued. Occasionally the wives and children of local Anglos managed to make a successful dash to refuge in the adobe fortress. The Rangers' supplies were running low, and nearly everyone inside was nearing collapse from fatigue.

On Monday, October 17, it seemed as though a solution might be found. The original uprising had started over a demand for forfeit of the $12,000 peace bond placed on Howard. Atkinson was now inside with the besieged Rangers, and Atkinson had $11,000 — proceeds from the sale of his store.

He called for a parley and offered to make a deal: $11,000 in cash, to take the place of the $12,000 bond, with everyone to go free. The insurgents agreed. The Rangers surrendered — the only such instance in Ranger history.

For a while there was a lull. The Rangers gave up their weapons and were herded into another building, where most of them slumped to the floor and sank into almost instant sleep.

But there was to be no freedom. On Tuesday, a group of about fifteen Mexicans entered the room and took Howard outside. A small, formal firing squad awaited him. Howard gave the command for his own execution:

"Fire!"

Then the committee came for Atkinson and McBride. Atkinson once had been a tax collector, too energetic and demanding in his work. McBride had been Howard's agent in handling fees for salt. Atkinson tried to talk the firing squad out of taking action.

"*Acábanlos!* (Finish them!)" shouted the crowd.

"When I give the word, fire at my heart," said Atkinson. "Fire."

Five bullets hit him, but none fatally.

"Higher! *Mas arriba, cabrones!*" he cried.

This time they made it. Then McBride met his death, with no heroics. Numbers five, six, seven.

Some of the insurgents wanted more deaths, but their leaders said the work was finished. No more killings. The crowd melted away; the last looting was done. The next day the Rangers were turned loose and headed back toward El Paso.

Now there was plenty of help available, when no one needed it. Sixty volunteers arrived from Silver City to aid the sheriff. A detachment of troops rode in, ninety strong.

There was little for them to do, but they rode back down through the river villages to San Elizario. They killed four Hispanos: Telles, Nunez, Durand, Aragon, most of them on the charge of "resisting arrest." Numbers eight through eleven. They helped themselves to chickens and also to at least one of the women, and shot a dog. A month later one of the sergeants shot a comrade in a quarrel. Some of the men who had come from Silver City were fine citizens; most of them were not, and the town was glad when the volunteers went back home.

A full dress investigation was launched, with hearings and depositions and statements, some signed by full committees and some signed only with an X. Then the whole report, a hundred and fifty-nine pages of small type, was printed at Congressional expense.

The wagons went again for salt, the drivers paid the fees, and there was no more trouble. At least not over salt.

12

What a Way to Go!

TEXAS had outlaws before it had Texans. They swarmed along the eastern borders of Spanish Texas thirty years before the Battle of the Alamo. Cleaned out by the U.S. Army, they came back to plague the Republic of Texas until Sam Houston called up the militia to restore order.

This happened in a strip of no-man's-land known as the Neutral Ground or Neutral Zone, and sometimes as the Twilight Zone. It was one of the strangest episodes in the history of western outlawry and, except for an incident near the end of its era, the least described in literature about badmen.

In 1804 the United States acquired Louisiana by purchase. Spain had never defined specifically the location of the boundary between Spanish Texas and Louisiana. It was assumed by the United States to be the Sabine River, which today is the boundary between the two states. The government of Mexico argued that the boundary traditionally ran along the Arroyo Hondo, a creek in Louisiana a few miles east of the Sabine.

General James Wilkinson, acting for the United States, parleyed with Lieutenant Colonel Simon de Herrera and on November 6, 1806, they agreed to regard the land between the Sabine and the Arroyo Hondo as Neutral Ground until their respective governments could settle the matter by formal treaty. The Adams-Onís treaty between the U.S. and Spain in 1819 placed the boundary along the Sabine River.

In the meantime, between 1806 and 1819, the Neutral Ground

was barred to all legal settlement. This made it a perfect haven for outlaws. Strictly speaking, all of the Neutral Ground lay in Louisiana, but for the outlaws' practical purposes there was an extension into Texas. Spanish and Mexican laws forbade settlement in a strip twenty leagues deep along any border with a foreign power; thus outlaws could roam freely along both banks of the Sabine River.

General Wilkinson and Lieutenant Colonel Herrera did not specify the northern boundary of the Neutral Ground, but it was generally accepted as the thirty-second parallel — or about where Mansfield, Louisiana, and Carthage, Texas, are today. From there it ran south to the Gulf of Mexico. At its lower end are forbidding swamps, still so desolate they are unforgettable to the traveler between the towns of Orange and Lake Charles.

At the northern end of the zone, in those early days, the Old San Antonio Road or El Camino Real ran from Natchitoches, on the Red River in Louisiana, southwest to San Antonio and on to Mexico City. From Natchitoches a trail meandered east toward the Mississippi across from Natchez, the end of the Natchez Trace coming west from Nashville in Tennessee. And Natchez, in 1804, was the crime capital of what was then the frontier of the United States.

There were land pirates along the Natchez Trace and river pirates plundering flatboats going down the Mississippi. Names such as Micajah Harpe, Wiley Harpe, Joseph Hare, Samuel Mason, and later John Murrel, were spoken with quiet venom in villages along the trace and the river. The law caught up with the leaders, but their lieutenants, their followers, and their imitators moved west into the refuge of the Neutral Ground.

During its heyday, the zone was a haven for the worst desperadoes, thieves, smugglers, fugitives, murderers, and adventurers of the Southwest. They plundered the travelers along every road and trail, killed casually, levied a toll of blood and booty, and laughed at any thought of punishment.

Not all of the fugitives were from the United States. The unsuccessful revolution of 1810 in Mexico sent men east in flight to the Neutral Ground. Finally a military expedition approved jointly by the United States and Mexico went in to clean out the nest. In command was Lieutenant Augustus Magee whose later career has been discussed in another chapter. Magee's soldiers shot some outlaws, hanged several more, and flogged others. For a time the zone was quiet, but only for a time. A military post, Fort Jesup, was established to maintain order and protect travelers — one of the few forts ever erected to guard immigrants against white savages. The Indians, at least, had a justification for their attacks; the white outlaws had only greed.

The lawlessness of the Neutral Zone remained in the spirit of many in the vicinity even after Texas became a republic. The night riders were especially troublesome in the village of Shelbyville, about thirty miles northwest of the Old San Antonio Road crossing of the Sabine River. In 1840 Charles W. Jackson killed Joseph G. Goodbread in a quarrel over land certificates. Jackson was acquitted, and he organized a band of thirty men resolved to suppress lawlessness. They called themselves Regulators, an old American term later replaced with "vigilante."

In time the over-zealousness of the Regulators led to the organization of a rival band called the Moderators, who set out to curb the excesses of the Regulators. Thus began the Regulators and Moderators War of Shelby county, the first significant "war" of its type in the West. By 1844 each side had a hundred and fifty men. In 1844 President Sam Houston of the Texas Republic had to call up six hundred militiamen to stop the lawlessness and give honest settlers some peace.

During this same year a boy named Cullen Baker was living with his family not far from Shelbyville. They had come from Tennessee, and Cullen was destined to become one of the first famous Texas outlaws, although there are those who say he was only opposing Yankee Reconstruction.

It is neither easy nor fair to label a man as an outlaw from any particular state. Rarely did a man's career run full cycle within his native borders; nearly always he rode the trail across two to a dozen states and territories. It would be futile to attempt any discussion of purely "Texas" outlaws or "Texas" lawmen and expect the list to be long or important.

Cullen Baker was chiefly but not entirely a Texas outlaw. He was born in 1835 in Tennessee, and in 1839 his family moved to Texas. Baker left home at the age of fifteen. He killed his first man in 1854, a witness against him in a court case where he was accused of beating another boy. Cullen fled to Kansas, started hanging around army forts, where soldiers taught the youth how to handle a six-shooter, and killed a trooper at a Kansas post. From there he fled to New Mexico and on to Utah. When the Civil War started, young Baker joined the Confederate forces but soon deserted. It was said that he later joined Quantrill's guerrilla forces aiding the Confederacy.

When the war ended and Union troops came to occupy Texas, Cullen Baker started a one-man guerrilla war of his own against Reconstruction. Others joined him, usually younger men such as Bill Longley, and before long Cullen Baker had acquired the luster and legend of a Robin Hood, avenging the loyal Southerners against the Yankee scalawags. It was a popular cause, and many people overlooked the occasional killings and robbings that were necessary for the gang's livelihood.

There was one man, however, who didn't see eye to eye with Baker. That was Thomas Orr, a young school teacher who was far from aggressive and was handicapped by a deformed right hand.

Their trouble started while they were crossing a small stream on a ferryboat. Cullen proffered a jug and asked Orr to take a social drink. Orr, a newcomer, was unaware of Baker's full reputation and unwisely refused the whiskey. Cullen clouted the youth with a pine branch and departed, leaving Orr unconscious and bleeding.

From that point on, Orr began to learn more about Baker, and he didn't like what he heard. In fact, he started to spread the word that Cullen Baker's acts should be considered treasonable.

Early in January, 1869, Baker finally went gunning for Orr. The young schoolteacher was frightened and tried to hide. Cullen's gang caught him and hanged him; as soon as it appeared that Orr was dead, Cullen had him cut down so the rope could be used to hang another. The gang rode off, and Orr recovered.

In a panic, Orr rallied five or six farmers, all armed with shotguns, and they trailed the unsuspecting Baker. The outlaw and a companion were found asleep "resting after refreshments" — which most people understood meant sleeping off a drunk. In one blast, Baker and his compadre were killed.

At the time of his death, Cullen Baker was wearing the unbelievable armament of four six-shooters, three derringers, and six knives, and was carrying two double-barreled shotguns. The terror of East Texas was killed in his sleep by a nervous schoolteacher. What a lousy way to go!

Tradition and television always have gunfighters dying with their boots on, preferably in a shoot-out or executed after capture. After all, John Wesley Hardin (1853-1895), perhaps the premier gunman in Texas, was killed in El Paso by a constable. William Preston "Wild Bill" Longley (1851-1878), who shared top Texas notoriety with Hardin, was legally hanged at Giddings, Texas.

Others across the West shattered all traditions and died in unlikely ways humiliating to their ghosts, and frustrating to writers who like to follow a formula.

Take the case of Ben Kilpatrick. He was raised down around Concho county, Texas, and by the time he was twenty he already had a record and was ready to head north to join up with the Wild Bunch. The story of that robber band is too well known to repeat here; their five-year rampage from 1896 to 1901 led Butch Cassidy, Kid Curry, the Sundance Kid, Will Carver, Ben Kilpatrick, and the others from Winnemucca, Nevada, to Saint Louis; from the Hole-in-the-Wall up where Utah, Colorado, and Wyoming join, down to West Texas. Their girls went with them, including Laura Bullion, who was usually Ben's girl.

In 1901 the gang scattered after robbing a Great Northern train. Ben and Laura were captured in Saint Louis. He drew a fifteen-year sentence and she received five years. Ben was released in 1911 and headed down to the Devil's River country in West Texas.

There Kilpatrick met up with Howard Benson, an outlaw also known as Ole Beck. The two men knew well the hills and mesas of West Texas, especially from the towns of Ozona and Sonora west to Sanderson and Fort Stockton. It was dry country, full of brush where a man could hide and with just enough water in places to support a man who knew where to find the streams. The two decided to rob the westbound Sunset Flyer on the Southern Pacific. Ben boarded the train at San Angelo and stopped it near Sanderson. Benson was waiting and climbed aboard.

Working their way forward to the express car, Benson stood guard while Kilpatrick entered. The surprised guard, D. A. Trousdale, was unarmed at the moment. He stalled for time when Ben ordered him to open the safe. When Kilpatrick's eyes shifted to look around the car. Trousdale picked up a huge mallet used to crush ice. He swung once and that was all — Ben dropped like a felled steer. Trousdale picked up Ben's gun and was ready when Benson peered into the car. One shot and Benson was dead. The train rolled on into Sanderson, where the two corpses were photographed, then buried.

Five years with Butch Cassidy, in a dozen scrapes, then eleven years in prison — only to die from a clout on the head with an ice mallet! What a lousy way to go!

Harry Tracy was another who had been part of the Wild Bunch in its early days. After a killing at Cripple Creek he was sentenced to prison but managed to escape while en route to the penitentiary. Around 1898 he turned up in Oregon, where he married the sister of a small-time gambler.

Tracy began a series of daring daylight holdups, and for several months lived high on the hog. Caught and imprisoned, he escaped again in June, 1902. Manhunters were soon on his trail, aided by bloodhounds and flanked by more than two hundred National Guardsmen ordered out by the Governor of Oregon.

For eight weeks the fugitive eluded his pursuers, unaware that he was front page news in cities all across the nation. Time after time he skinned out of a new trap, each time closer to capture.

They finally surrounded Tracy near Creston, Washington. A shot from a posseman's rifle hit his leg; Tracy put on a tourniquet but saw it was futile. That night he dragged himself out into a field and turned his gun upon himself.

Not many outlaws committed suicide, but some of the names were high on the list: Jim Younger, who killed himself in 1901 when he was unable to marry the woman of his choice; Johnny Ringo, who ended his own life in a spell of melancholy; Grant Wheeler, the Arizona train robber who shot himself when cornered; Charley Ford, a member of the James gang and whose brother killed Jesse, committed suicide in 1884. People said he never got over the way Jesse was killed.

There was Bill Hynson, up in Montana, who ended his own life in a dramatic manner. He was suspected of having robbed a Chinese woman of $1,000 and also had helped a condemned killer escape, plus other crimes and felonies enough to make a man's future look bleak. So in August, 1898, in the Montana town of Benton he hired a laborer to dig a grave. Then Hynson set up a tripod gallows of three logs. The next morning the townsfolk found him hanging beside his ready grave. In his pocket was a letter from his discouraged mother. What a way to go!

Some gunfighters met death in curious accidents. This happened to Clay Allison, the gentlemanly killer from the Washita. Born in Tennessee, he had been a spy for the Confederates. Later he turned to ranching, out in the Texas Panhandle then at Pope's Crossing, not far above Pecos, Texas.

Along the way he packed up a string of legends. In Dodge City he faced up to Bat Masterson and out-talked that marshal. Once in the town of Canadian, Texas, he lurched naked in the saddle on a drunken ride down the main street. In the Clifton House, a noted stage stop below the Colorado line, he killed Chunk Colbert in an argument over breakfast. The Allison legends grew: once in Las Vegas, New Mexico, Clay went to a dentist, who pulled the wrong tooth. Clay threw the dentist back into the chair and pulled out four teeth in revenge. Allison killed at least twelve men; some say twenty-one. But his one weakness was alcohol, and while in Pecos, Texas, he had several drinks too many and fell off his wagon. A wheel passed over his head, and that was the end of Clay Allison, aged thirty-seven.

Another who died in a freak accident was William E. Walters, who went under such aliases as Bill Anderson and Bronco Bill. He had worked cattle in Texas, Oklahoma, New Mexico, and Arizona, and had been in more than one brush with the law in each of those states. For a while he was with Black Jack Ketchum's gang, and at one time or another was trailed by such noted lawmen as George Scarborough and Jeff Milton. Walters claimed he had never killed a man. He was finally wounded, captured, and sent to prison, but was released because his health was poor. Walters went back to work at the Diamond A ranch near Hachita, New Mexico, and there he was killed — in a fall from a windmill ladder.

Hard luck also dogged another Southwesterner, one who was not an outlaw: Al Sieber, the famous government scout. Sieber was born in Germany and raised in Pennsylvania. During the Civil War he fought as a Union soldier at Gettysburg, where he was wounded in the leg. He went to Arizona in 1868 and became a scout and guide in the Indian-fighting army under General Crook and other commanders. Al served until the end of the Apache wars. In 1875, during a skirmish north of Phoenix, he was wounded in the arm. In 1887 at the San Carlos Indian agency he was shot in the other leg by an Apache. At the turn of the century Sieber "retired" and went to work as the foreman of an Apache road crew for the U.S. Bureau of Reclamation near Roosevelt, Arizona. In 1907, safe from Apache bullets at last, he was killed when a huge boulder rolled down upon him. A stone marker was carved from the fatal rock.

Earlier in Arizona, not every gunfighter at Tombstone died in the shootout at the OK Corral. There were four Clanton men there, and only one fell in the Earp-Clanton fusillade.

The patriarch was Newman H. "Old Man" Clanton, who went from Texas to California during the gold rush and stopped near Tombstone on his return east. There he became a cattleman and freighter. He brought his three sons from Texas: Joseph Isaac "Ike", Phineas "Fin", and the youngest, Billy. Their mother was dead.

As the students of Tombstone dig deeper and deeper into the archives, they come up with less and less to show that the Clantons were little more than a rough, unruly bunch. The evidence that they were outlaws at Tombstone shrinks every year. Wyatt Earp claimed that their ranch was a haven for rustlers and that they were smugglers, or worse. Yet there is no legal record of a single formal charge ever filed against them by Earp. Ike and Finn got into other legal difficulties later.

When the guns were drawn in the OK Corral fight, in 1881, Ike and Billy, along with the McLaurys, faced the Earps and Doc Holliday. Billy, aged about fifteen, was the only Clanton killed. Ike got away and was killed six years later by two deputy sheriffs. "Old Man" Clanton died before the corral fight; he was killed in August, 1881, when Mexicans ambushed his wagon train in Guadalupe canyon.

Phineas, or Finn, was captured later on another charge and was sent to the prison at Yuma for a term. Freed, he was charged with robbing a Chinese but was acquitted. Finn decided to lead a straight life, and became a goat rancher. While tending his herd in the Arizona mountains, he was caught in a sudden snowstorm and suffered from exposure. He died in 1906 of "congestive chills and fever" as a result of the storm.

Another Tombstone character, who might have been completely innocent, talked himself into being hanged. This was William Rogers

Tettenborn, known as Russian Bill. He turned up first at Fort Worth, where he got a bullet in his leg. Then he went to Denver and added a knife slash in his shoulder. From there he drifted down to the mining camp of Shakespeare, near Lordsburg, New Mexico, and lived off and on there and at Tombstone.

An old frontier lawyer, O. W. Williams, knew Bill and said his mother was the daughter of a Scotch sea captain who sailed the Baltic. Bill's father was a German subject of the Russian czar.

Bill was tall, blond, handsome, loved to dress well, and most of all liked to brag. He was considered to be a coward and a loafer, who always turned up ready to fight after the danger had passed or ready to work after the job was done. Near Tombstone he lived at the McLaury Ranch, where his boasting was considered entertainment.

Russian Bill spent barely two years in the Southwest. In 1880 he was in Deming when some horses were stolen from a railroad work camp. Bill bragged a little too close to the truth and was arrested as a horse thief because the railroad demanded action. The deputy sheriff who arrested Bill took him back to Shakespeare where the theft had occurred and locked him up in a room at the Grant House. There was another prisoner in the makeshift jail: a genuine bad man named Sandy King. Sandy was out on bail for murder and had been picked up on another charge.

That night a group of local characters decided to have a hanging party, so they strung Russian Bill from the rafters. Then they hanged Sandy King on the charge of "being a nuisance." Matters should have been handled the other way around; King was the genuine criminal and Bill might have gone free if he had kept his mouth shut.

There once was another horse thief, or rather a mule thief, who came to a strange end even though he was innocent. At least he was innocent at the moment.

Up in Kansas, in 1874, the Vail & Company stage line had a rich mail contract. A competitive outfit, the South Western Stage Company, decided to disrupt Vail's service by stealing mules from several stations along one stretch of the route. If the mails didn't get through, South Western might be given the contract. Several gunfighters were hired and assigned to raid specified stage stops.

Bill Watkins, Jasper Marion (alias Granger), and a couple of others were sent to hit the station at Kingfisher.

When the outlaws reached Kingfisher, they found it well guarded and decided to retreat. On the trail back they were ambushed by Indians in one of the relatively few genuine "cowboys and Indians" affairs on the plains frontier. Marion's horse was shot. Bill Watkins had even worse luck: he was killed and scalped.

Still another alleged horse thief, also in Kansas, met an undignified finish, about three years before the scalping of Watkins. This was J. E. Ledford, who owned the Harris House at Wichita in 1871. Whether or not Ledford was guilty was never proved, but Deputy U.S. Marshall Jack L. Bridges was out to arrest him. Along with Bridges went a man named Stewart and an Army officer named Hargous.

Ledford knew they were coming and hid in the two-holer outhouse that was a standard facility at frontier hotels in those days, out in back. When the lawmen approached, Ledford kicked open the door and fired before the others could draw their guns. He wounded Bridges, but before Ledford could get off another shot he was hit in the back by a slug from Stewart's gun. Altogether, it was not the best way to go.

A shot in the back ended more than one outlaw and lawman, and such a finish was seldom considered unusual. When it is part of a chain of six killings, this is something different. Yet this really happened.

Northfield, Minnesota, was quiet on the afternoon of that day in 1876 when soft-spoken Joseph Heywood greeted customers at the First National Bank. He looked up with little more than faint curiosity when four strangers came in around two o'clock. They didn't hesitate but moved directly toward him and leaped over the counter. One of them drew a knife and ordered Heywood to open the safe. He refused. Even when the man with the knife drew it lightly across Heywood's throat, leaving a thin red line of pain, he stood his ground.

One of the men lifted his gun and fired into Heywood's face. The banker slumped dead.

Gunshots flared outside as townfolk came up. Two outlaws fell; the others leaped into saddles and fled. It was Jesse James' first holdup killing.

But it was only the first of a strange chain of deaths that linked together brave man and coward, bad man and good. Jesse escaped the law, only to be killed by one of his own men.

Six years after the Northfield robbery a secretive sort of man moved into a cabin on the outskirts of St. Joseph, Missouri. He said his name was Thomas Howard, and with him were his wife, two children, and a friend, Charles Johnson. Neighbors saw little of the newcomers, but word got around that Johnson's brother, Robert, had joined the household.

That was all most people knew until April 3, 1882, when the whole country heard that Howard was really Jesse James and that he had been shot in the back by Robert "Johnson." The Johnsons were really Bob and Charley Ford, out for the $10,000 reward.

The Fords turned themselves in, were tried, sentenced to be hanged, then pardoned and rewarded. They made a tour of public appearances, traveling as far as New York.

But the chain still had four links to go.

The years passed and Bob Ford spent all of the reward money. He went to the mining camp of Creede, in Colorado, and opened a tent saloon in the boom town where people said, "It's day all day in the daytime, and there is no night in Creede."

The place was a bonanza for Ford until one day, ten years after Jesse's death, when a miner came into the saloon carrying a double-barreled shotgun. He walked up to Ford and said, "Hello, Bob, old pard!"

Ford turned and found himself staring into the double muzzles. Before Bob could say a word, the miner pulled both triggers.

Why? Some said it was over Ford's wife. Others said that the miner, Ed Kelly, had been an old friend of Jesse James, just biding his time. Still other said that Ford and Kelly had quarreled more than once and the shooting was the payoff.

Still that wasn't the end of the tale. Kelly was caught, tried, and sent to the Colorado State Penitentiary for twenty years. He was out in two. He drifted around the West and finally came to Oklahoma City. Without money or work, he loafed around the gambling houses by day and slept in railroad stations at night. Time after time, depot agents threw him out, but he always came back. One night the stationmaster called a policeman, Joe Burnette.

Joe tactfully asked Kelly if he were waiting for a train. When Kelly replied that it was nobody's business, Burnette had to arrest him.

On the way to the police station, Kelly tore loose from Burnette's grasp and drew a gun. The policeman grasped Kelly's gun with his own left hand. When Burnette drew his own weapon, Kelly grabbed it with *his* left hand. The two struggled in the darkness, both helpless but still holding off the other. Each managed to get off three shots, without effect. They fell to the ground and Burnette pulled the trigger again. Kelly died instantly.

First an innocent bank clerk; then an outlaw leader shot by a presumed friend; the friend slain by an angry miner; the miner killed by a lawman.

Burnette became an honored veteran on the police force. More years passed, each filled with risks, then in the routine arrest of a drunken Indian Burnette was killed.

The Indian was arrested, tried, sentenced, and executed. For the first time since the death of Heywood, one of the killers was brought to his end according to the procedures of law. It was as though Justice herself had entered the picture to break the death chain.

The story would have been just as strange even if Jesse James had not been involved, but some of the most famous outlaws seemed to attract legends. It was that way with Sam Bass, who was certainly Texas' most talked-about and sung-about robber even if he wasn't the gunfighter that Wes Hardin was.

In reality, Sam Bass had a short and stupid career. It lasted from September of one year until July of the next, and in all that time he made only one good haul — and that one was planned by someone else.

Sam had been born in Indiana, just as the ballad says, in 1851. He was nineteen when he turned up at Denton, Texas, where he made a little money racing a fast mare. In 1876 he and Joel Collins decided on a perfectly legitimate scheme to make some real money, quickly and legally. They would put together a trail herd of cattle, consigned by local ranchers and would drive this herd up to the Black Hills where hungry miners were paying well for beef.

They made the trip; they sold the herd for $8,000, but didn't head back south right away. Crooked gamblers clipped them for half of the cattle money; a devious mine promoter swindled them out of the rest.

So they robbed a stage for a few dollars, tried a second stage with little better luck, and then decided to rob a train. On September 18, 1877, they held up the train and found themselves richer by $60,000 — all in new twenty-dollar gold pieces dated 1877, easily traced.

The gang split up and went their various trails. Sam went back to Denton, where he swaggered and spent freely. One of Sam's old buddies was Frank Jackson, five years younger than the robber. Frank refused Sam's invitation to become a night rider. Jackson had killed a black desperado but found no taste for outlawry. Eventually he gave in and joined up with Sam.

Bass lined up a few more eager followers and in December, 1877, the gang rode down to San Antonio. They robbed two or three stages and held up perhaps four trains, with indifferent success. They played hopscotch with the Texas Rangers, but by the time June, 1878, rolled around the Rangers had planted a traitor in Sam's gang. This was Jim Murphy, whom Bass had known. The Rangers promised amnesty for Jim and his father for an earlier crime if Murphy would report on Sam's movements.

What happened afterward is common legend. On July 19, 1878, Sam and two of his men, including Jackson, went into the village of Round Rock, Texas, to study the layout for a bank robbery. Instead they ran into a Ranger ambush.

Frank Jackson helped the wounded Bass get away, and when Sam could go no farther he urged Jackson to flee for his own freedom. Reluctantly, Jackson galloped away and was never caught. When Sam was buried, a stranger rode up swiftly after the ceremony and threw a handful of earth on the grave. People still believe it was Frank Jackson.

All outlaws in their own time were not idolized; it takes the patina of time to build the legend. Just as the townsfolk of Las Vegas raised a purse to reward Pat Garrett after he shot Billy the Kid, so did Jim Murphy receive plaudits. But the applause died quickly and Jim began to worry about vengeance from those who rode with Sam Bass or who idolized him. He went back to Denton but had trouble sleeping at nights.

Finally he began to feel his eyes were affected, and about eleven months after the Round Rock finale Murphy went into a drugstore and asked for some eye drops. He was given a standard remedy of the time, but one that contained poison. Jim lay down on a cot in the back room to apply the drops. Somehow he awkwardly let a little of the medicine trickle down between his lips, and before the day was out he died in convulsions. What a way to go!

Frank Jackson met no strange death after he fled from the dying Sam Bass — or at least Frank met no death that was recorded. He vanished completely. The history of law and disorder in Texas and all the West is richly laced with tales of men who quit the outlaw trail to live out the rest of their days as upright citizens under a new name. None of these vanished gunfighters turned up in more places or under more names than did Frank Jackson of the Sam Bass gang.

There are those, of whom Arizona Ranger Tom Rynning was one and lawman Jim Herron was another, who were sure that Jackson went to Arizona and changed his name to Bill (or Bob) Downing. He joined Burton Alvord and others in robbing a Southern Pacific train at Cochise in 1899. Some said that Bill Downing had spent the previous years as a miner in Mexico and in the wood business around Willcox, Arizona. Other writers have credited Downing with as many as thirty killings. Rynning wrote that Downing was sentenced to ten years in the penitentiary at Yuma, was still in that rocky hell-hole when he (Rynning) became its warden, and that Downing revealed his true identity as Frank Jackson. After his release from Yuma, Downing became involved in a quarrel with an Arizona Ranger named Speed and the two killed each other in a gun duel. In further support of his case, Rynning claimed that while he was in charge at Yuma, the prison was visited by Dick Ware, the Texas Ranger who had fought Sam Bass, and that Ware had identified Downing as Jackson.

Contrary to this, William Sterling, himself a Texas Ranger long after the Downing episode at Yuma, told of receiving a letter from Jim Gillett, another famous Ranger, denying this. Gillett stated that Ware never visited Arizona at the time Rynning specified. Gillett was convinced that Jackson had followed Jim Murphy after the death of Sam Bass, seeking to revenge the death of the outlaw leader.

Charlie Siringo, the cowboy detective, was sure that Frank Jackson went to Montana and ran a big horse ranch there. Still another writer claimed that Jackson had gone to California, where he became a successful peace officer. Others said Frank became a traveling sales-man, working around Houston, Texas.

There were also reports that Jackson was in New Mexico. Governor James F. Hinkle of that state once said he had received some correspondence from people trying to secure amnesty for Jackson at Roswell. Eugene Manlove Rhodes was reported to have known Jackson well, even to the point of being able to forward mail to him. Another writer in Texas has claimed that the cowboy songwriter N. Howard "Jack" Thorp once admitted in a conversation that he (Thorp) was really Frank Jackson. This was impossible: Thorp was only eleven years old when Sam Bass was killed at Round Rock. Still others have placed Jackson in West Texas, in the vicinity of Big Spring, as a successful cattleman. This tallies up to seventeen variations of Frank Jackson's fate, and the legends continue to multiply.

The catalog of bizarre ends to gunfighter careers includes such entries as Jim Johnson, a cowboy in Arizona around 1880 when he shot himself in the leg, refused medical attention, and died of blood poisoning. It includes Bill Norris, who was sentenced to serve twenty-one years at Leavenworth and on the second day of his sentence butted his brains out against the stone walls. It includes Jim Bewley, in Oregon, who refused to be quarantined for smallpox. When he tried to dash for freedom he was shot.

But the top award for macabre endings must go to a tale discovered by Ed Bartholomew, one of America's most thorough researchers into badman lore. Ed tells of a Texas outlaw named Green McCullough who was being lynched at San Antonio. McCullough was guilty and he knew it. His last words were, "I've got to be hung, and I'm glad I'm going to be hung by friends."

What a way to go!

BIBLIOGRAPHY

GENERAL WORKS OF REFERENCE

Alessio Robles, Vito. *Coahuila y Texas, desde la Consumación de la Independencia hasta el Tratado de Paz de Guadalupe Hidalgo*. 2 vols. Mexico: Editorial Cultura, 1945.

American Guide Series. *Houston: A History and Guide*. Houston: The Anson Jones Press, 1942.

———— *Louisiana: A Guide to the State*. New York: Hastings House, 1941.

———— *New Mexico: A Guide to the Colorful State*. New York: Hastings House, 1940.

———— *Texas: A Guide to the Lone Star State*. New York: Hastings House, 1940.

Bancroft, Hubert Howe. *History of the North Mexican States and Texas*. 2 vols. San Francisco: The History Company, 1889.

Bolton, Herbert Eugene, and Eugene C. Barker, eds. *With the Makers of Texas: A Source Reader in Texas History*. New York: American Book Company, 1904.

Brown, John Henry. *History of Texas, from 1685 to 1892*. 2 vols. St. Louis: L. E. Daniell, Publisher, 1892.

Carter, Hodding. *Doomed Road of Empire: The Spanish Trail of Conquest*. New York: McGraw-Hill Book Company, 1963.

Castañeda, Carlos E., translator. *The Mexican Side of the Texas Revolution*. Dallas: P. L. Turner Co., 1928.

Evans, Clement A., ed. *Confederate Military History*. 12 vols. Atlanta: Confederate Publishing Company, 1899.

Fehrenbach, T. R. *Lone Star: A History of Texas and the Texans*. New York: The Macmillan Company, 1968.

Ford, John Salmon, and Stephen B. Oates. *Rip Ford's Texas*. Austin: University of Texas Press, 1963.

Fuermann, George. *Houston: Land of the Big Rich*. Garden City, N.Y.: Doubleday & Company, Inc., 1951.

Heitmann, Francis B. *Historical Register and Dictionary of the United States Army*. 2 vols. Washington, 1912; reprinted, Urbana: University of Illinois Press, 1965.

Hogan, William Ransom. *The Texas Republic: A Social and Economic History*. Norman: University of Oklahoma Press, 1946, 1969.

Hollon, W. Eugene. *The Southwest: Old and New*. New York: Alfred A. Knopf, 1961.

Jones, William M. *Texas Testimony Carved in Stone*. Houston: author, 1952.

225

Malone, Dumas, ed. *Dictionary of American Biography*. New York: Charles Scribner's Sons, 1935.

Perrigo, Lynn I. *Texas and Our Spanish Southwest*. Dallas: Banks, Upshaw and Company, 1960.

Richardson, Rupert N. *Texas: The Lone Star State*. New York: Prentice-Hall, Inc., 1943.

Sonnichsen, C. L. *Pass of the North: Four Centuries on the Rio Grande*. El Paso: Texas Western Press, 1968.

Texas Almanac and State Industrial Guide. Dallas: The Dallas Morning News, 1969 and earlier issues.

Warner, C. A. *Texas Oil and Gas Since 1543*. Houston: Gulf Publishing Co., 1939.

War of the Rebellion: A Compilation of the Official Records of the Union and Confederate Armies. 128 vols. Washington: Government Printing Office, 1880-1901.

Webb, Walter Prescott. *The Texas Rangers: A Century of Frontier Defense*. Boston: Houghton Mifflin Company, 1935.

———, editor. *The Handbook of Texas*. 2 vols. Austin: Texas State Historical Association, 1952.

Winsor, Justin, ed. *Narrative and Critical History of America*. Boston: Houghton Mifflin and Company, 1884.

Wortham, Louis J. *A History of Texas*. Fort Worth: Wortham-Molyneux Co., 1924.

Yoakum, Henderson. *History of Texas, from its First Settlement in 1685 to its Annexation to the United States in 1846*. 2 vols. New York: Redfield, 1855; reprinted, Austin: The Steck Company, n.d., in 1 vol.

CHAPTER SOURCES

BOOKS, ARTICLES, DOCUMENTS, AND PAMPHLETS

CHAPTER 1. *Cavalier on the Bayou.*

Bloom, Lansing B. "Grollet, Grole, Grule, Gurule." *New Mexico Historical Review*, Vol. 20, No. 2 (April, 1945), pp. 187-88.

Bolton, Herbert E. "The Location of La Salle's Colony on the Gulf of Mexico." *Southwestern Historical Quarterly*, Vol. 27 (1923-1924).

Brebner, John B. *The Explorers of North America, 1492-1806*. Meridian Books (Cleveland: World Publishing Co., 1946).

Chávez, Fray Angélico. *Origins of New Mexico Families*. Santa Fe: The Historical Society of New Mexico, 1954.

——— "The Archibeque Story." *El Palacio*, Vol. 54 (August, 1947), pp. 179-182.

Cole, E. W. "La Salle in Texas." *Southwestern Historical Quarterly*, Vol. 49 (1945-1946).

Cox, Isaac J., ed. *The Journals of La Salle and his Companions*. New York: Williams-Barker Co., 1906.

Dunbar, John B. "Massacre of the Villazur Expedition by the Pawnees on the Platte in 1720." *Collections of the Kansas Historical Society*, Vol. 9 (1909-1910), pp. 397-423.

Espinosa, J. Manuel. *First Expedition of Vargas into New Mexico, 1692*. Albuquerque: University of New Mexico Press, 1940.

Hackett, Charles Wilson. *Historical Documents Relating to New Mexico, Nueva Vizcaya, and Approaches Thereto, to 1773*. 3 vols. Washington: Carnegie Institution of Washington, 1937.

Lenk, Torsten. *The Flintlock: Its Origin and Development*. Translated by G. A. Urquart. New York: Bramhall House, n.d.

Loomis, Noel M., and Abraham P. Nasatir. *Pedro Vial and the Roads to Santa Fe*. Norman: University of Oklahoma Press, 1967.

Margry, Pierre, ed. *Découvertes et Etablissements des Francais dans le Sud et dans l'Ouest de l'Amerique Septentrionale, 1615-1754*. 6 vols. Paris: Maisonneuve et Cie., 1879-1888.

Parkman, Francis. *La Salle and the Discovery of the Great West*. Boston: Little Brown, and Company, 1879.

Peterson, Harold L. *Arms and Armor in Colonial America, 1526-1783*. New York: Bramhall House, n.d.

Russell, Carl P. *Guns on the Early Frontiers*. Berkeley: University of California Press, 1957.

Shea, John G., ed. *The Expedition of Don Diego Dionisio de Penalosa from Santa Fe to the River Mischipi in 1662*. Chicago: Rio Grande Press, 1964.

Terrell, John Upton. *La Salle: The Life and Times of an Explorer*. New York: Weybright and Talley, 1968.

Thomas, Alfred B. *After Coronado: Spanish Exploration Northeast of New Mexico, 1697-1727*. Norman: University of Oklahoma Press, 1935.

Twitchell, Ralph Emerson. "A Campaign Against the Moqui Indians." *New Mexico Historical Review*, Vol. 6, No. 2 (April, 1931), p. 183.

——— *The Spanish Archives of New Mexico*. 2 vols. Cedar Rapids: Torch Press, 1914.

Wharton, Clarence R. *L'Archeveque*. Houston: Anson Jones Press, 1941.

CHAPTER 2. *Filibusters West.*

Faulk, Odie B. *The Last Years of Spanish Texas, 1778-1821*. The Hague: Mouton & Co., 1964.

Garrett, Julia Kathryn. "Dr. John Sibley and the Louisiana-Texas Frontier, 1803-1814." *Southwestern Historical Quarterly*, Vol. 49, No. 3 (January, 1946), pp. 399-431.

——— "The First Constitution of Texas, April 17, 1813." *Southwestern Historical Quarterly*, Vol. 40, No. 4 (April, 1937), pp. 290-308.

———— "The First Newspaper of Texas: *Gaceta de Texas.*" *Southwestern Historical Quarterly.* Vol. 40, No. 3 (January, 1937), pp. 200-215.

———— "*Gaceta de Texas:* Translation of the First Number." *Southwestern Historical Quarterly,* Vol. 42, No. 1 (July, 1938), pp. 21-24.

———— *Green Flag Over Texas: A Story of the Last Years of Spain in Texas.* Dallas: The Cordova Press, 1939; reprinted, Austin: The Pemberton Press, n.d.

Gulick, Charles Adams, ed. *The Papers of Mirabeau Buonaparte Lamar.* Austin: Texas State Library, n.d.

Hatcher, Mattie Austin. "Joaquín de Arredondo's Report of the Battle of the Medina, August 18, 1813." *The Quarterly of the Texas State Historical Association,* Vol. 11, No. 3 (January, 1908), pp. 220-236.

Henderson, Harry McCorry. "The Magee-Gutiérrez Expedition." *Southwestern Historical Quarterly,* Vol. 55, No. 1 (July, 1951), pp. 43-61.

Hernandez y Davalos, J. E. *Colección de Documentos para la Historia de la Guerra de Independencia de Mexico.* Mexico: 1877-1882.

Jarratt, Rie. *Gutiérrez de Lara, Mexican Texan: The Story of a Creole Hero.* Austin: Creole Texana, 1949.

McCaleb, Walter Flavius. "The First Period of the Gutiérrez-Magee Expedition." *The Quarterly of the Texas State Historical Association,* Vol. 4, No. 3 (January, 1901), pp. 218-229.

Manning, William R. *Diplomatic Correspondence of the United States Concerning the Independence of Latin American Nations.* 3 vols. New York, 1925. Vol. I.

U.S. Department of State. *Consular Reports: Special Agents, 1794-1906.* National Archives, microfilm, Record Group 59, M-37.

Vigness, David M. *The Revolutionary Decades: The Saga of Texas, 1810-1836.* Austin: Steck-Vaughn Company, 1965.

Warren, Harris Gaylord. "José Alvarez de Toledo's Initiation as a Filibuster, 1811-1813." *The Hispanic American Historical Review,* Vol. 20, No. 1 (February, 1940), pp. 56-82.

———— *The Sword was their Passport: A History of American Filibustering in the Mexican Revolution.* Baton Rouge: Louisiana State University Press, 1943.

West, Elizabeth H., ed. "Diary of José Bernardo Gutiérrez de Lara, 1811-1812." *The American Historical Review,* Vol. 34, No. 1 (October, 1928), pp. 55-76; No. 2 (January, 1929), pp. 281-294.

CHAPTER 3. *Sailing the Texas Main.*

Barker, Eugene C. "Difficulties of a Mexican Revenue Officer in Texas." *The Quarterly of the Texas State Historical Association,* Vol. 4, No. 3 (January, 1901), pp. 190-202.

Binkley, William C., ed. *Official Correspondence of the Texas Revolution, 1835-1836.* 2 vols. New York: D. Appleton-Century Company, 1936.

Cox, C. C. "Recollections of ...." *Quarterly of the Texas State Historical Association,* Vol. 6, No. 2 (October, 1902), pp. 113-138.

Day, Donald, and Harry Herbert Ullom. *The Autobiography of Sam Houston.* Norman: University of Oklahoma Press, 1954.

Dienst, Alex. "The Navy of the Republic of Texas." *Quarterly of the Texas State Historical Association,* Vol. 12, No. 3 (January, 1909), pp. 165-203; also three succeeding issues.

Douglas, C. L. *Thunder on the Gulf, or The Story of the Texas Navy.* Dallas: Turner Company, 1936.

Franklin, Ethel Mary. "Memoirs of Mrs. Annie P. Harris." *Southwestern Historical Quarterly,* Vol. 40, No. 3 (January, 1937), pp. 231-246.

Fuller, George F. "Sketch of the Texas Navy." *Quarterly of the Texas State Historical Association,* Vol. 7, No. 3 (January, 1904), pp. 223-234.

Gulick, Charles Adams, ed. *The Papers of Mirabeau Buonaparte Lamar.* Austin: Texas State Library, n.d.

Haugh, George F., ed. "History of the Texas Navy." *Southwestern Historical Quarterly,* Vol. 63, No. 4 (April, 1960), pp. 572-579.

Hill, Jim Dan. *The Texas Navy in Forgotten Battles and Shirtsleeve Diplomacy.* Chicago: University of Texas Press, 1937; reprinted, New York: A. S. Barnes and Company, Inc., 1962.

Jenkins, John H. "The Texas Navy: Los Diablos Tejanos on the High Seas." *The American West,* Vol. 5, No. 3 (May, 1968), pp. 35-41.

Johnson, Howard P. "New Orleans Under General Butler." *The Louisiana Historical Quarterly,* Vol. 24, No. 2 (April, 1941), p. 466.

Kendall, John Smith. "The Successors of Lafitte." *The Louisiana Historical Quarterly,* Vol. 24, No. 2 (April, 1941), pp. 370-71.

Neu, C. T. "The Case of the Brig *Pocket.*" *Quarterly of the Texas State Historical Association,* Vol. 12, No. 4 (April, 1909), pp. 276-295.

Vigness, David M. *The Revolutionary Decades: The Saga of Texas, 1810-1836.* Austin: Steck-Vaughn Company, 1965.

Wells, Tom Henderson. *Commodore Moore and the Texas Navy.* Austin: University of Texas Press, 1960.

————— "An Evaluation of the Texas Navy." *Southwestern Historical Quarterly,* Vol. 63, No. 4 (April, 1960), pp. 567-571.

Winthrop, John. *Report of the Trial of Thomas M. Thompson for a Piratical Attack upon the American Schooner* San Felipe, New Orleans, 1835.

25th Congress, 2nd sess., House Doc. 351. Vol. XII (Serial 332). Washington, 1837. (Report on relations between U.S. and Mexico.)

30th Congress, 1st sess., Senate Misc. Doc. 62 (Serial 511). Washington, 1848. (Admission of Texas Navy officers into U.S. Navy.)

31st Congress, 1st sess., House Report 238, Vol. II (Serial 584), Washington, 1850. (Admission of Texas Navy officers into U.S. Navy.)

32nd Congress, 1st sess., Senate Report 347, Vol. II (Serial 631). Washington, 1852. (Admission of Texas Navy officers into U.S. Navy.)

35th Congress, 1st sess., House Misc. Doc. 27, Vol. I. Washington, 1858. (Concerning Capt. John G. Tod of the Texas Navy.)

40th Congress, 2nd sess., Senate Report 110. Washington, 1868. (Petition of widow of Commodore Moore.)

CHAPTER 4. *Draw Black for Death.*

Barton, Henry W. "The United States Cavalry and the Texas Rangers." *Southwestern Historical Quarterly,* Vol. 63, No. 4 (April, 1960), pp. 496-510.

Bell, Thomas W. *A Narrative of the Capture and Subsequent Sufferings of the Mier Prisoners in Mexico* . . . De Soto County, Miss.: R. Morris & Co., 1845; reprinted, Waco: Texian Press, 1964.

Binkley, William Campbell. "New Mexico and the Texan-Santa Fe Expedition." *Southwestern Historical Quarterly,* Vol. 27, No. 2 (October, 1923), pp. 85-107.

Bloom, Lansing. "New Mexico under Mexican Administration." *Old Santa Fe,* Vol. 2, No. 6 (October, 1914), pp. 143-156.

Carroll, H. Bailey. "The Texan Santa Fe Trail." *Panhandle-Plains Historical Review,* Vol. 24, 1951.

Chabot, Frederick C. *The Perote Prisoners: Being the Diary of James L. Trueheart.* San Antonio: The Naylor Company, 1934.

Day, Donald, and Harry Herbert Ullom. *The Autobiography of Sam Houston.* Norman: University of Oklahoma Press, 1954.

Day, James M., ed. "Diary of James A. Glasscock, Mier Man." *Texana,* Vol. 1, No. 2 (Spring, 1963), pp. 85-119.

Duval, John C. *The Adventures of Big Foot Wallace, the Texas Ranger.* Philadelphia, 1870; reprinted, Lincoln: University of Nebraska Press, 1966.

Falconer, Thomas. *Letters and Notes on the Texan Santa Fe Expedition, 1841-1842.* New York: Dauber & Pine Bookshops, Inc.; reprinted, Rio Grande Press.

Friend, Llerena, ed. "Thomas W. Bell Letters." *Southwestern Historical Quarterly,* Vol. 63, No. 1 (July, 1959), pp. 99-109.

Green, Thomas Jefferson. *Journal of the Texian Expedition Against Mier.* New York: Harper and Brothers, 1845; reprinted, Austin: The Steck Company, 1935.

Gulick, Charles Adams, ed. *The Papers of Mirabeau Buonaparte Lamar.* Austin: Texas State Library, n.d.

Hernandez y Davalos, J. E. *Colección de Documentos para la Historia de la Guerra de Independencia de Mexico.* 6 vols. Mexico, 1877-1882.

Igleheart, Fanny Gooch Chambers. *Boy Captive of the Texas Mier Expedition.* San Antonio: Passing Show Publishing Company, 1918.

Kendall, George W. *Narrative of the Texan Santa Fe Expedition.* London: Wiley & Putnam, 1844; reprinted facsimile, Austin: The Steck Company, 1935.

Loomis, Noel M. *The Texan-Santa Fe Pioneers*. Norman: University of Oklahoma Press, 1958.

McGrath, J. J., and Wallace Hawkins. "Perote Fort — Where Texans Were Imprisoned." *Southwestern Historical Quarterly*, Vol. 48, No. 3 (January, 1945), pp. 304-345.

McHenry, J. Patrick. *A Short History of Mexico*. Garden City: Dolphin Books, reprint, 1962.

Maverick, Rena M., ed. *Samuel Maverick, Texan, 1803-1870*. San Antonio: privately printed, 1952.

Nance, Joseph Milton. *Attack and Counter-Attack: The Texas-Mexican Frontier, 1842*. Austin: University of Texas Press, 1964.

Nielsen, George. "Mathew Caldwell and the Texan Santa Fe Expedition." *Southwestern Historical Quarterly*, Vol. 63, No. 4 (April, 1960), pp. 580-583.

Smith, George Winston, and Charles P. Judah. *Chronicles of the Gringos: The U.S. Army in the Mexican War, 1846-1848*. Albuquerque: University of New Mexico Press, 1968.

Spellman, L. U. "Letters of the Dawson Men from Perote Prison, Mexico." *Southwestern Historical Quarterly*, Vol. 38, No. 4 (April, 1935), pp. 246-269.

Stapp, William Preston. *The Prisoners of Perote, Containing a Journal Kept by the Author . . .* Philadelphia: G. B. Zieber and Company, 1845; reprinted, Austin: The Steck Company, 1935.

CHAPTER 5. *Confederates on the Rio Grande*.

Colton, Ray C. *The Civil War in the Western Territories: Arizona, Colorado, New Mexico, and Utah*. Norman: University of Oklahoma Press, 1959.

Craig, Reginald S. *The Fighting Parson: The Biography of Colonel John M. Chivington*. Los Angeles: Westernlore Press, 1959.

D'Hamel, Enrique B. *The Adventures of a Tenderfoot*. Reprinted, Waco, Texas: W. M. Morrison, n.d.

Emmett, Chris. *Fort Union and the Winning of the Southwest*. Norman: University of Oklahoma Press, 1965.

Ganaway, Loomis M. *New Mexico and the Sectional Controversy, 1846-1861*. Santa Fe: Historical Society of New Mexico, 1944.

Giese, Dale F., editor. *My Life with the Army in the West: Memoirs of J. E. Farmer*. Santa Fe: Stagecoach Press, 1967.

Griggs, George. *History of the Mesilla Valley; or, the Gadsden Purchase, Known in Mexico as the Treaty of Mesilla*. Mesilla, N.M.: author, 1930.

Hall, Martin Hardwick. *Sibley's New Mexico Campaign*. Austin: University of Texas Press, 1960.

Harris, Gertrude. *A Tale of Men Who Knew Not Fear*. San Antonio, Texas: Alamo Printing Company, 1935.

Heyman, Max L., Jr. *Prudent Soldier: A Biography of Major General E. R. S. Canby.* Glendale, Calif.: Arthur H. Clark Company, 1959.

Hollister, Ovando James. *History of the First Regiment of Colorado Volunteers.* Denver: Thos. Gibson & Co., 1863. Reprinted as *Boldly They Rode;* Lakewood, Colo.: The Golden Press, 1949.

Hughes, W. J. *Rebellious Ranger: Rip Ford and the Old Southwest.* Norman: University of Oklahoma Press, 1964.

Hunt, Aurora. *The Army of the Pacific: Its Operations in California, Texas, Arizona, New Mexico, . . . 1860-1866.* Glendale, Calif.: Arthur H. Clark Co., 1951.

——— *Major General James Henry Carleton, 1814-1873: Western Frontier Dragoon.* Glendale, Calif.: Arthur H. Clark Co., 1958.

Johnson, Robert U., and Clarence C. Buel, editors. *Battles and Leaders of the Civil War.* New York: The Century Company, 1887-1888.

Jolly, John P. *History: National Guard of New Mexico, 1606-1963.* Santa Fe: Adjutant General's Office, 1964.

Keleher, William A. *Turmoil in New Mexico, 1846-1888.* Santa Fe: The Rydal Press, 1952.

Kerby, Robert L. *The Confederate Invasion of New Mexico: 1861-1862.* Los Angeles: Westernlore Press, 1958.

Lewis, Oscar. *The War in the Far West, 1861-1865.* Garden City, N.Y.: Doubleday & Company, Inc.

McKee, James C. *Narrative of the Surrender of a Command of U.S. Forces at Fort Fillmore, N.M., in July, A.D., 1861.* Prescott, Ariz.: author, 1878.

McMaster, Maj. Richard K. *Musket, Saber, & Missile: A History of Fort Bliss.* El Paso: author, 1962.

Marchand, Ernest, editor. *News From Fort Craig, New Mexico, 1863: Civil War Letters of Andrew Ryan.* Santa Fe: Stagecoach Press, 1966.

Mozer, Corinne C. "A Brief History of Fort Fillmore." *El Palacio,* special Fort Fillmore issue, Vol. 74, No. 2 (Summer, 1967), pp. 5-18.

Noel, Theophilus. *Autobiography and Reminiscences of Theophilus Noel.* Chicago: Theo. Noel Company Print, 1904.

——— *A Campaign from Santa Fe to the Mississippi.* Shreveport: Shreveport News Printing Establishment, 1865; reprinted, Houston: Stagecoach Press, 1961.

Pettis, George H. *The California Column.* Santa Fe: Historical Society of New Mexico, 1908.

Petty, Joseph W. *Confederate Campaign in New Mexico.* Houston: The Houston Civil War Round Table, 1955.

Sabin, Edwin L. *Kit Carson Days, 1809-1868.* 2 vols. Chicago: A. C. McClurg & Co., 1914.

Shinkle, James D. *Fort Sumter and the Bosque Redondo Indian Reservation.* Roswell, N.M.: Hall-Poorbaugh Press, 1965.

Walker, Charles S. "Causes of Confederate Invasion of New Mexico." *New Mexico Historical Review,* Vol. 8, No. 2 (April, 1933), p. 97.

Watford, W. H. "Confederate Western Ambitions." *Southwestern Historical Quarterly,* Vol. 44, No. 2 (October, 1940), p. 168.

White, Owen. *Out of the Desert: The Historical Romance of El Paso.* El Paso: The McMath Company, 1923.

Whitford, William C. *Colorado Volunteers in the Civil War: The New Mexico Campaign in 1862.* Denver: The State Historical and Natural History Society, 1906. Reprinted, Boulder, Colo.: Pruett Press, Inc., 1963.

CHAPTER 6. *Black Day for the Navy.*

Barr, Alwyn. "Texas Coastal Defense, 1861-1865." *Southwestern Historical Quarterly,* Vol. 45, No. 1 (July, 1961), pp. 1-31.

Bartholomew, Ed E. *The Houston Story.* Houston: Frontier Press of Texas, 1951.

Cushing, E. H. *New Texas Reader.* Houston: E. H. Cushing, 1864.

Mahan, Alfred T. *The Gulf and Inland Waters.* New York: Charles Scribner's Sons, 1883; reprinted, New York: Jack Brussel, Publisher, n.d.

Manucy, Albert. *Artillery Through the Ages.* Washington: U.S. Government Printing Office, 1949; reprinted, 1962.

Muir, Andrew Forest. "Dick Dowling and the Battle of Sabine Pass." *Civil War History,* Vol. 4, No. 4. (December, 1958), pp. 399-428.

Noel, Theophilus. *A Campaign from Santa Fe to the Mississippi.* Shreveport: Shreveport News Printing Establishment, 1865; reprinted, Houston: Stagecoach Press, 1961.

Official Records of the Union and Confederate Navies in the War of the Rebellion. Series I, Vol. 20. Washington, 1905. (Major source.)

Pray, May M. (Mrs. R. F.) *Dick Dowling's Battle: An Account of the War Between the States in the Eastern Gulf Coast Region of Texas.* San Antonio: The Naylor Company, 1936.

Sackett, Frances Robertson. *Dick Dowling.* Houston: Gulf Publishing Company, 1937.

Scharf, J. Thomas. *History of the Confederate States Navy.* New York: Rogers & Sherwood, 1887.

Tolbert, Frank X. *Dick Dowling at Sabine Pass.* New York: McGraw-Hill Book Company, 1962.

Welles, Gideon. *Diary of Gideon Welles.* 3 vols. Boston: Houghton Mifflin Company, 1911; reprinted, New York: W. W. Norton & Company, 1960. Vol. I, pp. 441-42, quotation by permission of publishers.

Young, Jo. "The Battle of Sabine Pass." *Southwestern Historical Quarterly,* Vol. 52, No. 4 (April, 1949), pp. 398-409.

CHAPTER 7. *Confederate Victory — After Appomattox.*

Barr, Alwyn. "Texas Coastal Defense, 1861-1865." *Southwestern Historical Quarterly,* Vol. 45, No. 1 (July, 1961), pp. 1-31.

Delaney, Robert W. "Matamoras, Port for Texas During the Civil War." *Southwestern Historical Quarterly,* Vol. 58, No. 4 (April, 1955), pp. 473-485.

Elliott, Claude. "Union Sentiment in Texas, 1861-1865." *Southwestern Historical Quarterly,* Vol. 50, No. 4 (April, 1947), pp. 449-477.

Hughes, W. J. *Rebellious Ranger: Rip Ford and the Old Southwest.* Norman: University of Oklahoma Press, 1964.

Jones, Allen W. "Military Events in Texas During the Civil War, 1861-1865." *Southwestern Historical Quarterly,* Vol. 64, No. 1 (July, 1960), pp. 64-70.

Lea, Tom. *The King Ranch.* 2 vols. Boston: Little, Brown and Company, 1957.

Oates, Stephen B. *Confederate Cavalry West of the River.* Austin: University of Texas Press, 1961.

———— "John S. 'Rip' Ford." *Southwestern Historical Quarterly,* Vol. 64, No. 3 (January, 1961), pp. 289-314.

Pierce, Frank Cushman. *A Brief History of the Lower Rio Grande Valley.* Menasha, Wisc.: George Banta Publishing Company, 1917.

Smith, George Winston, and Charles Judah. *Chronicles of the Gringos: The U. S. Army in the Mexican War, 1846-1848.* Albuquerque: University of New Mexico Press, 1968.

CHAPTER 8. *Comancheros of the Staked Plains.*

Abel, Annie Heloise, ed. "The Journal of John Greiner." *Old Santa Fe,* Vol. 3, No. 11 (July, 1916), pp. 189-243.

———— *The Official Correspondence of James S. Calhoun, while Indian Agent at Santa Fe and Superintendent of Indian Affairs in New Mexico.* Washington: Government Printing Office, 1915.

Adams, Eleanor B., and Fray Angélico Chávez. *The Missions of New Mexico, 1776: A Description by Fray Francisco Atanasio Dominguez.* Albuquerque: University of New Mexico Press, 1956.

Bannon, John Francis. *Bolton and the Spanish Borderlands.* Norman: University of Oklahoma Press, 1964.

Binkley, William Campbell. *The Expansionist Movement in Texas, 1836-1850.* University of California Publications in History, Vol. 13. Berkeley: University of California Press, 1925.

Cabeza de Baca. Fabiola. *We Fed Them Cactus.* Albuquerque: University of New Mexico Press, 1954.

Carroll, H. Bailey. "Some New Mexico-West Texas Relationships, 1541-1841." *West Texas Historical Association Year Book,* Vol. 14, 1938, pp. 92-102.

————, and J. Villasana Haggard, editors. *Three New Mexico Chronicles,* Albuquerque: The Quivira Society, 1942.

Chávez, Fray Angélico. *Origins of New Mexico Families.* Santa Fe: The Historical Society of New Mexico, 1954.

Cook, John R. *The Border and the Buffalo.* Topeka: Crane and Company, 1907; reprinted, New York: Citadel Press, 1967.

Duval, John C. *The Adventures of Big Foot Wallace, the Texas Ranger.* Philadelphia: 1870; reprinted, Lincoln: University of Nebraska Press, 1966.

Faulk, Odie B. *The Last Years of Spanish Texas, 1778-1821.* The Hague: Mouton & Co., 1964.

Foster, James Monroe, Jr. "Fort Bascom, New Mexico." *New Mexico Historical Review,* Vol. 35, No. 1 (January, 1960), pp. 30-62.

Gregg, Josiah. *Commerce of the Prairies.* 1844; reprinted, Norman: University of Oklahoma Press, 1954.

Hackett, Charles Wilson, ed. *Historical Documents Relating to New Mexico, Nueva Vizcaya, and Approaches Thereto, to 1773.* 3 vols. Washington: Carnegie Institution of Washington, 1937.

Haley, J. Evetts. "The Comanchero Trade." *Southwestern Historical Quarterly,* Vol. 38, No. 3 (January, 1935), pp. 157-176.

Harrison, Lowell H. "Three Comancheros and a Trader." *Panhandle-Plains Historical Review,* Vol. 38, 1965, pp. 73-93.

Jones, Oakah L., Jr. *Pueblo Warriors & Spanish Conquest.* Norman: University of Oklahoma Press, 1966.

Kendall, George W. *Narrative of the Texan Santa Fe Expedition.* 2 vols. London: Wiley & Putnam, 1844; reprinted facsimile, Austin: The Steck Company, 1935.

Kenner, Charles L. *A History of New Mexican-Plains Indian Relations.* Norman: University of Oklahoma Press.

Leckie, William H. *The Military Conquest of the Southern Plains.* Norman: University of Oklahoma Press, 1963.

Loomis, Noel M., and Abraham P. Nasatir. *Pedro Vial and the Roads to Santa Fe.* Norman: University of Oklahoma Press, 1967.

Moncus, Herman H. *Prairie Schooner Pirates: The Story of the Comancheros.* New York: Carlton Press, 1963.

Pike, Albert. *Prose Sketches and Poems Written in the Western Country.* Boston, 1834; reprinted, Albuquerque: Calvin Horn Publisher, Inc., 1967.

Reeve, Frank D. "The Federal Indian Policy in New Mexico." *New Mexico Historical Review,* Vol. 13, No. 1 (January, 1938), pp. 14-62.

Richardson, Rupert Norval. *The Comanche Barrier to South Plains Settlement.* Glendale, Calif.: The Arthur H. Clark Company, 1933.

Rister, Carl Coke. *Border Captives: The Traffic in Prisoners by Southern Plains Indians, 1835-1875.* Norman: University of Oklahoma Press, 1940.

Simmons, Marc. *Border Comanches: Seven Spanish Colonial Documents, 1785-1819.* Santa Fe: Stagecoach Press, 1967.

———— *Spanish Government in New Mexico.* Albuquerque: University of New Mexico Press, 1968.

Thomas, Alfred Barnaby. *After Coronado: Spanish Exploration Northeast of New Mexico, 1697-1727.* Norman: University of New Mexico Press, 1935.

———— *Forgotten Frontiers: A Study of the Spanish Indian Policy of Don Juan Bautista de Anza, Governor of New Mexico, 1777-1787.* Norman: University of Oklahoma Press, 1932.

———— *The Plains Indians and New Mexico, 1751-1778: A Collection of Documents.* Albuquerque: University of New Mexico Press, 1940.

Twitchell, Ralph E. *The Spanish Archives of New Mexico.* Cedar Rapids: Torch Press, 1914.

Wallace, Ernest. "Ranald S. Mackenzie on the Texas Frontier." *The Museum Journal,* Vols. 7-8 (in one), 1963-64. Lubbock: West Texas Museum Association.

———— "Ronald S. Mackenzie's Official Correspondence Relating to Texas, 1871-1873." *The Museum Journal,* Vol. 9, 1965.

Williamson, Harold F. *Winchester: The Gun That Won the West.* Reprinted, New York: A. S. Barnes and Company, Inc., 1967.

Worcester, Donald E. "The Spread of Spanish Horses in the Southwest, 1700-1900." *New Mexico Historical Review,* Vol. 20, No. 1 (January, 1945), pp. 1-13.

CHAPTER 9. *Slaughter on the Plains.*

Branch E. Douglas. *The Hunting of the Buffalo.* New York: D. Appleton and Company, 1929; reprinted, Lincoln: University of Nebraska Press.

Cook, John R. *The Border and the Buffalo.* Topeka: Crane and Company, 1907; reprinted, New York: Citadel Press, 1967.

Dixon, Olive K. *Life of "Billy" Dixon, Plainsman, Scout and Pioneer.* Guthrie, Okla., 1914; reprinted, Dallas: P. L. Turner Company, 1927.

Dobie, J. Frank. *On the Open Range.* Dallas: Southwest Press, 1931.

Dodge, Richard I. *The Plains of the Great West and Their Inhabitants.* New York: G. P. Putnam's Sons, 1877.

Gard, Wayne. *The Great Buffalo Hunt.* New York: Alfred A. Knopf, Inc., 1959.

Garrard, Hector Lewis. *Wah-To-Yah and the Taos Trail.* Cincinnati, 1850; reprinted, Norman: University of Oklahoma Press, 1935.

Garretson, Martin S. *The American Bison.* New York: New York Zoological Society, 1938.

Grinnell, George Bird. *When Buffalo Ran.* Norman: University of Oklahoma Press, 1966.

Haley J. Evetts. *Charles Goodnight: Cowman and Plainsman*. Boston: Houghton Mifflin and Company, 1936.

Hill, J. L. *The Passing of the Indian and the Buffalo*. Long Beach, Calif.: W. Moyle Publishing Co., 1917.

Holden, W. C. "The Buffalo and the Plains Area." *West Texas Historical Association Year Book*, Vol. 2 (June, 1926), pp. 8-17.

———— "Robert Cypret Parrack, Buffalo Hunter and Fence Cutter." *West Texas Historical Association Year Book*, Vol. 21 (1945), pp. 29-49.

Hornaday, William T. *The Extermination of the American Bison*. In: Smithsonian Report, N. S. National Museum, 1887. Washington, 1889.

Kincaid, Naomi H. "Rath City." *West Texas Historical Association Year Book*, Vol. 24 (October, 1948), pp. 40-46.

Knight, Oliver. *Fort Worth: Outpost on the Trinity*. Norman: University of Oklahoma Press, 1953.

McCarty, John L. *Adobe Walls Bride: The Story of Billy and Olive King Dixon*. San Antonio: The Naylor Company, 1956.

Monaghan, Jay, ed. *The Book of the American West*. New York: Julian Messner, Inc., 1963.

Mooar, J. Wright. "The First Buffalo Hunting in the Panhandle." *West Texas Historical Association Year Book*, Vol. 6 (June, 1930), pp. 109-111.

———— "Frontier Experiences of J. Wright Mooar." *West Texas Historical Association Year Book*, Vol. 4 (June, 1928), pp. 89-92.

Powers, Alfred. *Buffalo Adventures on the Western Plains*. Portland, Ore.: Binfords & Mort, 1945.

Rister, Carl Coke. *Fort Griffin on the Texas Frontier*. Norman: University of Oklahoma Press, 1956.

———— "The Significance of the Destruction of the Buffalo in the Southwest." *Southwestern Historical Quarterly*, Vol. 33, No. 1 (July, 1929), pp. 34-49.

Rye, Edgar. *The Quirt and the Spur*. Chicago: W. B. Conkey, Co., 1909.

Sandoz, Mari. *The Buffalo Hunters*. New York: Hastings House, 1954.

Strickland, Rex W., editor. "The Recollections of W. S. Glenn, Buffalo Hunter." *Panhandle-Plains Historical Review*, Vol. 22 (1949), pp. 15-64.

Waters, L. L. *Steel Trails to Santa Fe*. Lawrence: University of Kansas Press, 1950.

Webb, William E. *Buffalo Land: Authentic Account of . . . Scientific and Sporting Party in the Wild West*. Philadelphia: McLean Publishing Co., 1874.

Wheeler, Homer W. *Buffalo Days: Forty Years in the West*. Indianapolis: The Bobbs-Merrill Company, 1923.

CHAPTER 10. *Log Jam — Texas Size.*

Bell, John. *Documents from the War Department.* 27th Congress, 1st sess., House Document No. 1 (Serial 392). Washington, 1841.

Caldwell, Norman W. "The Red River Raft." *Chronicles of Oklahoma,* Vol. 19, No. 3 (September, 1941), pp. 253-268.

Dorsey, Florence L. *Master of the Mississippi: Henry Shreve and the Conquest of the Mississippi.* Boston: Houghton Mifflin Company, 1941.

Flint, Timothy. *Recollections of the Last Ten Years . . . in the Valley of the Mississippi.* Boston: Cummings, Hilliard & Co., 1826; reprinted, New York: Alfred A. Knopf, Inc., 1932.

Foreman, Grant. "River Navigation in the Early Southwest." *Mississippi Valley Historical Review,* Vol 15, No. 1 (June, 1926), pp. 34-55.

Fuller, C. A. *Report on Survey of Red River.* 33rd Congress, 2nd sess., Senate Exec. Doc. No. 62, Vol VII (Serial 752). Washington, 1855.

Jones, Victor Harlan. *Sedimentation in Red River Below the Mouth of Washita River.* University of Iowa Studies in Natural History, Vol. 15, No. 4.. Iowa City: University of Iowa Press, 1933.

Marcy, Randolph B. *Exploration of the Red River of Louisiana, in the Year 1852.* 32nd Congress, 2nd sess., Senate Exec. Doc. No. 54. Washington, 1854.

Marshall, Thomas M. *A History of the Western Boundary of the Louisiana Purchase.* Berkeley: University of California Press, 1914.

Neville, A. W. *The Red River Valley, Then and Now.* Paris, Texas: North Texas Publishing Company, 1948.

Noel, Theophilus. *A Campaign from Santa Fe to the Mississippi.* Shreveport: Shreveport News Printing Establishment, 1865; reprinted, Houston: Stagecoach Press, 1961.

Norman, H. Philip. "The Red River of the South." *Louisiana Historical Quarterly,* Vol. 25, No. 2 (April, 1942), pp. 397-535.

Peck, J. M. *Memorial Regarding Snag-Boats.* 28th Congress, 1st sess., Senate Doc. No. 141, Vol III (Serial 433), Washington, 1844.

Shreve, Henry M. *Report on Obstructions in Red River.* 24th Congress, 2nd sess., Senate Doc. No. 197, Vol. III (Serial 281). Washington, 1836.

Sibley, Dr. John. In: *American State Papers, Indian Affairs,* Vol. I, pp. 725-731. Washington, 1832. (Letter to Secretary of War Henry Dearborn.)

Swanton, John R. *Source Material on the History and Ethnology of the Caddo Indians.* Smithsonian Institution, Bureau of American Ethnology, Bulletin 132. Washington, 1942.

Woodruff, Lieut. Eugene A. "Removal of the Red River Raft." In: *Report of the Secretary of War,* 43rd Congress, 1st sess., House Exec. Doc. No. 1, Part 2, pp. 613-620, 635-676. Washington, 1873. (Major source.)

Wright, Muriel H. "Early Navigation and Commerce Along the Arkansas and Red Rivers in Oklahoma." *Chronicles of Oklahoma,* Vol. 8, No. 1 (March, 1930), pp. 65-88.

23rd Congress, 1st sess., House Report No. 509, Vol. IV (Serial 263). Washington, 1834. (On petition of Henry M. Shreve.)

26th Congress, 2nd sess., House Report No. 141 (Serial 388). Washington, 1841. (On appropriation for removal of Red River Raft.)

27th Congress, 2nd sess., Senate Doc. No. 112, Vol. III (Serial 397). Washington, 1842. (Resolutions on improvement of Western rivers.)

27th Congress, 2nd sess., House Report No. 648, Vol. III (Serial 409). Washington, 1842. (Adverse to payment of Thomas B. Lee and H. Cheatham for work on raft removal.)

29th Congress, 1st sess., Senate Doc. No. 31, Vol. III (Serial 472). Washington, 1845. (Memorial on Red River Raft.)

33rd Congress, 1st sess., House Exec. Doc. No. 24, Vol. V (Serial 640). Washington, 1854. (Report on obstructions in Red River.)

34th Congress, 1st sess., House Report No. 85, Vol. I (Serial 868). Washington, 1856. (Report on Red River Raft.)

CHAPTER 11. *The Peppery Little War Over Salt.*

Alfredo, Don (Alfred M. Perkins). "Halite." *Rocks and Minerals,* Vol. 30 (1955), pp. 115-120.

Bartlett, John Russell. *Personal Narrative of Explorations and Incidents in Texas, New Mexico, California, Sonora, and Chihuahua, connected with the United States and Mexican Boundary Commission, during the years 1850, '51, '52, and '53.* 2 vols., 1854. Reprinted, Chicago: Rio Grande Press, 1965.

Christiansen, Paige W., and Frank E. Kottlowski, editors. *Mosaic of New Mexico's Scenery, Rocks, and History.* Socorro, N.M.: State Bureau of Mines and Mineral Resources, 1967.

Darton, N. H. *Permian Salt Deposits of the South Central United States.* U. S. Geo. Survey Bulletin 715. Washington: Government Printing Office, 1921.

Dobie, J. Frank. *A Vaquero of the Brush Country.* Dallas: Southwest Press, 1929; reprinted, New York: Bantam Books, Inc., 1954.

Ellis, Robert W. *New Mexico Mineral Deposits Except Fuels.* University of New Mexico Bulletin No. 167. Albuquerque: El Palacio Press, 1930.

El Paso Troubles in Texas. 45th Congress, 2nd sess., House Exec. Doc. No. 93 (Serial 1809). Washington, 1878.

Gibson, Arrel M. *The Life and Death of Colonel Albert Jennings Fountain.* Norman: University of Oklahoma Press, 1965.

Gillett, James B. *Six Years with the Texas Rangers, 1875 to 1881.* New Haven: Yale University Press, 1925.

González, Nancie L. *The Spanish-Americans of New Mexico: A Heritage of Pride*. Albuquerque: University of New Mexico Press, 1969.

Jones, Billy M. *The Search for Maturity: The Saga of Texas, 1875-1900*. Austin: Steck-Vaughn Company, 1965.

Kibbe, Pauline R. *Latin Americans in Texas*. Albuquerque: University of New Mexico Press, 1946.

Lowrie, Samuel H. *Culture Conflict in Texas, 1821-1835*. New York: Columbia University Press, 1932.

Maverick, Maury. *A Maverick American*. New York: Covici Friede Publishers, 1937.

Maverick, Rena M. *Samuel Maverick, Texan: 1803-1870*. San Antonio: privately printed, 1952.

Northrop, Stuart A. *Minerals of New Mexico*. Albuquerque: University of New Mexico Press, 1959.

Puckett, Fidelia M. "Ramon Ortiz: Priest and Patriot." *New Mexico Historical Review*, Vol. 25 (1950), pp. 265-295.

Sanchez, George I. *Forgotten People: A Study of New Mexicans*. Albuquerque: University of New Mexico Press, 1940.

Schroeder, Albert H., and Dan S. Matson. *A Colony on the Move: Gaspar Castaño de Sosa's Journal, 1590-1591*. Santa Fe: School of American Research, 1965.

Sonnichsen, C. L. *The El Paso Salt War, 1877*. El Paso: Carl Hertzog and the Texas Western Press, 1961.

Strickland, Rex W. *Six Who Came to El Paso*. Southwestern Studies, Vol. I, No. 3. El Paso: Texas Western College Press, 1963.

Treutlein, Theodore E., editor. *Pfefferkorn's Description of Sonora*, Albuquerque: University of New Mexico Press, 1949.

Utley, Robert N. *The International Boundary: United States and Mexico*. Santa Fe: U.S. Department of the Interior, National Park Service, 1964.

White, Owen. *Out of the Desert: The Historical Romance of El Paso*. El Paso: The McMath Company, 1923.

CHAPTER 12. *What a Way to Go!*

Barnes, Will C. *Arizona Place Names*. Tucson: University of Arizona Press, 1935.

Bartholomew, Ed E. *The Biographical Album of Western Gunfighters*. Houston: The Frontier Press of Texas, 1958.

——— *Cullen Baker: Premier Texas Gun Fighter*. Houston: The Frontier Press of Texas, 1954.

——— *Wyatt Earp: The Untold Story*, and *The Man and the Myth*. 2 vols. Toyahvale, Texas: Frontier Book Company, 1963, 1964.

Burroughs, John R. *Where the Old West Stayed Young*. New York: William Morrow and Company, 1962.

Chrisman, Harry E. *Fifty Years on the Owl Hoot Trail: Jim Herron, the First Sheriff of No Man's Land, Oklahoma Territory.* Chicago: Sage Books, 1969.

Coates, Robert N. *The Outlaw Years: The History of the Land Pirates of the Natchez Trace.* New York: Pennant Books, 1954.

Coolidge, Dane. *Fighting Men of the West.* New York: Bantam Books, 1952.

Cunningham, Eugene. *Triggernometry: A Gallery of Gunfighters.* Caldwell, Idaho: The Caxton Printers, Ltd., 1947.

Farber, James. *Texans With Guns.* San Antonio: The Naylor Company, 1950.

Gard, Wayne. *Sam Bass.* Lincoln: University of Nebraska Press, 1969.

Gillett, James B. *Six Years with the Texas Rangers, 1875 to 1881.* New Haven: Yale University Press, 1925.

Haggard, J. V. "The Neutral Ground Between Louisiana and Texas." *Louisiana Historical Quarterly,* Vol. 28 (1945).

Hayes, Jess G. *Sheriff Thompson's Day: Turbulence in the Arizona Territory.* Tucson: University of Arizona Press, 1968.

Hendricks, George D. *The Bad Man of the West.* San Antonio: The Naylor Company, 1959.

Hertzog, Peter. *A Directory of New Mexico Desperadoes.* Santa Fe: The Press of the Territorian, 1965.

Horan, James D. *Pictorial History of the Wild West.* New York: Crown Publishers, Inc., 1954.

―――― *The Wild Bunch.* New York: New American Library, 1958.

Langford, Nathaniel P. *Vigilante Days and Ways.* Boston: J. G. Cupples Co., 1890.

Marshall, Thomas M. *A History of the Western Boundary of the Louisiana Purchase.* Berkeley: University of California Press, 1914.

Martin, Douglas D. *An Arizona Chronology: The Territorial Years, 1846-1912.* Tucson: University of Arizona Press, 1963.

―――― *Tombstone's Epitaph.* Albuquerque: University of New Mexico Press, 1951.

Miller, Nyle H., and Joseph W. Snell. *Great Gunfighters of the Kansas Cowtowns, 1867-1886.* Lincoln: University of Nebraska Press, 1963.

Myres, S. D. *Pioneer Surveyor-Frontier Lawyer: The Personal Narrative of O. W. Williams, 1877-1902.* El Paso: Texas Western College Press, 1966.

Rynning, Captain Thomas H. *Gun Notches: The Life Story of a Cowboy-Soldier.* New York: Frederick A. Stokes Company, 1931.

Shirley, Glenn. *Six-gun and Silver Star.* Albuquerque: University of New Mexico Press, 1955.

―――― *Toughest of Them All.* Albuquerque: University of New Mexico Press, 1953.

Sterling, William W. *Trails and Trials of a Texas Ranger.* Norman: University of Oklahoma Press, 1968.

Wilson, Edward. *An Unwritten History: A Record from the Exciting Days of Early Arizona.* Santa Fe: Stagecoach Press, 1966.